The FLN in Algeria

The FLN in Algeria

PARTY DEVELOPMENT IN A REVOLUTIONARY SOCIETY

Henry F. Jackson

Contributions in Afro-American and African Studies, Number 30

 GREENWOOD PRESS
Westport, Connecticut • London, England

Burgess

JQ
3298
.J2
J32
1977

c. 1

Library of Congress Cataloging in Publication Data

Jackson, Henry F
    The FLN in Algeria.

    (Contributions in Afro-American and African studies; no. 30)
    Bibliography: p.
    Includes index.
    1. Jabhat al-Tahrir al-Qawmi. 2. Algeria—Politics and government.
I. Title. II. Series.
JQ3298.J2J32   1977   329.9'65   76-47889
ISBN 0-8371-9401-6

Library of Congress Catalog Card Number: 76-47889
ISBN: 0-8371-9401-6

First published in 1977

Greenwood Press, Inc.
51 Riverside Avenue, Westport, Conn. 06880

Printed in the United States of America

This book is dedicated to
Dr. Wilburn H. Weddington,
the man who taught me the power of human goodness
by his own living example.

Contents

List of Illustrations and Tables

Preface

This examination of the Algerian party movement from revolution to independence is the product of research work that spanned three years. Motivating my interest from beginning to end was a conviction that the Algerian party experiment, despite its uniqueness and peculiarities, offers instructive insights for the study of liberation parties in general. The research material used in the analysis was derived from a wide variety of sources, including interviews, unpublished primary sources, and on-the-spot observations (in 1963 and 1966-67) of particular events discussed in the text. Works in French have been used extensively, and all translations are the author's unless otherwise indicated.

I am pleased to acknowledge the persons and institutions whose assistance was crucial to the completion of this work. For scholarly criticisms and intellectual insights, I am most grateful to Professors Jacob C. Hurewitz and Hollis R. Lynch of Columbia University. I send a special thanks to Professor Mohamed Farès of the University of Algiers, who provided me with invaluable source materials. David and Marina Ottaway also assisted me in obtaining useful information, as did another long-time colleague Hossein Kired (of Algiers). My good friend and former assistant, Thomas S. Williamson, Jr., read and ruthlessly criticized every page of the manuscript while it was in the working stages. The John Hay Whitney Foundation, New York City, supported my work in Algeria and at the Centre de recherches sur les affaires méditerraneennes of the University of Aix-en-Provence, France. The Regents Faculty Program of the University of California, Berkeley, provided a small stipend that enabled me to put the study into final shape.

My gratitude goes also to my friends who are not mentioned here, but whose minds and other resources I often strained in the long course of my labor.

Henry F. Jackson
May 2, 1976
Berkeley, California

Introduction

This study analyzes the development of the Algerian *Front de libération nationale* (FLN) from its beginning in 1954 to its demise in 1965. The FLN was the spearhead of the war against French colonialism and developed as the central force behind the Algerian revolution. This revolutionary party movement enabled Algerian nationalists to wage one of the most violent and successful wars of national liberation on the African continent, and indeed in the Third World generally. Evolving out of unique historical conditions, the FLN reemerged after independence as the focal point of Algeria's provocative experiment in party building, a process that continued until the party's collapse in the wake of a military coup d'etat.

Colonialism in Algeria was deep-rooted. It originated in 1830 from a desperate effort by Charles X, the reigning French monarch, to save his fledgling dynasty by forcing the coastal states of North Africa to stop interfering with French maritime trade.[1] The territory that is now Algeria then belonged to the Ottoman system and was ruled by the dey of Algiers, an Ottoman administrative official. When, in the midst of an altercation, the dey literally smacked the French consul with a fly whisk, the Paris regime had a convenient pretext for massive military reprisal. In came the French expeditionary forces, who soon prepared the foundation for a colonial system that lasted 130 years.

The colonial system in Algeria differed greatly from that in most other European colonies due to the fact that the Paris government legalized the conquered territory as an integral part of France. Most importantly, large numbers of Frenchmen actually settled in the territory and in time transformed the indigenous Muslim-Arab society by superimposing the French language, French culture, and French rule on the colonized people. Algeria's fertile land originally attracted the settlers, but their material appetites were whetted more by the discovery of oil just before the outbreak of the rebellion in 1954. By that time, the well-entrenched Europeans had come to regard Algeria's wealth and promise as their own.

The FLN consisted of a small guerrilla force when the rebellion erupted. In the next seven years, however, the FLN succeeded in mobilizing the great majority of the native population in support of the nationalist objective: political independence through the total elimination of the colonial system. The strength of the movement was later demonstrated by the fall of the Fourth Republic, which was a direct consequence of the political disintegration the FLN precipitated in metropolitan France, and by the neutralization of the modern French army which had been sent to Algeria to suppress the rebel upheaval.

Early in the war, FLN leaders recognized the need for creating political units within the guerrilla fighting force. At a clandestine meeting held in the summer of 1956, they organized the FLN into political and military divisions, establishing a hierarchy of leadership to command the separate but related activities of both. Among the new political institutions was an FLN directorate, or party executive, whose role was to assure the priority of political over military issues in the FLN's later development. FLN leaders then organized nonmilitary groups like trade unionists and students to support the struggle. These changes elevated the FLN from a narrowly based guerrilla force to a party movement, or nascent political party.

The FLN forces, initially concentrated in urban areas, were eventually distributed over most of Algeria's 920,000 square miles.[2] To mobilize the native population, the FLN employed classic techniques of guerrilla warfare,[3] including political indoctrination and organization of communities into party cells. Ultimately, the FLN's broadened popular base and new political institutions enabled it to achieve national unity and triumph in the anticolonial war.

What the FLN lacked after the 1956 meeting was a well-defined party ideology and program. Politically, this omission appeared to be critical, for sustaining consensus among FLN leaders necessitated a clear-cut program of political, economic, and social objectives for Algeria after independence. In the absence of an ideological program, the foundation of national unity basically rested on common hostility toward the enemy and did not transcend military objectives. For the duration of the war, FLN leaders tended to identify politics with warfare and made only unsuccessful efforts to differentiate politics from war up to the eve of independence.

The development of FLN institutions followed a distinctly military pattern. Few FLN components were created that were not primarily adapted to the exigencies of a colonial war. The FLN failed to develop political institutions partly as a result of the counterinsurgency strategy of the French army, which caused frequent discontinuity in leadership. Rebel leaders who escaped death were often imprisoned or forced into exile, and this involuntary attrition frustrated the establishment of a stable party command. But the fundamental obstacle to the movement's political development was divisiveness among the FLN leaders themselves. Of necessity, the leaders contained their political and personal differences in the confrontation against the French. Yet, the latent conflicts were never resolved in wartime and persisted even after independence was won.

Through a variety of techniques, the leaders succeeded in maintaining sufficient unity to continue the war, despite the fact that conflict in leadership precluded general agreement on the further development of institutions within the party. Lacking a well-defined domestic political program, they acted without any guidelines for organizing an enlarged party constituency beyond the immediate imperatives of war. The consolidation of a stable political party in wartime was likely to guarantee incumbents power in the postindependent political system; hence, the FLN leaders in general refused to agree on the institutionalization of any system that might ensure the future domination of one over the other. To the extent that the FLN moderated dissension at all, it was in the military, not the political, arena.

From its inception the FLN adopted the principle of collegial leadership. This principle required the leaders to decide collectively all important issues affecting the movement's wartime development as well as the terms of any settlement with France. Collective authority was instrumental in regulating the leadership conflicts during the struggle. But just before independence the party movement itself divided into opposing camps as different leaders enlisted supporters to compete in a factional struggle for power. Consequently, the principle of collective leadership succumbed to factionalism at the very time it would have been most useful in promoting the rise of a cohesive and representative party.

Algeria became independent in July 1962, following a negotiated settlement between France and the Gouvernement provisoire de la république algérienne (GPRA), the official Algerian government-in-exile formed in wartime. The cease-fire settlement attested to the success of the anticolonial struggle. Among FLN leaders, however, the cease-fire signaled the beginning of a domestic struggle for power that threatened to thrust the new nation into civil war. Ahmed Ben Bella and Houari Boumedienne, respectively the chief political and military leaders of the movement, joined ranks against the GPRA incumbents to seize control of Algeria's first government after independence. With their superior forces, Ben Bella and Boumedienne overthrew the GPRA and then established a regime based upon Ben Bella's status as a national hero and Boumedienne's claim on the loyalty of the army.

The FLN emerged from the war as a highly fragmented, almost nonexistent entity. Its only effective agency was the Political Bureau, the new party executive formed by the Ben Bella faction during its struggle against the GPRA. Although party elements did formulate a broadly stated party ideology and program prior to independence, the FLN continued to lack supportive institutions and an organized constituency. On independence the triumphant revolutionary movement resembled, as it were, a head without a body.

Shortly before independence, FLN leaders decided that the party should be the national guide and authority of the new political system. What was required after independence, therefore, was a massive commitment to party building. However, Ben Bella promoted as his first priority a centralized governmental bureaucracy, or state system, to provide a foundation for the FLN of the future. Through his control of the state administration, he gained a monopoly of political power, creating in the process a system of personal rule whose policies were predicated on his prerogatives as the supreme political leader. The system of personal rule was qualified only by Ben Bella's dependence on Boumedienne who, as chief of the armed forces, sustained governmental authority and the FLN's hegemony over competing political groups.

While Ben Bella concentrated on establishing the state system, the task of party building was advanced by Mohammed Khider, the first secretary general of the Political Bureau. Khider shaped the FLN as an institutionalized mass party by reorganizing its structure and by integrating or coopting popular constituent groups such as trade unionists into the resuscitated party organization. A persistent problem that afflicted the party-building process was Ben Bella's insistence that the FLN's emerging institutions integrally reflect his personal leadership. When Ben Bella saw that Khider's direction of the party posed a threat to personal rule, he forced Khider out of office and took direct responsibility for party building himself. The development of the FLN continued, but always in the shadow of Ben Bella's militarily enforced prerogatives.

The FLN grew in constituency and structure under Ben Bella's direct leadership. Trade unionists, women, students, and youths in general were obliged to enlist in the party organization. Ben Bella also sought to mobilize Algerian peasants, the country's vast majority, into party participation. After the national constitution was ratified, the Algerian political system came under the single-party rule of the FLN, and this change established the party as the only legitimate political organization in the system. Finally, a party congress was called to fully systematize the FLN's structure and to define a party ideology and program.

With the government's assistance, the FLN entered a process of reorganization and ideological redefinition that promised to accelerate the growth of a viable mass political party. This possibility was enhanced by Ben Bella's belated willingness to reduce his personal prerogatives in favor of the FLN's institutional power. But a military coup, three years after independence, destroyed Ben Bella's regime and terminated official efforts at political party development in Algeria. What had begun as a commitment to establish a government under a revolutionary mass party ended in complete failure.

The disaster that befell the FLN in 1965 must be correlated with the many advantages it possessed on independence. From the war, it gained a fairly large body of leaders who were able political and military organizers. There was a not insignificant number, including Ben Bella, who had previously demonstrated their competence while serving in colonial institutions, such as the French army or French political parties, long before the rebellion. Independent Algeria could also boast a sizable educated class that included university graduates and committed ideologists. Although Europeans had long exploited the resources of the country, it was far from impoverished. Such assets, then, seemed to favor the possibility of an early and effective restoration of the party system. The FLN was the driving force behind the successful anticolonial struggle, and its continuing legitimacy provided the new leaders with a sound basis for asserting their authority. Such advantages were there; but in a short time, they were turned irreversibly into liabilities.

In this analysis, two different but closely related themes explain why the FLN did not succeed as a mass political party. First, the destiny of the FLN was determined to a large extent by the failure of its leaders during the struggle for independence to develop enduring political institutions, as distinguished from military institutions that were essentially adapted to waging an anticolonial war. Of particular importance in exploring this hypothesis is the role of ideology in the development of political parties in developing societies. Ideology can be understood as a set of ideas and beliefs that characterize the nature and order of a political system. For political leaders, it functions as a more or less comprehensive set of principles, disposing them to certain objectives and decisions as they exercise authority. Without a systematic ideology, FLN leaders had little vision of what goals, institutions, and functions the party movement should develop in wartime to facilitate its consolidation after independence.

The second theme is that Ben Bella's subordination of an institutionalized party system to the imposition of personal rule weakened the FLN's development in the early years after independence. The concept of personal rule essentially describes a political system wherein an individual diffuses his authority by requiring personal loyalty to him as the primary criterion for selecting and promoting political leaders at all levels of the system. This system of authority usually contradicts the institutionalization of a party system, which requires mobilizing people to support and participate in a functionally specific or goal-oriented organization based on a well-defined ideology, that is, on ideas and values that transcend the preferences of any individual leader. The recurring question underlying this theme is whether Ben Bella's priorities were consistent with the needs of a party organization aspiring to mobilize and systematically regulate the interests of diverse social and economic groups.

The colonial background from which the FLN emerged is

examined in Chapter 1 of this study. Chapters 2 and 3 focus on the wartime FLN to show how it helped FLN leaders maintain a relatively united front against the common external enemy. Chapters 4 through 9 demonstrate how personal rule, untempered by a willingness to share power, inhibited the FLN from becoming a viable political party in the initial years after independence. Because Ben Bella's regime depended on his alliance with Boumedienne, the government, like the party, became susceptible to a military takeover. The conclusion brings this analysis on the FLN up to date and compares the FLN with other parties of liberation.

The FLN in Algeria

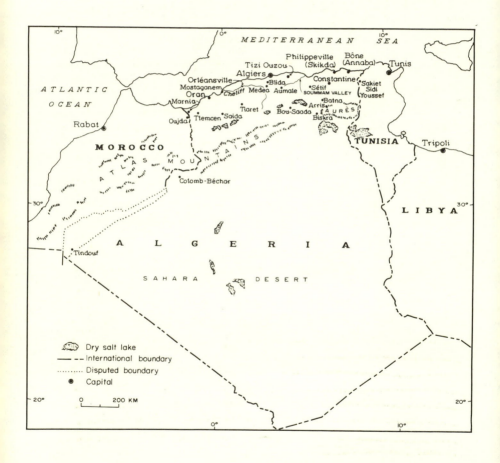

MEDITERRANEAN SEA

ATLANTIC
OCEAN

Philippeville
(Skikda)

Bône
(Annaba)

Tunis

Tizi Ouzou

Algiers

Orléansville

Constantine

Sakiet
Sidi
Youssef

Mostaganem

Blida

Oran

Cheliff Medea Aumale

Sétif

Marnia

SOUMMAM VALLEY

Batna

Oujda

Tlemcen

Saida

Tiaret

Bou-Saada

Arris

AURÈS

Biskra

Rabat

MOROCCO

ATLAS MOUNTAINS

TUNISIA

Tripoli

Colomb-Béchar

LIBYA

Tindouf

ALGERIA

SAHARA

DESERT

Dry salt lake

International boundary

Disputed boundary

Capital

0   200 KM

Colonialism: Background to Revolution

The French conquest of Algeria in 1830 was qualified by a pledge from the Paris government to respect the property, religion, and customs of the indigenous Muslim population. By the end of the nineteenth century, however, a policy of direct colonial rule had resulted in the uprooting of the native economy, the displacement of Arabic with French, and the settlement of thousands of Europeans on Algerian soil. When Muslim nationalists emerged in the early twentieth century, they recalled the breach of the 1830 pledge and began the organization of native party movements that paved the way for the FLN. At bottom, therefore, French colonialism provided the necessary stimulus for the Algerian revolution and for the insurrectionary forces who led it.

France's imperial conquest of Algeria was signaled by the capitulation of the dey of Algiers soon after the invasion. Official French sources did not refer to the conquered territory as a colony at that time, nor at any point during the entire history of French rule. Instead, the French introduced legalisms that portrayed Algeria as an integral part of France and Muslims as accessible to the rights and privileges of Frenchmen. But the economic, political, and social relationships between the native inhabitants and the Europeans partitioned this new society into two sharply distinct categories: the colonized and the colonizers.

Algeria as a Colonial Territory

Algeria's Muslim population totaled approximately three million persons in 1830[1] and could be separated into two principal ethnic groups, Berbers and Arabs. Berbers, the country's original inhabitants, formed about 30 percent of the population. A people whose ancestry remains obscure, the Berbers were assimilated into Arab society after the seventh century through conversion to Islam and contact with Arab culture. Berbers resided mainly in villages in Kabylia and the Aurès mountains where they continued to speak Berber, their mother tongue (which remains an oral, unwritten language).

Arabs, the majority ethnic group, comprised about 70 percent of the native inhabitants. They were descendants of the Arab conquerors who invaded and occupied North Africa in the seventh century, establishing Islam and the Arabic language as permanent elements in Algerian society. Bedouins, or Arab nomads, predominated in this group and were dispersed throughout the hinterlands of Algeria. The balance of the Arab conquerors settled in the few coastal towns like Oran, Algiers, and Bône.[2] Nearly all Arabs belonged to the Sunni, or orthodox branch of Islam, which prevailed over the society as a whole.[3]

Traditional or native institutions fused the Berber and Arab peoples in many ways. For instance, the agnatic extended family, which involved the lineage of all family members over generations from a common male ancestor, caused the traditional social structure to operate as a series of interlocking communities. Indeed, Algeria in 1830 could be described as a country of villages and communal ethnic groups tied together by different clans or family cells. The social system built upon family membership also determined economic relations, which were always personal and direct.[4] Land, like most property, was held in common, and a hierarchy of authority headed by a dominant father (who was usually the communal chief) regulated the labor and participation of all members in its cultivation.

Islam constituted the most prevalent bond between Arabs and Berbers. It controlled a Muslim's life in all important respects, including law, government, marriage, and inheritance.[5] No Arab or Berber community escaped the influence of religious officials, such as the *qaids* (communal judges or chiefs) or the *'ulama* (legists or doctors of Islamic laws), and education remained limited to the madrasat, or Quranic schools. More than any other force, Islam integrated the culture of precolonial Algeria.

To be sure, some cultural differences did persist between Arabs and Berbers, but centuries of acculturation, intermarriage, and socialization blurred sharp distinctions between them so that it became "almost impossible to divide the Arab element from the Berber element with any degree of certainty."[6] Consequently, a single Muslim-Arab culture characterized the indigenous population at the time of the French conquest: all Algerians embraced Islam as a religion and way of life, spoke Arabic, and identified with the historic Arab civilization and culture.

The European population increased rapidly after the conquest of 1830 in response to "free land" which France offered to Europeans willing to emigrate to Algeria. The French government was determined to control the territory through the Europeans who lived there, with the result that a whole class of settlers came into being. From a small community of 3,000 town dwellers in 1831,[7] the colonizers grew to some 131,000 town and rural residents by 1851.[8] The *colons*, as the settlers were known, benefited upon arrival from the rich farmlands sequestered or expropriated from the *fallahin*, the Muslim peasant farmers. The plantation system and commercial agriculture blossomed in the countryside as metropolitan interest in creating an overseas market and in producing raw resources for sale in France coincided with settler interest in the profits of private enterprise.

Before colonization, the types of Muslim agricultural production were generally traceable to particular geographical locations, whether the fallahin were Arabs or Berbers, sedentary or nomadic. Berbers in Kabylia produced wheat, figs, and olives, and practiced small-scale livestock raising. Arab farmers, especially those in the north and west of Algeria, cultivated cereals, barley, and wheat, and raised sheep. It took only a few years of European domination, under the cataclysmic impact of the new system of commercial agriculture, for the native system to virtually collapse.

An abundance of good land, according to Adam Smith, is an essential condition for the survival of a new colony.[9] The French settlers found just such a condition in the vast, fertile regions of northern Algeria, such as the rich plains of the Mitidja and Cheliff valleys. There they transformed the Muslim economy from production for consumption to production for commercial sale and profit. With the advent of commercial agriculture came the development of a staple crop economy whose produce consisted of wine grapes and citrus fruits which, as export commodities, enabled the French in Algeria to trade with the French in France. Meanwhile, the primordial custom of land held under communal ownership succumbed to the European system of private property, and Muslims were suddenly converted into hired wage laborers on lands they used to work essentially for themselves. Export trade arose to suit the tastes and material interests of the colonizers, who eventually earned as much as a billion French francs ($200 million) annually from their new acquisitions.[10]

The settler population consisted of many who were neither French in citizenship nor French in origin. As late as 1896, for example, the colon population approximated 318,000 Frenchmen (of whom 50,000 were naturalized) and 212,000 others.[11] The others included Italians, Corsicans, Maltese, Germans, and especially Spaniards, the most numerous foreign group. Algeria's Jews, many born in the colony, received French citizenship en bloc by the Crémieux decree of 1870. A law of 1889 enabled all foreigners born in Algeria to acquire automatic naturalization upon legal maturity. Progressively assimilated into French culture, the colons became the major protagonists of Algeria's administrative and political integration into the French system.

France reacted to colon pressure in 1871 by adapting in Algeria the centralized administrative system that governed the *métropole*, or mother country. In Algiers, Oran, and Constantine, the French established new *départements*, or administrative subdivisions, that were directly responsible to the Paris government. Each département functioned with its own prefect, elected general, and municipal councils which the metropolitan minister of the interior supervised. Since the Algerian départements were administered like départements in France, the French applied metropolitan laws of political representation and established a judiciary in the image of France. Later, a governor general was appointed to head the départements.[12] As a result of these measures, Algeria became an integral part of the French system.

This process was reinforced by the Warnier law of 1873, which was sometimes labeled the "colons' law" because it permitted settlers to confiscate indigenous farm properties when the fallahin could not show "good title" to them. Except for traditional elites like the *qaids*, no Muslims held property under titled ownership; hence, the confiscation of Muslim lands became widespread. The colons had accumulated about 481,000 hectares between 1830 and 1870; under the Warnier law, within twenty years they obtained a million hectares of the country's most arable land.[13] In the towns, the colons enjoyed a complete monopoly of Algeria's commercial and administrative facilities.

The legal and political integration of Algeria into metropolitan France culminated in the French army's rout of local resistance waged by several Muslim chiefs, the most famous of whom was Amir Abdelkader.[14] This marked the beginning of the pacification period, which extended to 1870, and the expansion of European immigration to Algeria. The French continued the geographic expansion of the territory, steadily enlarging it from the series of Mediterranean coastal cities (e.g., Algiers, Oran), which had defined Algeria in 1830, to the territorial boundaries it had reached by independence.[15]

The settlers disrupted native society most intensively by building industries in the towns, creating the necessary conditions for modern business and an industrial labor class. "In the cities when they established themselves in great numbers," Le Tourneau wrote, the Europeans "needed more and more manual labor as their activities developed, and the towns, both traditional and newly founded, became powerful centers of attraction."[16] The internal migration of Muslims from the *bled* (country) led to the formation of an indigenous labor force. The political importance of such migration, as Hodgkin found in his study of African nationalism, was the discovery of new points of contact and interest that for the first time enabled the colonized to perceive their problems as social rather than personal.[17]

Statistically, the Europeans recognized Muslim urbanization around 1930 when they began to publish studies on the *bidonvilles*, or tin-can shanty settlements built in Algiers and other cities by uprooted and homeless individuals seeking employment.[18] The process had begun in the nineteenth century, continued through World War II, and accelerated during the war of independence. The overall population of Algiers, for instance, increased from 500,000 in 1954 to more than 800,000 in 1960; the rapid increase resulted from newly arrived Muslim residents.[19]

Absentee landlordism enabled the Europeans to control agriculture from the towns. Nearly 60 percent of the European population lived in the towns as early as 1870, and only an eighth remained on the land when the rebellion broke out in 1954.[20] Since the Europeans branched their industrial and commercial enterprises in Algiers,

Oran, Bône, and Constantine, the Muslims flocked to these areas in large numbers. About 30 percent of the Muslim population was urban in 1963, as compared with less than 20 percent two decades earlier. [21] Colonial disruption of traditional society was in part responsible for the men, skills, and ideas that would challenge European domination.

The Muslims maintained a numerical superiority in hectares of farmlands, but these were generally on the most mountainous, least productive terrain. The social and economic condition of the indigenous population deteriorated steadily as European techniques of agricultural production and marketing overwhelmed the crude, subsistence-oriented practices of peasant farming. Although the introduction of modern medical and sanitary techniques checked epidemics and disease in Algeria, the Muslim population (which had grown to almost nine million by 1954 [22]) suffered new material disadvantages as declining infant and adult mortality exacerbated the scarcity of foodstuffs and consumption goods. French manufactured products, meanwhile, supplanted the traditional artisan crafts that survived only in a few towns of the interior.

Politically, colon discrimination and French laws combined to impede the evolution of Muslim society. Perhaps most indicative of the colons' suppression of Muslim political development was the *code de l'indigénat* of 1881 which denied Muslims basic civil rights, such as trial by jury, and excluded them from almost all civil administrative posts. In theory, Muslims could acquire French citizenship and the legal prerogatives of Frenchmen after 1865. Such relief from the code de l'indigénat, however, involved many complicated procedures incomprehensible to most of the population, which was roughly 95-percent illiterate as late as 1914. Furthermore, Muslims could not accede to citizenship without renouncing their personal status under Quranic law, including the important Islamic canons on marriage, divorce, inheritance, and religion. Since Islam constitutes a totality of commands regulating a Muslim's life in all aspects, the Muslims had to abandon their entire cultural heritage and identity to become French citizens. Citizenship required, as it were, that Muslims assume a French personality. This is why Frantz Fanon, analyzing the psychological dimension of colonization, stated that "in the colonial context the settler only ends his work of breaking in the native when the latter admits loudly and intelligibly the supremacy of the white man's values."[23] Not surprisingly, few Muslims ever aspired to French citizenship.

The French policy of direct colonial rule disrupted all segments of the Muslim population. As Bourdieu discovered, the Arabs, the majority group, were most traumatized by the direct shock of colonization and the weakening of the old social structures.[24] From a family-based agrarian economy, in which production was geared to the needs of consumption by the producers, the Algerian society was transformed into a wage labor system where Muslims now worked on property owned by the colonists. French had replaced Arabic as the *lingua franca* of the territory. In place of the old institutions, French administration and government dictated the order of society. Most importantly, French citizens, settled by the thousands across the country, governed Algeria as if it were their own homeland. In short, the country had developed a new identity: French Algeria.

Assimilation Versus Self-Determination: The Muslim Choices

Muslim political participation in the colonial system was negligible until 1919 when France eased the requirements for Muslims to qualify for the rights of citizenship, primarily as a concession based on Muslim service in the French military and industry during World War I. The postwar generation of Muslim Algerians, influenced by notions of nationalism current in Europe during World War I, resolved to alter the colonized status of their population. Some adopted assimilation into French society as their goal and looked to political organization as the means to achieve it. Others, embracing the same means, aspired to autonomy or self-determination. These essentially nonviolent progenitors of nationalist activity were ultimately succeeded by the militants who ignited the anticolonial rebellion in 1954 and formed the leadership of the FLN.

A few Muslims entered political activity through an Algerian branch of the Parti communiste français (PCF).[25] Radical European intellectuals dominated the Parti communiste algérien (PCA) and limited their efforts to seeking social and economic reform for the Muslim society. Algerian communists viewed nationalism as a reality of industrial Europe and argued that it had no relevance to a non-industrial country like Algeria. For this reason, they rejected the Comintern's instruction in the early 1920s to undertake a movement calling for decolonization. Even so, a small number of Muslims rallied to the PCA because they then had no other outlet for organized political activity.

The real groundwork for a broad-based nationalist movement was inadvertently laid by France itself during World War I when Muslims were recruited to support the French war effort. The Algerians usually volunteered for services in the French army in large numbers, but some were conscripted under duress. In either case, they became exposed to techniques of modern warfare and learned organizational skills that later benefited nationalist activity in Algeria. Military service significantly contributed to the development of Muslim nationalism by introducing Algerians from diverse backgrounds and regions to each other. For the first time, they had a forum to discuss the national, and not simply local, aspects of colonization.

France rewarded Muslim military participation after 1919 by revoking many restrictions on Algerian political activity. The Algerians then organized the first Muslim political organization: the Etoile nord-africaine (ENA). The movement was led by Hadj Abdelkader, a former member of the PCF's central committee, and it recruited most of its members from the large group of Algerians working in France. Some 5,000 Muslims had emigrated to France voluntarily by 1912 in search of employment, but between 1914 and 1918 the French often used force to ensure an adequate supply of workers producing goods in metropolitan factories essential to the war effort.[26] As a result, nearly 100,000 Muslims worked in France by the war's end. The ENA drew on these laborers to develop a constituency that contained some of the most skilled and politicized elements in the Muslim population.

Like the PCA, the new Muslim organization demanded certain radical reforms, such as a redistribution of colon lands, in the interest of the peasant farmers. The ENA distinguished itself by making the unprecedented call for Algerian independence, a goal that it promoted among Algerian workers in France and urban workers in Algerian cities. In 1927, the movement came under the leadership of Hadj Ben Ahmed Messali, popularly known as Messali, an Arab nationalist whose background reflected a number of important French institutions including the Sorbonne, the French army (in World War I), and especially the PCF.

From the French communists Messali had learned techniques of modern party organization that he now began to apply in the development of the ENA. For instance, he adopted the PCF's structure of well-knit party cells closely controlled by a central committee.[27] The

PCF was probably the most cohesive civilian institution in France after the war; this fact prompted Messali to try duplicating the PCF's example, organizationally at least, in the service of Algerian national-ism. Messali maintained contact with French communists, but ideo-logically he was fast substituting Algerian nationalism for Marxism-Leninism. The success of his program seemed evident in 1929 when the ENA claimed a following of 4,000 active members, and the Paris government, alarmed by the party's burgeoning anticolonial influ-ence, demanded its suppression.[28]

A strong rival to Messali and the ENA was the Fédération des élus musulmans d'Algérie (FEMA). The composition of this group, mainly French-educated intellectuals and former Muslim officers of the French army, marked it as a decidedly elite, middle-class minority. Because it advocated cultural assimilation with France, the FEMA was also in the curious position of sharing one of the colons' objec-tives. The FEMA adopted a strategy of nonviolence in promoting Algeria's further integration with France. Thus, in class background as well as in political objectives, the FEMA assimilationists were sharply pitted against the ENA.

Ferhat Abbas, a pharmacist from the town of Sétif, became the most prominent leader of the FEMA elites. He articulated the essence of assimilationism in an article entitled "La France, c'est moi:"

> If I had discovered the "Algerian nation," I would be a national-ist. . . . But I will not die for the Algerian fatherland because it does not exist. I have questioned history, the living, and the dead. . . . Nobody spoke to me about it. Of course, I did dis-cover the "Arab empire," the Muslim empire which honored Islam and our race, but these empires are dead. . . . Therefore we have cast aside all foggy ideas and idle fancies to bind our future definitively to that of French endeavor in this country.[29]

Abbas' position clearly put him at odds with Messali. These two leaders representing contradictory objectives (self-determination versus assimilation) emerged as the pillars around whom Muslim Algerians organized in the interwar period.

Quite apart from Messali and the ENA, the assimilationist position also came under attack from the Association of Reformist 'Ulama, a small group of Quranic scholar-legists. It was organized in 1931 by

Shaykh Abdelhamid Ben Badis who, more than any other religious
figure, promoted Islamic nationalism in Algeria, achieving wide influence among the educated and peasants alike.[30] The 'ulama combined traditionalist (Islamic) and modern nationalist aspirations in
their program, demanding political independence, adoption of
Arabic as the official language, and rejection of French culture.
     The Islamic doctors contributed to the rise of nationalism in the
interwar period by undermining the authority of French-sponsored
marabouts.[31] The marabouts, mystics who fostered an animistic cult
embracing variants of Islam, had blocked nationalism in the countryside by indoctrinating the fallahin in superstitious notions and curs-
ing the new political ideas. Under the leadership of Ben Badis, the
'ulama caused Islam to serve as a unifying element in the development
of nationalism, thereby facilitating the growth of secular nationalist
organizations.
     Despite the progress of the Muslim nationalist leaders after World
War I, the Europeans' economic and political monopoly of Algerian
society was not seriously questioned until the 1930s. France opened
the door to Muslim political participation in 1919 in Algeria's general
councils (where Muslims held one-fourth of the seats), in the municipal councils (where token Muslim representation was tolerated), and
in mayoral elections (in which Muslims voted). Muslims were also
accepted in the *délégations financières*, advisory bodies chosen by restricted suffrage to vote the Algerian budget. Muslim representation
consisted of middle-class elements dedicated to the FEMA position in
all of these institutions.
     The colons dominated the entire system economically. In agricul-
ture, for instance, European farmers owned nearly all of the country's
irrigated lands. Few proprietors with large, fertile farms were Muslim.
In administration, the Europeans accounted for 86 percent of all civil
servants.[32] Industry, which began to develop after 1930, belonged to
Europeans completely.
     Léon Blum's Popular Front came to power in France in 1936
promising to alter the relationship between the Europeans and Algerians. The Blum-Viollette plan proposed to grant rights of citizenship
to an estimated 20,000 to 25,000 Muslims.[33] If passed, the bill would
have reinforced the assimilationists' position. But colon opposition
condemned the plan to failure, as manifested by the resignation of all
the European mayors in Algeria. The colons then intensified their

pressure on the Blum government by demanding suppression of the nationalist parties; the ENA, which had been revived by Messali in 1933, was then dissolved again. In their reaction to the Blum-Viollette plan, the Europeans revealed the intransigent stance they were to hold against Muslim political development throughout the history of French Algeria.

Messali counteracted Blum's dissolution of the ENA in March 1937 by regrouping his followers into a new party called the Parti du peuple algérien (PPA). The communists in Blum's government refused to defend the ENA, especially its call for independence; consequently, Messali broke all ties with the communists and began to organize the PPA with Muslim nationalists exclusively. The PPA program was less aggressive and secular than the ENA program, but still advocated national independence together with Pan-Arabism (Arab unity) and the Islamic goals of the 'ulama. Its emphasis on agrarian and economic reform attracted Algerian workers (in France and Algeria) from whom the PPA recruited most of its following. Before the PPA could acquire a significant hold on the general Muslim population, however, the French arrested Messali and other PPA leaders. Messali was detained in 1937 and convicted of sedition two years later, but the PPA kept together its 10,000 members under secondary leaders and went underground during World War II.

The assimilationists, greatly disillusioned by the colons' refusal to endorse the Blum-Viollette plan, began to turn toward the nationalist positions of Messali and the 'ulama. Mohammed Salah Bendjelloul, a Constantine physician and founder of FEMA, resigned from the assimilationists' party in 1938 to form a radical faction called the Rassemblement franco-musulman algérien (RFMA). Like the FEMA, the new movement drew its support from the small Muslim middle class; unlike the FEMA, it adopted an independent nationalist program demanding Algerian autonomy. The RFMA also pressed for abolition of laws discriminating between Muslims and Europeans.

Ferhat Abbas also abandoned FEMA and organized the Union populaire algérienne (UPA), a movement similar to its predecessor but more explicit in its demand for progressive Muslim enfranchisement. Abbas did not, however, call for Algerian independence. Neither of the new assimilationist factions was as militant as the PPA, but both reflected the growing strength of the nationalists.

The French condemned the Muslim movements generally and regarded the PPA and the 'ulama association as the most intolerable. France outlawed both immediately after the outbreak of World War II. The FEMA and the UPA were allowed to continue activity, but they too encountered European hostility when the Vichy regime took power in June 1940. Increasingly, the assimilationists realized that their positions had become untenable, not only in nationalist but also in European circles. The experience of Abbas was a case in point: the French prohibited Muslim participation on the few advisory committees then functioning, and Abbas, on December 16, 1940, attempted to protest the new restriction. He quickly found himself ejected from the governor general's office and impugned publicly as anti-French. [34] Precisely because the Vichy regime discredited the assimilationists, it unintentionally expedited their conversion to nationalism.

When the Free French provisional government sought to recruit Algerians for the French army, Muslim leaders demanded certain concessions as a condition for their participation. The Algerian Manifesto, as their proviso was entitled, had been authored by Abbas in collaboration with PPA and 'ulama leaders. It represented the first act of unity among the Muslim movements and established the most refined statement of their goals since the beginning of nationalist organization. The Manifesto's key demands included the abolition of colonialism; the elimination of the colons' land monopoly and redistribution of their farms among the peasants; the institution of Arabic as an official language; and the acceptance of Muslims in the new Algerian government. It did not demand full self-determination and instead called for federal autonomy between Frenchmen and Muslims in Algeria. Nonetheless, the Manifesto revealed growing nationalist militancy among all Algerian leaders.

In response to the ultimatum, General Charles de Gaulle, leader of the Free French National Liberation Committee, agreed in December 1943 to admit certain categories of Muslims to French citizenship without requiring them to renounce their Quranic civil status. The French acted on this agreement in March 1944 by extending voting rights to most adult Muslim males (though for a separate college) and raising the proportion of Muslim representatives in local assemblies. The first electoral college, which had previously excluded Muslims, was opened to some 60,000 Muslim lycée and university graduates, former army officers, war veterans, and civil service bureaucrats. [35] France enlarged the proportion of Muslims elected by the second college for the assemblies, including the French parliament, to parity with the Europeans. Muslims also gained the right to elect 40 percent of the members of city and regional councils and the same percentage of the délégations financières.

The Gaullist measures did little to decrease the Europeans' overwhelming superiority in both electoral colleges, in local assemblies, and in the municipal governments. The laws also failed to satisfy either the Muslims or the Europeans. The Algerians rejected them as inadequate since they fell short of the Manifesto's demands; the Europeans first denounced them as excessive concessions to the nationalists, then nullified the proposed changes by simply refusing to enforce them.

The defeat of the Gaullist proposals fell like a death blow to Abbas' stature in the Muslim community. In an effort to regain lost influence, he replaced the UPA with the Amis du manifeste et de la liberté (AML) for the express purpose of leading the campaign for the Manifesto's original demands. The AML recruited freely in 1944 after de Gaulle authorized all Muslim organizations to operate again. Soon the AML claimed a membership of 500,000. [36] Abbas maintained formal leadership of the movement but gradually lost control to the urban middle class and the workers of Messali's PPA who pressed for greater militancy. Under Messalist influence, the AML veered from its initial goal of federalism in the French system to the demand for an Algerian state associated with any system it chose. The Messalists confirmed their nationalist leadership position at the AML congress of 1945 when they won adoption of a resolution proposing an Algerian parliament and government. In effect, Abbas' assimilationist movement had come very close to advocating independence.

What ultimately catalyzed the nationalists into an unequivocally militant movement were the events occurring at an armistice celebration in Sétif, Algeria, on May 8, 1945. In the parade Muslims hoisted the flags of green and red Algerian nationalism while shouting demands for Messali's release. The French police attempted to seize the flags and thereby incited a bloody clash between Muslim and European demonstrators. The ensuing riot produced heavy Muslim fatalities as the police often fired indiscriminately into Muslim crowds. Both sides reported significant casualties, the French claiming 197 killed or wounded, and the nationalists estimating Muslim losses at 50,000. [37] If a date clearly marking a turning point in nationalist development can be set, it must be that of the Sétif massacre because it formed a wedge between the choices of assimilation and Algerian self-determination. In fact, choices scarcely existed because the balance had shifted irrevocably to the side of political independence.

Governor General Yves Chataigneau sought to appease the Algerians by proposing general amnesty for all convicted of political crimes and other acts classified as inimical to the sovereignty of Algeria. The first Constituent Assembly, meeting in Paris on March 16, 1946, swiftly passed the bill. The governor later released Abbas and several AML partisans who had been detained after the Sétif riots. The French arrested the most militant leaders, but it was Messali's detention that really intensified nationalist fervor among PPA forces.

Abbas, who believed the PPA was partly responsible for the Sétif episode, abandoned the 'ulama-PPA-AML coalition and founded a third organization, the Union démocratique du manifeste algérien (UDMA). This party aspired to an autonomous Algerian republic federated with France and attracted most of its support from the Muslim intellectuals and professionals. The UDMA seemed to reveal its strength in the second Constituent Assembly elections of June 1946 when it won eleven out of the thirteen seats in the second college. This victory was deceptive, however, because neither the PPA nor the RFMA participated in the elections. Bendjelloul withdrew from the race in favor of Abbas, and the PCA, defeated in an earlier election, threw its support to the UDMA. The party's electoral success belied its potency, for the UDMA, still led by middle-class elites, had lost its rank and file to Messali. Not yet a nationalist, Abbas never regained his prestige among the Muslim leaders or masses.

The Paris government released Messali in October 1946. He returned immediately to the political front to organize the Mouvement pour le triomphe des libertés démocratiques (MTLD). The new movement demanded a sovereign Algerian constituent legislature and the evacuation of French troops. From Bouzarea, site of the MTLD headquarters, Messali recruited the more militant nationalists, most of whom were urban workers or former members of the French army, and deliberately shunned the middle-class groups supporting Abbas. The PCA attempted to recoup its losses in previous elections by proposing to Messali that a national coalition of the MTLD, PPA remnants, the UDMA, and the PCA be formed to run as a unit in the forthcoming

November elections for the French National Assembly. Messali, however, had at this time come to view himself as the paramount chief among the nationalist leaders and increasingly assumed a dictatorial stance in the movement. He rejected the joint-front proposal and, on his insistence, the MTLD contested the elections alone, winning only five of the fifteen seats. [38]

Rise of the Insurrectionists

Messali reacted to the later nationalist disaffection by adding more militant demands to the MTLD program, including universal suffrage, abolition of French control over religion and education, and complete independence. His response did not attract a militant following in his own movement, for political participation was not the main interest of the MTLD's newest elements.

The newcomers, young nationalists who did not derive from middle-class backgrounds, had entered political activity through the PPA during and after World War II. They followed Messali when he created the MTLD but were already resolved to use armed action for winning independence. The MTLD leader, still clinging to nonviolent, legalistic methods, found his position threatened by the young militants. This tension was evident at the MTLD convention of March 1947 when Messali barely managed to get his proposal for nonviolent reform endorsed. The militants failed in their bid for the establishment of a paramilitary force, but it seemed clear that the nationalist thrust was moving toward armed insurrection.

The young nationalists achieved ascendance in the nationalist movement after the enactment of the Algerian statute. The new law, voted by the French National Assembly in September 1947, repudiated the notion of progressive assimilation and ordered the creation of two separate communities in Algeria, one European and the other Muslim. It classified Algeria as a group of French départements having separate civil status, financial autonomy, and a common administrative structure. To harmonize decision-making, the statute proposed that a Council of Government and an elected Algerian Assembly (each composed of sixty members) assist the governor general in policy matters. Some 464,000 Europeans and 58,000 Muslims with French civil status would elect the first college, while some 1,400,000 Muslims would elect the second college. [39] Although the law discriminated in favor of the *évolués* (elite Muslims), it did not propose significant changes for muslim representation.

Like the Gaullist measures three years earlier, the Algerian statute failed to appease any of the interested parties. It satisfied neither the Messalists, who demanded independence, nor the Europeans, who were determined to maintain "French Algeria," nor even the UDMA, which advocated assimilation. In the face of demands ranging from sovereignty to no change at all, the law represented a desperate effort by the Fourth Republic to assert its authority in the colony. France's ambivalent gesture, coupled with the colon-rigged (Algerian) Assembly elections of April 1948, directly promoted the rise of the young militants in the nationalist movement.

It is unlikely that any liberal French policy could have deflected the militants, for late in 1947 they had resolved to advance the nationalist cause through armed struggle. Rejecting Messali's leadership, they split from the MTLD and organized, in May 1948, a clandestine paramilitary force called the Organisation spéciale (OS).[40] The architect of the OS was nationalist intellectual Hocine Ait Ahmed. Then twenty-two years old, he was a militant who had grown impatient with the MTLD's nonviolent methods. The other core members of the OS included Belkacem Krim, twenty-four years old, a soldier in the French army during World War II; Mohammed Boudiaf, twenty-seven years old, also a former French soldier, and the man who first proposed the formation of a paramilitary force; Rabah Bitat, twenty-one years old, a newcomer to nationalist activity; Ahmed Ben Bella, twenty-eight years old, a former master sergeant in the French army; and Mohammed Khider, a former PPA nationalist who at thirty-four was the oldest member of the OS vanguard.

All were relatively unknown in the nationalist leadership, and all had entered into nationalist activity largely through the PPA and the MTLD. Khider stood out as the most politically experienced member of the OS because he had previously represented the Muslim district of Algiers (i.e., the Casbah) in the French Chamber of Deputies. Except for Ait Ahmed and Boudiaf, none of the OS men was college-educated or considered an intellectual. The distinguishing characteristics of the insurgent group were its youth, its repudiation of reformist methods, and its determination to realize complete independence.

The OS began its activity by amassing arms and funds to supply a guerrilla force. For instance, Ben Bella organized a holdup of Oran's central post office in April 1949 which netted over 3 million French francs (about $9,000);[41] this exploit soon enabled him to replace Ait Ahmed as the OS commander. In preparing for insurrection, the OS men established cells in central and western Algeria and in the eastern regions around the Aurès mountains. A plan for a secret army with a nine-man general staff was discussed but never implemented. For the time being, the militants concentrated on drilling new recruits in the essentials of guerrilla warfare. The OS had gained about 1,800 members when the French secret service uncovered its existence in March 1950 and arrested about a hundred of its members,[42] forcing others into hiding.

The future revolutionaries started critical collaboration with Gamal Abdel Nasser of Egypt during this time. Nasser, who came to power in 1952, was emerging as the leader of the Arab world, particularly as the spokesman against European imperialism in Arab countries from west to east.[43] With his support, the Maghrib Office was established in Cairo to promote the anticolonial movements of Morocco, Tunisia, and Algeria. The Arab League, with headquarters in Cairo and dominated by Nasser, participated in the development of the Maghrib Office.[44] Cairo gave the OS leaders another advantage that would become important strategically during the revolution: there they met leaders of the Moroccan and Tunisian nationalist parties from whom the Algerians later received crucial military and material support. Egypt, then, was a haven where "the Algerian nationalists could go, a place where the architects of rebellion could draft plans and start to build without fear of arrest."[45]

Policy differences agitated relations between the OS and Nasser for a while because the Algerians pressed for their goal of Algerian independence in opposition to Nasser's Pan-Arab proposal for the liberation of the entire Maghrib through the unified action of nationalists in the three Maghrib countries. Ben Bella, who had escaped from prison following the French arrests of 1950, reached Cairo in 1953. He reinforced the argument of other OS leaders, like Khider, who maintained that the anticolonial movements of North Africa represented *national*, as opposed to Pan-Arab, sentiments and that therefore the establishment of a supranational (Maghrib) organization was both impractical and unrealistic. In the end, Nasser yielded to the Algerians' position and directed chiefs of his military staff to assist Ben Bella in preparing the Algerian rebellion.[46] The Algerians gained from Egypt not only organizational support, but eventually diplomatic, military, and financial assistance as well.

Inside Algeria, meanwhile, the OS's suppression caused grave repercussions on the UDMA-MTLD alliance. Abbas broke with Messali's remaining faction, fearing that continued association might implicate him with former MTLD members in the OS. A split occurred between Messali and Hocine Lahouel, who was a militant and secretary general of the MTLD's central committee. In part, the differences between them involved conflicting perspectives on policy. Messali, having made the jump from communism to Pan-Arabism since the 1920s, opposed the use of violence; Lahouel, an advocate of Maghrib unity and a nationalist much younger than Messali, endorsed the OS program. But their dispute was essentially a conflict of personality resulting from Messali's self-proclaimed status as "the father of Algerian nationalism."[47] Lahouel abhorred his leader's egoism, insisting that the nationalist movement could not tolerate a cult of personality.

The split deepened at the second MTLD convention held in Belgium in July 1954. Messali apparently sought to preclude OS members from attending and, with the backing of about 150 close followers,[48] had himself elected MTLD president for life. The Messalists passed a resolution abolishing the central committee and then resolved to recover MTLD funds held by Lahouel. It is believed that Lahouel did not attend the Belgium meeting, but he convened a third MTLD convention in Algiers a month later. The new convention, stacked with militants supporting Lahouel, introduced the principle of collective leadership to guide nationalist organization and voted full powers to a restored central committee.

Thus, there emerged two conflicting factions in the MTLD: one composed of Lahouel's partisans and known as the Centralists; the other supporting Messali and popularly called the Messalists. This fissure became more critical later when the OS reorganized its forces and finalized a plan of insurrection.

By 1954, certain economic and political factors in Algeria reinforced the Muslim inclination to insurrection. The material conditions of the Europeans had been improving since 1952 as a result of Marshall Plan assistance. In contrast, Muslim conditions had either remained relatively stagnant or had absolutely deteriorated. For example, the Europeans monopolized Algerian industry and continued to dominate the civil bureaucracy. Some 21,650 colons, constituting a mere 2 percent of the total European population of 984,000 settlers,[49] controlled at least a third of the country's farmlands, or five million acres of the most fertile and cultivated soil.[50] At the same time, two-thirds of the Muslim population eked out an existence from some of the worst farm regions. While the Europeans could be considered fully employed, only 570,000 Muslims held gainful employment in industry, commerce, or administration,[51] and a mere 200,000 worked regularly in agriculture.[52] Muslim unemployment was estimated at two million.

While such factors constituted the immediate background to the Algerian revolution, in a larger sense the whole history of French colonialism lay behind the Muslims' decision to revolt. The Europeans' long disruption and control of Algerian society had also brought into existence the leaders whose education and political and military experience enabled them to successfully challenge the colonial system. To the militant Muslim vanguard violence appeared to be the ultimate response. As Fanon notes in his analysis of Algerian colonialism, this was the same force that the Europeans had always used to maintain their hegemony over the colonial society.[53]

Assimilation ceased to be a viable alternative among Algerians after the Sétif massacre. Young militants in the PPA and the MTLD assailed it vigorously, and by 1947 they had succeeded in reducing nationalist options to violence or nonviolence. When the nationalists polarized over the ends and means of their movement, the result was the emergence of the young OS insurrectionists. Add to these factors the impact of two World Wars, Muslims in the French army acquiring new ideas of nationalism, the promulgation of the Atlantic Charter, the nationalists' demands for an Arab-Islamic cultural revival, and France's defeat at Dienbienphu, and the stage is set for the entry of the FLN as a violent, revolutionary party.

2

Emergence of the FLN

The outbreak of the Algerian rebellion in 1954 heralded the death of colonialism and the rise of the FLN as the guiding force in the nationalist movement. Very soon after the rebellion, this incipient party movement achieved military and political monopoly over the nationalist struggle by utilizing a variety of weapons, including coercion and cooptation of the existing Muslim and communist organizations. The FLN rebels were convinced that winning independence necessitated the unity of all Muslims, a task that could be best accomplished through a single organization. Developing functional institutions within the FLN became their principal priority since the institutional development of the party movement was integrally related to the goals of national unity and waging the anticolonial war.[1]

This initial phase of the FLN's development foreshadowed the attempts at party building after independence. From the crucial FLN meeting in Soummam in 1956 sprang all the dominant problems concerning the party's wartime organization, leadership, and ideology. The Soummam meeting resolved some of the problems and postponed others, although the success of the anticolonial struggle and the FLN's viability after independence hinged upon a resolution of all. In their drive to defeat the French, FLN leaders concentrated on developing military institutions at the expense of political institutions and thereby largely determined the future destiny of the FLN.

Persuasion and Terror: The Making of Nationalist Unity

Shortly before the outbreak of rebellion, an alliance was formed between a faction of the Centralists and a new organization called

the Comité révolutionnaire d'unité et d'action (CRUA). A paramilitary force and predecessor to the FLN, the CRUA regrouped the OS
insurrectionists who had remained underground after the French
banned the movement in 1950. The CRUA adopted the Lahouelist
principle of collegial leadership, hoping to achieve nationalist unity
before staging the rebellion.

Six members of the defunct OS constituted the core of CRUA leadership: Ben Bella, Ait Ahmed, Khider, Boudiaf, Krim, and Bitat.
Three new militants of obscure backgrounds—Larbi Ben M'Hidi,
Mourad Didouche, and Mustapha Ben Boulaid—aligned with the
CRUA. The nine leaders, later known as the "historic chiefs," represented a group unwilling to compromise on the necessity of violence
for gaining independence. Their commitment distinguished them
from nationalists like the Messalists who intended to maintain the old
leadership's cautious, legalistic policies. Like Messali, Ferhat Abbas
did not join the insurgents and apparently had no part in the crucial
decisions that followed.

The CRUA leaders sought a realignment of nationalist forces early
in 1954 by urging militants among the Centralists and Messalists to
join them in resolving the division in the nationalist movement. The
insurrectionists presented them with a plan of direct armed action in
order to provoke general agreement on the timing of the rebellion.
Gradually, the CRUA attracted the support of militant Centralists,
but the moderates, perhaps a majority, refused to take an affirmative
position.[2] The moderate Centralists stipulated that nationalist unity
and a specific timetable of strategy should precede the rebellion.
CRUA leaders rejected this proposition, insisting that action itself
would catalyze the desired unity. A growing number of Centralists
eventually yielded to the CRUA's determined, unequivocal position,
whereas Messali and his group remained intransigent to the end.

The CRUA leaders then conducted a series of clandestine meetings
at home and abroad to set a date for the revolt. On the night of November 1, 1954, a small but coordinated band of insurgents struck some
seventy French military and police garrisons, depots, and other strategic targets.[3] The critical region of violence centered in the Aurès
mountains. Perhaps only a dozen persons died in the assaults in this
area, yet these initial incursions provided the rebels with temporary
control of several small towns such as Batna and Arris.[4] Greater

Kabylia, regional homeland of the Berber population, became a major theatre of war. The insurrectionists had coordinated the uprisings with their North African allies and, upon the outbreak of rebellion, Cairo radio broadcast far and wide the emergence in Algeria of the FLN.

In unison with the military action, the rebels distributed a tract to the Algerian people outlining their political objectives. The tract declared that the FLN's principal objective, political independence, required the "restoration of the sovereign democratic Algerian state within the framework of the principles of Islam."[5] The proclamation described the rebels' domestic objectives as forging "political renewal by redirecting the national revolutionary movement on its true path" and "unifying the efforts of the Algerian people to liquidate the colonial system."[6] It also set forth the FLN's foreign and diplomatic objectives which included, inter alia, "making the Algerian problem one of international concern."[7] For the first two objectives, the FLN organized a guerrilla army drawing upon all regional and ethnic groups of the Muslim population. For the third, Ben Bella set up an external munitions delegation in Libya, and Ait Ahmed headed a diplomatic delegation to present the Algerian case to the United Nations.

The FLN proclamation stressed the fact that the rebels acted "completely independent of either of the two factions which are struggling for power."[8] This statement, referring to the dissident Centralists and Messalists, asserted that the FLN group, a "team of young men and active supporters, after careful and due consideration, joined forces with other groups of true and active supporters in order to take advantage of this propitious moment to rescue our nationalist movement from its impasse—an impasse into which it has been dragged by clashing interests and personal rivalry."[9] As for the local population, the FLN considered all Muslims duty-bound to promote the FLN charter "so that we may save our country and regain our freedom."[10] Thus, the FLN shaped its program to appeal politically and psychologically to the indigenous population.

The extent to which the FLN political program drew upon aspects of Algerian political culture should be noted. The goal of independence was partly predicated upon the religious principles of Islam. At no time did the rebels publicize the insurrection as a *jihad*, or Muslim holy war, but it cannot be doubted that the inclusion of the Islamic proviso expanded nationalist appeal among the peasant masses and the more traditional elements in urban areas. The Islamic imprimatur contrasted with every other feature of the proclamation's thoroughly rational, Western political concepts. The chapter on independence, for instance, recognized respect for "the basic rights of man without distinction of race and creed." [11] The whole tenor of the FLN proclamation reflected the secular revolutionary notions of the Westernized insurrectionists.

The military component of the FLN was named the Armée de libération nationale (ALN). Ben Bella and Ben Boulaid began preparations for the rebel army during a secret meeting in Tripoli in late summer 1954; Ben Bella, chief of munitions, and Ben Boulaid, chief of the underground in the Aurès mountains, appeared to be its major architects. The army then consisted of about 2,500 guerrillas, [12] and most commandos in charge of the guerrilla forces had gained fighting experience in the French army during World War II or later in the OS. On the whole, however, the guerrillas were poorly armed, inadequately supplied, and unprofessional in modern warfare.

ALN guerrillas generally resided among the Algerian masses and thereby obtained provisions for themselves and communal support for the revolutionary cause. Neutrality ceased to exist as a Muslim option, for the guerrillas subjected politically moderate Algerians to acts of terror and persecution, and often murdered those who collaborated with the French (the *harki*). For example, Krim and Amar Oumrane, another founding member of the CRUA, directed twenty-one different assassinations in the rural town of Tazmalt against local Muslim bureaucrats in the French administration; the assassinations totally eliminated Muslim officeholders in that town. [13] As an insurgent force fighting an unconventional war, the ALN applied guerrilla warfare techniques against pro-French Muslims as well as the Europeans. The ranks of the FLN increased greatly in later years, generally because of voluntary commitment to the nationalist program but sometimes as the result of coercion or terror.

In an effort to systematize military organization, the FLN leaders divided the country into six *wilayat*, or military districts, each under the militant vanguard of the army. [14] Weapons were scarce in the early days, but daring raids and aid from abroad (from Egypt and Tunisia especially) augmented the supplies. From such modest beginnings, the ALN developed into a highly organized military force, receiving contraband arms from abroad and subsistence and recruits from the local population.

The FLN rebellion, which the French authorities initially dismissed as a minor, localized incident, accelerated so rapidly that the Paris government managed to have its state of emergency bill approved by the National Assembly in April 1955. The increase in French troops dispatched to contain the rebellion attested to the success of the ALN; in 1954, about 50,000 French soldiers were stationed in Algeria as compared to nearly 400,000 at the close of the war. This last figure represented nearly eight times the number of men officially under the ALN. [15] In a strictly military sense, France probably could have won the war if it had been willing to suffer the costs in human and material resources, but it had no means whatever of dissevering the commitment of most Muslims to the FLN. The success of the ALN, therefore, must be attributed not simply to military exploits, but also to the political and psychological strategy of the FLN.

Once the rebellion was a *fait accompli*, the issues previously separating the CRUA from the Messalists and the dissident Centralists became moot points. The moderate groups had seen the FLN take the initiative and now felt compelled to accommodate themselves to its program and leadership. The FLN undercut the constituency of other nationalist factions by restricting membership in the FLN to those militants who had broken organizational ties with the other factions. Hence, the FLN's drive for supremacy in the nationalist movement transcended past bickering over the possibility of unified action by the various nationalist parties.

Diplomatically, the FLN's ascendancy held paramount significance because the Algerians would have to delegate an *interlocuteur valable*, or genuine spokesman, to negotiate with France in the event of a cease-fire. Since the FLN insurrection preempted all programmatic designs of the Messalists, the UDMA, and the Centralists, it became increasingly evident that the FLN would be the single valid interlocutor for the whole nationalist movement.

The Messalists and the Centralists initially resisted FLN overtures and then attempted to maintain separate identities in the nationalist movement. But because the FLN had undertaken independent action and owed no debts to either faction, the two groups were forced to deal with the FLN on its terms. As a result, Lahouel ordered his supporters to unite behind the FLN when he yielded to the rebels late in November 1954. Among the more prominent in his entourage were Mohamed Yazid, a former leader of Algerian students in France, who soon replaced Ait Ahmed in the diplomatic delegation; Mohamed Lamine Debaghine, the ex-secretary general of the PPA; Abdelhamid Mehri, a political organizer from Constantine and a specialist in Arab affairs; and Benyoussef Benkhedda, a former Lahouelist member of the MTLD's Central Committee, who joined Krim and Ramdane Abane (a new guerrilla chief) in wilaya IV during May 1955. With the major Centralist leaders now on the side of the FLN, a major part of the FLN's early opposition disappeared.

If the Centralists accepted the FLN's appeal for unity, Messali did not. He repudiated the FLN's claim to political supremacy and went so far as to organize an opposition *maquis* (underground movement), the Mouvement national algérien (MNA). The new group consisted of Messali's old MTLD partisans (i.e., the Messalists) under another name. Early in 1955, FLN leaders began to condemn the MNA openly, charging it with collusion with the French police. FLN terror exterminated several small MNA maquis in Algeria. In France, where the MNA gained support from the emigrant Algerian workers, FLN advocates clashed with Messali's forces in 1957. The FLN directed these assaults not only to diminish the opposition, but also to acquire exclusive control of the monetary resources the Messalist workers sent to the MNA in Algeria. Under the constant threat of potential and actual violence, some MNA partisans in Algeria sought refuge among the harki while others surrendered to the FLN. Ultimately, the FLN's terrorism destroyed Messali's movement, and he himself fled the country, never to return.

After the FLN coopted the Centralists and eliminated the MNA, only two important leaders remained outside the party movement: Ferhat Abbas, still head of the UDMA, and Tewfik El Madani, an Islamic leader. Madani had succeeded Ben Badis as chief of the Association of Reformist 'Ulama and, after 1954, became the most active religious leader in the nationalist movement. Abbas continued to be important because he was universally recognized as a national public figure. Moreover, his party had demonstrated its strength in the 1951 Assembly election by garnering 11 percent of the vote (or about a fourth more than the MTLD and more than double the tally of the PCA).[16] The insurrectionists scoffed at the elections, but they recognized that the UDMA vote represented a sizable following in the Muslim middle class. To lure this constituency into the FLN, the rebels needed to win Abbas' support. Similarly, they had to obtain the endorsement of Madani to attract the traditionalist elements in the Muslim population.

Abbas' assimilationist policy became increasingly indefensible after the Sétif massacre, and the UDMA itself disappeared from nationalist decision-making centers after the FLN appeared on the stage with its revolutionary program. Such factors compelled Abbas to abandon his pro-French orientation and to take a definite stand on revolution. He was soon assisted in this conversion by the French police who arrested and tortured his brother-in-law. The decline of the UDMA and personal pressures explained why Abbas, standing beside Ben Bella and Khider at a press conference in Cairo on April 25, 1956, acknowledged his affiliation with the FLN.

The 'ulama, of course, had been prominent in the evolution of Algerian nationalism since the time of Shaykh Ben Badis. Through Madani, the FLN hoped to invest its movement with an aura of religious sanction. Shaykh Ibrahimi, president of the 'ulama, endorsed the rebel program shortly after the rebellion but later retracted his support because of the rebels' use of terror (which he opposed as a matter of moral principle). The Ibrahimi wing of the Muslim teachers did not actively oppose the FLN but still refused to support it. Then, as the rebellion grew in violence and intensity, a militant *alim*, [17] Madani, ascended the ranks of the 'ulama defending the Muslim war against France. Thus, he became the FLN's obvious and logical choice to represent the Islamic forces in the party movement.

On April 5, 1956, Madani made his way to Cairo (which had grown as a center of rebel organization owing to security risks inside Algeria) and joined the FLN. Like other notable converts to the party, such as Lahouel and Abbas, Madani provided the FLN with another national personality and with elements of the group he represented. Each conversion, in turn, created a potent psychological pull to attract noncommitted individuals who embraced the leader's particular ideological (or religious) views. The inclusion of the traditionalist leadership established the FLN as the only representative of all major Muslim groups in Algeria.

The PCA alone remained outside the FLN by 1956. The Algerian communists, like the Messalists and the UDMA, were astonished by the outbreak of rebellion and had just begun to perceive it dimly as the onset of an anticolonial revolution. In fact, the PCA opposed the struggle during its initial stages because wars of liberation, from the communists' perspective, belonged to industrial working-class societies. Victims of their own ideology, they failed to understand either the blend of nationalism and Islam in the FLN's program or the possibility of revolution in a peasant society.

When the PCA headquarters in Algiers later recognized and endorsed the FLN struggle, communists began to participate in it but insisted that their activity should be independent of the FLN. As explained by the PCA directorate, organic structures of nationalist unity "are not necessary and are even unjustified. In the event that the Front is hostile to a dual association, unity of political action at every echelon between the Front and our Party seems to us the most effective formula."[18] The PCA position was ironical because the communists, who followed orders from Moscow via the PCF in Paris, held little autonomy over their own internal party affairs and policies. Thus, the PCA's resistance to nationalist unity rested less on political and ideological grounds than on their strategic concern of going the way of the Centralists and the UDMA, namely, absorption into the FLN.

The contradictory demands on Algerian communists from the FLN and the PCF further undermined the PCA position. Whereas the official party line dictated a policy of separate involvement in the struggle, the FLN accepted communists into the movement only on the condition that they renounce their PCA membership, an act that they had to manifest symbolically by tearing up their PCA membership cards. The PCA dilemma was not resolved until March 1956 when the party relinquished its joint-front policy and decided to rally behind the FLN; this decision did not come until after the USSR recognized the FLN. Until then, Algerian communists had vacillated between a political kind of Scylla and Charybdis: between orders opposing the rebellion from abroad and demands imposed by the FLN at home.

Ideological differences aside, the PCA also differed greatly from the FLN in constituency. The native Jewish minority constituted the most dedicated proponents of Algerian communism;[19] their French citizenship and often European background made them suspect in the eyes of the FLN militants. Dr. Saddock Hadjares, an Algerian Jew, presided over the PCA in this period because Moscow had not yet decided whether the organization ought to be directed by a French-man or a Muslim. [20] This question was being deliberated at a time when most Muslim communists had abandoned the PCA for the FLN.

The one outstanding Muslim leader of the PCA, Amar Ouzegane, became its most eloquent detractor. In his book, *Le Meilleur Combat*, he refuted the entire record of nationalist participation that the party claimed upon independence:

> the PCA engaged only thirteen combatants for the zone of Algiers, 150-200 for the whole of the Algerian-Saharan territory, a figure which is a bit meager for a revolution on the very soil of the fatherland when the same PCA was able—once upon a time—to find two thousand Algerian volunteers to fight in the International Brigade. [21]

Like Muslim dissidents, the communists were permitted entry into the FLN only on an individual basis and never as a party en bloc.

In contrast to the PCA as a body were the Algerian communists who, as individuals, made important contributions to the nationalist struggle. Henri Alleg, editor of the PCA newspaper, *Alger républi-cain*, reported the only fairly accurate accounts of the rebellion to be found in the European press of Algeria; the French police banned the paper in 1955 and, two years later, threw Alleg into an interment camp on charges of jeopardizing the state. He continued his indirect support to the FLN struggle from prison by writing *La Question*, [22] an exposé of his (and others') torture at the hands of French soldiers. The book was smuggled into France where it awakened liberal and radical opinion to the horrors of repression practiced by the French in Alge-ria. To a great extent, Alleg's book helped to turn metropolitan public opinion against the colons' war campaign.

The FLN fashioned the *modus operandi* guiding its political strat-egy to accomplish two results: unity, or absorption of the nationalist forces under the FLN; and an alignment of special groups that could serve the party movement in nonmilitary spheres. By mid-1956, the first had been accomplished. Therefore, the rebels began to extend their organizational range to encompass other national groups, such as students and the trade unionists.

Of the civilian Muslim groups, the trade unionists easily qualified as the most important because they formed a substantial numerical force and were still divided between Messali's MNA and the metropolitan French trade unions. Most Algerian workers, whether in Algeria or France, belonged to the Confédération générale du travail (CGT), a French union associated politically with the PCF. Other French unions with Algerian workers included the Confédération française des travailleurs chrétiens (CFTC), a Catholic labor movement, and the Force ouvrière (FO), which was aligned with the French Socialist party. [23]

As noted earlier, the communists initially opposed the rebellion, a position that tended to deter Muslims in the CGT from joining the FLN. Messali further confounded the FLN's unity effort by organizing, in February 1956, the Union syndicale des travailleurs algériens (USTA), which was the very first Muslim labor organization. The USTA's immediate recognition by the International Confederation of Free Trade Unions (ICFTU) reinforced Messali's preemptive act against the FLN. The FLN reacted to the MNA initiative on February 24, 1956, by organizing the Union générale des travailleurs algériens (UGTA), the nationalist trade union. Aissat Idir and Rabah Djermane, Muslim unionists in Algeria, took leading roles in structuring the UGTA. The UGTA inaugurated its activity by organizing Algerian workers in the hospital, dock, tobacco, and railway trades, which existed almost exclusively in the urban areas. As a result of the FLN's terroristic activities against the USTA, the UGTA gained immediate successes in this effort.

The FLN, seeking to tighten the links between Muslim labor and the revolutionary party, clarified the mission of Algerian workers: "You, the Algerian workers are veritable political commissaries in the non-clandestine arena; your principal mission is overt struggle and legal promotion of the objectives of the FLN whose national revolutionary authority must be proclaimed." [24] The UGTA appropriated the Algiers office of the UDMA and soon prepared the strategy required to effect its mission. Labor militants Aissat Idir, Djermane, Boualem Bourouiba, Ali Majid, and others met in early 1956 to elect Idir as the first secretary general; five executive officers were also chosen to head the new organization. [25] Together this group developed the labor strategy that followed.

The UGTA implored all Muslim workers to withdraw from the French trade unions, and it began to establish itself rapidly in the major cities. Three weeks after its founding, the UGTA created regional unions in Algiers, Blida, and Oran, and recruited 110,000 workers. [26] Workers in Constantine and Bône set up other UGTA federations. Another feature of the UGTA strategy aimed at overriding the ICFTU's recognition of the USTA and gaining the international body's endorsement of the UGTA. The UGTA triumphed as the dominant spokesman of Algerian workers after a few months of organizational activity, as verified by the general strike of July 5, 1956.

The strike disabled French businesses in every urban area of the country. The most severely affected facilities included the shipping and port businesses where the UGTA vanguard, the dockers, took action. The success of the strike confirmed the UGTA's authority over Algerian workers nationally; this fact prompted the ICFTU to admit the nationalist trade union to full membership (on July 7, 1956) and simultaneously to expel the USTA. From this time onward, the organized Algerian workers received their orders from the UGTA, and therefore from the FLN.

Thus, two years after the November rebellion, a series of political and military developments had transformed the splintered nationalist movement into a unitary political organization. Because the FLN confronted the rival factions with a *fait accompli* by the act of rebellion, each became obliged to make a specific response to it. Some organizations, like the MNA and the PCA, reacted by resisting consolidation under the FLN, while others, like the Centralists and the UDMA, succumbed to it. At the same time that the FLN managed its rivals, through political suasion or terror, it also moved to channel their (nominally) nonpolitical constituencies into its own structures. It remained for the FLN to institutionalize the movement it had unleashed.

The Soummam Valley Congress

The revolutionaries' agreement on the indispensable need for unified military action had enabled them to continue the war against France and to establish the FLN's supremacy in the nationalist movement. But it did not suffice to resolve a wide range of outstanding political questions, such as the form and structure of leadership authority, whose resolution was essential to the FLN's wartime development and its continued development after independence. The FLN leaders had not even discussed these questions. As will be seen, this was no coincidence because any attempt to settle them was certain to expose certain intraleadership conflicts that had existed in the FLN command since 1954. In short, the leadership's preoccupation with waging war concealed the problems on which no common agreement could be reached.

A major question was whether leaders of the interior (i.e., the movement within Algeria) ranked above the external leaders (i.e., FLN representatives abroad) in decision-making authority. Likewise, the sharing of power between FLN political leaders and the ALN guerrilla chiefs remained in question. The FLN's relationship to supportive civilian groups such as trade unionists and students had not been defined. Finally, the FLN, which was represented as a national revolutionary party, still lacked an ideology as well as political institutions and objectives.

The latent intraleadership conflicts were directly related to these questions. For instance, the absence of clear lines of authority between the internal and external leaders coincided with a competition for power between Ben Bella and the external delegation on the one hand, and Ramdane Abane (the new chief in wilaya IV) and his allies of the interior on the other. As head of the external delegation in Egypt, Ben Bella had become Nasser's close friend. This association strengthened Ben Bella's political influence abroad, and the internal leaders suspected that he would exploit it to usurp personal control of the movement. Abane, meanwhile, had risen in the echelon of internal leadership authority following the death of the "historic chief" Mourad Didouche (who was killed by the French early in 1955). He was now widely acknowledged as the interior's chief political leader, [27] and he was not willing to relinquish his new authority to Ben Bella.

The irresolution of such issues explained why the Soumman Valley Congress, which promised to resolve them, held such crucial importance. For the first time since the rebellion, almost all of the FLN's internal leaders met to create party institutions and to settle the important outstanding questions. The meeting began on August 20, 1956, and according to Duchemin:

> The Soummam Congress . . . constituted the most important event in the history of the FLN. It was from this Congress that the relations of the Front were defined with the trade unionists

of the UGTA and the students of the UGEMA. It was there also
that the ALN could draw lessons from twenty months of war and
finally establish the political objectives of the revolution. [28]

It should be pointed out that much remains unknown about what
really happened at the Soummam Congress because the revolutionaries withheld details of the meeting. Reasons of security often necessitated such action, but sometimes it resulted from the leaders' effort
to conceal intraleadership differences. The motive at Soummam
seems to have been a combination of the two.

Approximately fifty delegates attended the Soummam Congress. It
had been planned by Abane and the interior leaders while the entire
exterior delegation under Ben Bella was still abroad. The Soummam
delegates inaugurated their activity by creating the FLN's first political institution, the Conseil national de la révolution algérienne
(CNRA), a legislative body authorized to consider and approve the
FLN's general decisions. The CNRA had a total of seventeen full
voting members, eight of whom were the surviving "historic chiefs" of
the CRUA (i.e., all but Didouche), plus nine new leaders. [29] The group
represented a diversity of political views; it included "historic chiefs"
like Ben Bella and Krim, ex-Centralists like Benkhedda and Yazid,
moderates like Abbas, and the alim Madani. To this body of seventeen regular members, the congress appointed seventeen deputy
members who would replace any of the regulars felled or incapacitated by the hazards of war. [30]

The FLN's executive organ was named the Comité de coordination
et d'exécution (CCE). Five members of the CNRA belonged to this
decision-making agency: Abane, Krim, Benkhedda, Saad Dahlab,
and Larbi Ben M'Hidi, all leaders of the interior. They distributed its
ministerial duties entirely among themselves, with Abane in charge of
organization, Krim controlling liaison between the CCE and the
wilayat, Dahlab and Benkhedda, directing foreign relations and information (or propaganda) respectively, and Ben M'Hidi responsible
for general strategy. The distribution of power was a personal
triumph for Abane and the interior leaders.

Fairly distinct lines of jurisdiction were delineated between the two
party organs in the *Plateforme de la révolution algérienne*. The CCE,
a war council, commanded all political, diplomatic, military, and
administrative agencies of the FLN; the six wilaya chiefs received

their orders from the executive body and were directly responsible to it. Ultimate authority for making decisions relative to Algeria's future political status rested exclusively with the CNRA. When the CCE implemented policies determined by the CNRA in intervals between (CNRA) meetings, it could not act on such issues as negotiations, cessation of hostilities, an international solution to the Algerian problem, or the intervention of a third party into the Franco-Algerian conflict. As the supreme body, the CNRA could give the CCE wide powers or abolish it altogether by a two-thirds majority vote.

The congress enacted a provision expressly prohibiting any negotiations with the French until France recognized Algeria's independence. This specification was much more than a policy position; it was the Abane group's response to Ben Bella. They feared that he would seek a negotiated settlement on his own authority, without consulting the interior leaders, and this provision was designed to preclude it.[31] On the question of negotiations, as on others at Soummam, FLN policy was inseparably associated with the interior leaders' personal interests.

Institutionalization of the party movement was also a major concern of the Soummam delegates. As a guideline to decision-making in the FLN, they adopted the principle of collegial leadership as established by the CRUA in 1954. The proviso for collective authority reflected Abane's opposition to Ben Bella, who was accused of dereliction in his duties and failure to procure the arms and money necessary for the fighting forces.[32] The adoption of the collegial leadership principle was an implicit criticism of Ben Bella. Also apparently aimed at Ben Bella was the congress's declaration of independence from all foreign powers, including Egypt, which seemed to refer obliquely to his ties with Nasser. However, none of the political and military leaders possessed sufficient strength, either in following or resources, to monopolize the movement. Given their relative weaknesses, all could agree on the principle banning a "cult of personality," thereby assuring that no single leader would dominate the party apparatus.

Another high priority on the agenda related to the predominance of political over military matters. The congress decided that political prerogatives would prevail over the military, emphasizing that this provision affirmed "the essentially political aim of our struggle: national independence."[33] It recalled the fact that the revolution, sparked by men who qualified as much as politicians as militarists (i.e., the CRUA), had been joined at this time by others whose sole status was military; these included, in particular, the deputy wilaya commanders such as Said Mohammedi and Slimane Dhiles. This guideline was adopted to prevent the militarists from controlling major posts in the FLN, and, likewise, to guarantee that strictly military issues would be subordinated to the political. The principle gained majority acceptance, which indicated that the conduct of the movement remained in the hands of the militant politicians.

The Soummam Congress also determined the relationship between the internal and external leaders. Leaders actually directing the struggle inside Algeria formed the interior leadership, and those whose responsibilities required them to operate abroad (such as Ben Bella in charge of munitions or Ait Ahmed in the diplomatic mission) composed the exterior leadership. In the event of conflict between internal and external activities or needs, the delegates decided that the internal took priority.[34]

Was this decision based upon personal interest alone or upon strategic necessity, or both? Clearly, the internal leaders dominated the entire meeting, for the principals there included Abane, Krim, Ben M'Hidi, Amar Oumrane, and Youcef Zirout. Another interior leader Omar Ben Boulaid, who later replaced his brother (Mustapha Ben Boulaid) as head of wilaya I, did not attend the congress, although he had participated in its preliminary arrangements. Owing to various technical or security reasons preventing travel, however, the exterior delegation—which included Ben Bella and Khider in particular—did not appear. Ben Bella and Khider seemed to play no special role in the preliminaries which had been engineered by Zirout and his allies in wilaya II.[35]

The congress assigned the absent external leaders to positions either in the CCE or the CNRA, while reserving real authority for the internal leaders and their close lieutenants. Thus, Abane and company assumed control of the CCE. The most telling aspect of the internal leadership monopoly related to the sudden elevation of two men virtually unknown at this time: Lakhdar Ben Tobbal, who was Zirout's assistant (and son-in-law), and Abdelhafid Boussouf, who benefited from the patronage of Ben M'Hidi.[36]

Inevitably, the subject of leadership appointments raises the question of whether the internal leaders' control of the congress, especially the influence of Berbers like Krim and Abane, resulted in the formation of a narrow, self-interested cabal. Force of circumstances prevented the external leaders from attending; but this explanation fails to resolve the question because other important factors were simultaneously at play. One French critic, Bromberger, has described the congress as "a Kabyle affair, led from end to end by Krim and Abane."[37] While it cannot be doubted that they managed the meeting, it does not follow necessarily that they exploited it for the benefit of the Berber group. Too many Arabs participated and too much remained at stake nationally to substantiate this argument of ethnic conspiracy. Ethnic considerations may help to shed light on the existence of personal and family ties (owing to regional or village relations) among some of the major Berber leaders—such as Krim and Ben M'Hidi, or Zirout and Ben Tobbal—but not to determine the CCE's composition.

Rather, the answer seems to be that the internal leaders succeeded in gathering authority among themselves simply because they were the only FLN chiefs then on the battlefield. In the context of war, decisions had to be made rapidly, and therefore time worked to the advantage of the internal leaders. The principle of collegial rule survived but its scope was constricted greatly. For the first time, the internal-external division in the FLN leadership became generally acknowledged within the movement.

Reorganization of the ALN figured as another major item in the Soummam proceedings. The delegates maintained the system of six wilayat, expanding each to cover a specific locality under the command of a second lieutenant. Each command post was regulated by a political and a military representative of the FLN. A popular consultative assembly, chosen by direct election in each wilaya, discharged such responsibilities as fiscal allocations, legal and Islamic procedures, and police duties. In addition, the congress approved new programs to enhance the FLN's psychological warfare strategy; these included, notably, social services to dependent families. This social and military system operated with varying degrees of efficiency under the command of the ALN general staff.

Meanwhile, the absence of the external leaders caused difficulties in determining the personnel of the military leadership. In this matter, as on the question of political leadership, the internal leaders settled the issue. Krim, for instance, appropriated Ben Bella's former title as chief military commander; Krim's deputy, Oumrane, received the post of chief of supply. The internal leaders and their allies also gained command in other key positions. From time to time, new designations shifted to new men because of the exigencies of war; thus, when the ALN general staff later took refuge in Tunis, Moham-medi replaced Krim, who in turn was replaced by a wilaya captain named Amirouche. The predominance of the interior leaders charac-terized political leadership throughout the war.

The Soummam platform formalized the role of the UGTA and its relation to the party in an important section on the Algerian labor movement. The nationalist trade union was represented as different from its French antecedents (i.e., the CGT, the CFTC, and the FO) in all aspects, especially in the structure of leadership and ideological orientation. Several political directives were presented to the UGTA: the creation of FLN-UGTA groups in French business establish-ments, the civil service, and on the farms; and the concentration of UGTA forces in strategic and technical areas, like the utility or trans-portation outlets, where they could engage in sabotage or serve as liaisons to the political-military leaders.

The document noted that the UGTA's "backbone" was formed not by a "labor aristocracy" but by the most numerous and exploited labor classes, namely, the dockers, miners, and other urban workers. But this assertion glossed over the fact that Algeria's *organized* work-ers already comprised a labor aristocracy. At a time when more than 80 percent of Algerian workers subsisted on agriculture,[38] the UGTA executives by contrast could be considered an urban privileged caste among Muslim workers as a whole. For example, Aissat Idir worked as chief of personnel in a French business firm, Bourouiba as a rail-wayman, and Djermane as a docker. By Western industrial stand-ards, these were modest occupations, but not so in an underdeveloped country where the masses of the population remained unskilled, il-literate, and peasant.

A related, and perhaps more important, element of future conflict deriving from the Soummam platform involved its provision for trade union autonomy: "The FLN must not neglect the *political* role that it can play in supporting and consummating the *independent* action of the UGTA towards its consolidation and reinforcement."[39] [Empha-sis added.] Whether the FLN leaders genuinely envisaged the evolu-tion of an autonomous labor movement, or simply postscripted this provision as a matter of political expediency, has not been ascertained. But there can be no doubt that they failed to accurately gauge this vital element in the trade unionists' orientation, i.e., the French syndicalist background of the workers. This background determined the Algerians' ideological reference point originally and continued to guide their actions after the formation of the UGTA.

Substantial financial assistance from Algerian workers in France heightened the importance of the UGTA to the FLN. As the national labor organization, the UGTA represented the 600,000 workers in France, [40] and FLN leaders established the Fédération de France du FLN (FFFLN) in 1956 to direct them just as the FLN directed UGTA members in Algeria. Adapting FLN practices to the metropolitan context, the FFFLN "provided judicial services to the Algerians in France, paid monthly allowances to the families of political prisoners, set up commissions of hygiene to improve the living conditions of the workers, and organized armed groups to carry out police actions against the MNA or repressive landlords." [41] No exact figures on the FFFLN's monetary contributions have been obtained, but one UGTA official stated that over 1 million AF ($500,000) were received by FLN representatives in 1958; [42] another source reported that the total sum had risen to 450 million AF ($900,000) by 1961. [43] So important did the FLN leaders consider the FFFLN that, after 1958, they granted it representation on the CNRA that equaled that of the wilayat.

Because of their close rapport with the UGTA, the Soummam leaders rewarded the trade unionists by appointing Aissat Idir to the CNRA. Other important trade unionists like Amar Ouzegane and Ali Yahia Abdennour later held prominent posts in the FLN. However, after the French intensified the war in early 1957, it became increasingly dangerous for UGTA members to wage covert operations. Each strike led to arrests of UGTA militants and a consequent turnover of trade union leaders; in 1957, for example, seven different persons occupied the post of national secretary as arrests eliminated one leader after another. Toward the end of the war, the UGTA lost most of its influence in FLN decision-making centers because guerrilla leaders took control of the interior struggle.

Another important nonmilitary group that the Soummam delegates integrated into the new party structure was Algerian students. For this purpose, they turned to the Union générale des étudiants musulmans algériens (UGEMA), the Muslim student organization

organized by the FLN in July 1955 to mobilize Algerian students
behind the nationalist movement. UGEMA regrouped Algerian
students into a strictly Arab-Muslim organization, terminating their
affiliation with the liberal French student organization, the Union
nationale des étudiants français (UNEF). Although few students
played significant roles in the war or in the FLN organization proper,
Youssef Khatib, a medical student who used the pseudonym Si
Hassan, rose to the command of wilaya IV.

The participation of students was limited mainly to the university
milieu and to actions they could perform successfully. There were only
589 Algerian students at the University of Algiers when the rebellion
began.[44] They represented about one-tenth of the predominantly
European student body. Approximately 300 additional Algerian
students were enrolled in metropolitan French universities. In numbers, therefore, UGEMA represented a small constituency, a fact explaining why its members restricted their actions to situations that
minimized their vulnerability to the dangers of war. The students
called their organization a "unit of combat" in the nationalist struggle and dispatched diplomatic missions pleading the Algerian cause
to international student councils, specifically to the International
Student Conference (ISC) in the West and the Soviet-sponsored International Union of Students (IUS). The UGEMA and the UGTA
together constituted the FLN's national interest group organizations,
or its civilian constituency.

Viewed as a whole, the Soummam decisions advanced considerably
the institutional development of the FLN. From its pre-congress state
as a guerrilla organization, the FLN emerged after Soummam as a
party movement. An incipient party apparatus came into being with
the establishment of the CCE, the FLN's executive committee, and
the CNRA, its representative body. Clear lines of decision-making
authority were adopted to separate the political from the military
components of the organization. The party hierarchy was also differentiated between its civilian and military units. Thus, two years after
the rebellion, the FLN spawned a visible and growing party structure.

The components of the FLN after Soummam are shown in Figure 1.

The success of the Soummam delegates in establishing political
institutions contrasted with their attempt to formulate a party program of specific political and economic objectives that could be promoted both in wartime and, more significantly, after independence.

Figure 1. Organization of the FLN as Established at the Soummam
Valley Congress, August 1956

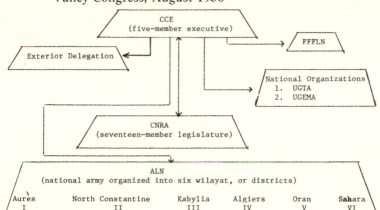

The Soummam platform set forth the minimal goals of the party
movement as follows: "The doctrine is clear. National independence
is the goal, and the means to its attainment is revolution destroying
the colonial regime."[45] "National independence" as a keystone of
policy negated the colonial regime but failed to articulate the specifics
of a domestic program. Beyond the immediate necessities of war, the
delegates undertook no further action to develop plans and preparations for future policy. Moreover, except for its grounding in nationalism, the platform failed to define the FLN's ideological perspectives.

Political policies could have been proposed at this time, but the tension between the internal and external leaders precluded serious
deliberations on this subject. Rather than propose policies that the
external delegation might subsequently oppose, the internal leaders
decided to make none at all. Consequently, leadership conflict caused
the congress to settle for a mere restatement of the FLN's original
broad objectives.

Meanwhile, in a different matter, a personal power struggle
developed between Ramdane Abane and Ferhat Abbas. This conflict
ostensibly arose over the so-called *préalable*, or whether France
should guarantee Algerian independence before the FLN agreed to
undertake negotiations for a cease-fire. The political disagreement,
however, disguised what at heart was a clash of personalities.

Abane and Krim, who distrusted Abbas' commitment to the FLN's revolutionary orientation, objected to the opening of negotiations without an advance guarantee. Abbas, on the other hand, favored negotiations in the absence of such a stipulation. He contended that insistence upon a préalable might cause France to refuse even to negotiate. Once the two belligerents began to negotiate seriously, Abbas believed, independence would surely follow. Two important FLN moderates—Mohamed Yazid and Ahmed Mehri (liaison chief for the Arab countries)—seconded Abbas' position. Complications of this nature tended to divert the congress's attention away from political policy to military strategy, a subject that all factions could accept as urgent.

The dispute between Abane and Abbas continued until early 1958 when the Abbas group gained temporary control of the movement and won majority acceptance of their view. The influence of Habib Bourguiba, president of Tunisia, helped to sway the FLN nationalists toward Abbas in this development. Bourguiba had sectioned off a part of Tunisian territory as a sanctuary for the Algerian rebels. In February 1957, he concluded an arms agreement with Ouzegane. The French retaliated by constructing "the Meurice-Challe Line,"[46] an electrified barbed-wire barricade, on the Algerian-Tunisian frontier; they further declared the right of hot pursuit into Tunisian territory. Bourguiba then pressed the case for negotiations, fearing that the war might spread into his own country, which had just become independent in 1956.[47] Since the FLN leaders depended on the continued support of this neighboring country, many heeded Bourguiba's counsel when he sided with Abbas.

The FLN forces at Soummam adhered to the basic principle of collective leadership, but at the end of the congress lacked a design of future political objectives. Indeed, the question of the préalable was the only instance in which they entertained any serious policy issue. The Soummam platform accorded political matters priority over military issues, but in practice the FLN leaders relegated political ends to military strategy. At this juncture, the FLN had not yet created a conceptual framework that could facilitate the development of the country's political values and organization after independence.

The leadership's preoccupation with military objectives, which assured a further prosecution of the war, had the indirect effect of retarding the FLN's political development. Any comprehensive effort to secure the establishment of political institutions, on the other hand, was certain to bring the intraleadership antagonisms more danger-ously into the open. Thus, two years after the November rebellion, a profound dilemma faced the FLN leaders: whether to proceed with the emphasis on military strategy or whether to risk the dissolution of the whole movement by trying to reach agreement on the consolida-tion of political institutions and definition of ideology. In the end, the FLN leaders opted for the military solution, and this choice sealed the wartime destiny of the FLN.

3

Politics and War

The FLN's executive council, the CCE, expanded the FLN throughout Algeria in the aftermath of Soummam. Party leaders had hitherto concentrated on organizing guerrilla forces in the countryside, but they now turned their attention to the urban areas, especially to Algiers, the capital city. Existing party cells were enlarged and new ones were created to bring recruits into the organization. In each wilaya, or military district, one or more cells operated under the command of an ALN commander and an FLN political officer. The objective was to mobilize the entire Muslim population behind the party movement. These developments immediately after Soummam constituted the most dynamic period of the FLN's institutional growth in wartime. Yet, this burst of institutional development was soon eclipsed by French military escalation and by intensified intraleadership strife resulting from an FLN decision to organize a formal government in exile.

Political independence, the basic objective of FLN leaders since 1954, became a foregone conclusion in June 1960 when de Gaulle agreed to begin discussions with the Gouvernement provisoire de la république algérienne (GPRA). Algerian nationalist unity, which the FLN had forged in the preceding years of struggle, was primarily responsible for inducing the French president to accept a negotiated settlement of the war. On the eve of independence, however, the latent conflicts and divisions in the FLN leadership erupted violently, culminating in the virtual disintegration of the FLN.

These fateful events occurred at a final CNRA meeting held in Tripoli in June 1962, the first general leadership meeting since the

Soummam Congress. The Tripoli Conference formed the background for the postindependence history of the FLN because it determined the outcome of the future political system and produced the first general statement of the FLN's program and ideology. Many of Soummam's unresolved problems surfaced again at this time and prevailed with an adverse effect on the FLN's development under the new independent regime.

Organization of the Masses

The political-military cells created after Soummam often reached whole communes or villages in the countryside, and usually some members of most families in urban areas. The cells performed a network of military, political, communications, and related functions. In addition to assisting the guerrillas, the majority in every unit, the cells maintained training schools for recruits, paramedical facilities, and quasi-judicial tribunals in which an FLN political officer settled disputes in accordance with the Soummam program and directives from the CCE. A system of mandatory taxation was imposed on the local population as another means of requiring Muslims to support the struggle. Through the cells, FLN members sometimes perpetrated acts of terror against Muslims who equivocated in response to the party organization or continued to collaborate with the French.[1]

Progressively, the new FLN structures functioned as an alternative political system to the colonial regime for the general Muslim population. Thomas Hodgkin has identified the political significance of the bourgeoning party movement:

> Following the classic pattern of revolutionary wars, what has come into being during these last years is not simply a new kind of army but also the rudiments of a form of state—with its clandestine (or semi-clandestine) local authorities, courts of justice, police schools, medical services, communications, and taxation.[2]

The FLN organization directly or indirectly affected the lives of most of the Muslim population. For the first time, large numbers of Algerian women entered the struggle in various supportive capacities, as suppliers of food or clothing, as messengers, and in some instances as saboteurs.[3]

Illustrative of the new cell-type organization was the Zone Autonome d'Alger (ZAA), a special FLN unit operating within wilaya IV
(Algiers). Together with military operations, the ZAA performed
several guerrilla-warfare functions under the direction of political
officers, a special bomb squad, and committees that included Muslim
intellectuals, businessmen, and other skilled persons.[4] While the
guerrillas and bomb squad conducted various strategic operations,
such as sabotage and armed assaults, the committees maintained,
among a number of useful noncombat activities, an extensive taxation
system that eventually netted the FLN as much as $300,000 annually.[5]
The ZAA contained less than 1,500 active members, but it succeeded
in holding the Europeans of Algiers in a state of terror for nearly a
year.

The FLN party movement was rapidly evolving into a political party
which, according to Coleman and Rosberg, can be defined as an association "formally organized with the explicit and declared purpose of
acquiring and/or maintaining legal control, either singly or in coalition or electoral competition with other similar organizations, over
the personnel and the policy of the government of an actual or prospective sovereign state."[6] Through cooptation, coercion, and recruitment, the FLN had developed as a mass-based party, integrating
military and civilian groups into the organization. It mobilized most
of the peasant masses either as guerrillas or as noncombat participants. The FLN political officer shared decision-making authority
with the wilaya commander in most of the military districts (especially
in wilaya II), which operated independently of each other.

FLN leaders at Soummam prepared the party movement to develop
as a strong, cohesive institution that would be sufficiently authoritative and representative to serve as the transitional link between war
and independence. It could be said that the basis for the new state
existed in the new structures of the FLN by 1957.

The CCE leaders' first important political decision came in early
1957 when they called a national labor strike "to show in a decisive
way the adhesion of the whole Algerian people to the FLN, its sole
representative."[7] The recently organized UGTA helped to organize
and lead the strike, which lasted from January 28 to February 4, 1957.
It succeeded in mobilizing large segments of the Muslim (especially
urban) population into the struggle; in Algiers, for example, 71

percent of the Muslim personnel stopped work in the postal and tele-
graph services, as compared with an almost total walkout in the railway system.[8] A secondary effect of the strike was to strengthen the
Algerians' case for independence in their appeals before the United
Nations. The strike provided concrete evidence that the local populace supported the FLN.

This "insurrectional strike," so called by the UGTA, appeared at
first sight to assure the FLN's future development as an expressly political institution. But this forceful show of the FLN's strength marked
the point at which the party was being increasingly diverted from its
political development to policies, strategies, and institutional forms
that were uniquely adapted to the exigencies of fighting a colonial
war. The immediate cause of this critical redirection was the famous
Battle of Algiers,[9] the massive assault that the French staged against
the residents of the Algiers' Casbah as a reprisal for the eight-day
strike. The cellular party organization was temporarily shattered by
the French campaign of destruction and brutality; many of its members were detained or killed, and survivors of the CCE fled to Tunis to
escape the oppression.

Elsewhere, the French hastened the FLN's disintegration by building the Meurice-Challe Line on the Algerian-Moroccan frontier. A
barricade of electrified barbed wire and mine fields had already been
erected on Algeria's eastern boundary (with Tunisia) in 1957. This
extension created two strategic impediments to FLN organization:
guerrilla activity was confined thereafter within Algeria's territorial
boundaries, and quite abruptly the external army was forced into involuntary withdrawal. Perhaps as many as 35,000 ALN troops sat out
the war in Tunisia, while about 10,000 remained in Morocco.[10]

More critical to the FLN's political consolidation was the discontinuity in party leadership caused by French counterinsurgency.
Probably the most crippling event occurred in October 1956 when the
French intercepted the four leaders of the exterior delegation (Ait
Ahmed, Ben Bella, Boudiaf, and Khider) during their secret flight
from Rabat to Tunis. A fifth passenger on the plane was Dr. Mostefa
Lacheraf, a historian, who served as an FLN information officer. As
their plane crossed Algiers, the French forced it to land and then
quickly conveyed the five men to prisons in France, where they stayed
for the balance of the war. With the regular army in enforced exile and

the external leaders in jail, responsibility for fighting the war fell completely upon the wilaya guerrillas and the few FLN leaders still in the
country.

The CCE leaders under Abane established new headquarters in
Tunis, striving to retain control of FLN units in Algeria. They hoped
to diminish the problem of fragmented leadership (between internal
and external leaders) from this liaison base, which was more accessible to FLN leaders but less vulnerable to French assaults. In Tunis,
the CCE executives arranged a second CNRA meeting to reorganize
the political leadership as a first step toward coordinating military
policies between the guerrillas in Algeria and those exiled in Tunisia
and Morocco.

The CNRA meeting actually took place in Cairo during August
1957 and was intended as a sequel to the Soummam Congress. To re-
vamp the FLN's political machinery, the Cairo delegates enlarged the
CNRA from thirty-four to fifty-four members, each holding full
voting rights, and increased the CCE from five to nine members. The
new CCE consisted of the pro-préalable group led by Abane and
Krim, the anti-préalable faction of Abbas, and other political and
military men favored by these two interests.[11] They appointed the
four imprisoned external leaders and Rabah Bitat (jailed in Algiers)
as ex-officio members of the CCE.

In what appeared to be a unilateral act, the CCE assumed wider
decision-making authority in the FLN. Only twenty-two members of
the old thirty-four member CNRA attended the meeting, and there is
no evidence that the Cairo delegates consulted the full CNRA membership before expanding the CCE's authority. To this extent, the
principle of collegial rule was compromised. The extension of CCE
authority to such matters as foreign policy suggested that the FLN
leaders intended to elevate themselves into an oligarchy over the general movement. If this was indeed the case, the oligarchy they created
still reflected nationalist contradictions, since the new CCE embraced
the disparate groups represented by Abane, Krim, and Abbas. This
eclecticism was necessary because neither faction then held sufficient
power to dominate the movement alone.

A fundamental shift in FLN policy was made when the CNRA affirmed that "all those who participate in the liberating struggle, *with
or without uniform*, are equal."[12] This principle, unopposed by all
leaders except Abane and Colonel Slimane Dhiles, reversed the pre-

vious one giving priority to political over military matters. Here was
sure evidence that Abane, who led in enforcing political decisions at
Soummam, was losing ground to ALN officers in the CCE. Among
them, Belkacem Krim and Abdelhafid Boussouf (the former heads of
wilayat three and four, respectively) demanded a military emphasis on
the FLN's policies and development. These militarists captured leadership of the movement in May 1958 when Abane was killed, apparently by his opponents in the CCE.[13]

In addition to the conflict between the FLN's political and military
factions, another dispute arose between CCE leaders and the traditional Islamists on the doctrinal nature of the future independent
state. The Islamists were represented by Madani, who insisted on an
Islamic state based upon Quranic Law, whereas the more Westernized CCE leaders proposed a liberal parliamentary regime patterned
after European models. The issue was not resolved at the Cairo meeting and would, like other important questions, reappear to aggravate
the FLN's development after independence.

The GPRA: Crisis in Leadership

The CCE leaders convened another FLN conference in Tangier in
April 1958. There the FLN leaders, concluding that the CCE had
grown ineffective because of the conflicts within it, decided to create a
government-in-exile to replace the CCE and to represent the FLN in
any eventual negotiations with France. On September 19, these leaders proclaimed at Tunis the establishment of the Gouvernement provisoire de la république algérienne (GPRA). The new government was
promptly recognized *de jure* by Peking and eight Arab states.[14] The
announcement of the GPRA symbolized Algeria's final separation
from France. It was also the last political institution to grow out of
FLN decision-making in wartime.

The timing of the proclamation suggested that the Algerians were
reacting to the Gaullist coup in Paris. The FLN leaders proposed to
deal diplomatically with the new Paris government, which had just
emerged from the French militarists' revolt of May 13 and the concomitant demise of the Fourth Republic.[15] The GPRA satisfied the
revolutionaries' need for an entity to meet France on an official gov-
ernment-level basis.

The composition of the GPRA's nineteen-member cabinet reflec-

ted the relative prominence of the FLN's political and military leaders. Ferhat Abbas presided over the GPRA as prime minister while
Ben Bella, still in prison, was designated deputy prime minister. The
other members of the GPRA included:

Belkacem Krim—*minister of defense and deputy premier*
Mohamed Lamine Debaghine—*minister of foreign affairs*
Lakhdar Ben Tobbal—*minister of internal affairs*
Mahmoud Cherif—*minister of armaments and supply*
Abdelhafid Boussouf—*minister of communications*
Benyoussef Benkhedda—*minister of social affairs*
Abdelhamid Mehri—*minister of North African affairs*
Ahmed Francis—*minister of economy and finance*
Mohamed Yazid—*minister of information*
Tewfik El Madani—*minister of cultural affairs*
Lamine Khene—*secretary of state*
Omar Oussedik—*secretary of state*
Mustapha Stambouli—*secretary of state*

Four other imprisoned FLN leaders—Ait Ahmed, Bitat, Boudiaf, and
Khider—were appointed honorary ministers of state.

Three important leadership divisions could be discerned in the
GPRA. Krim, Ben Tobbal, and Boussouf represented the ALN (i.e.,
military) faction of the movement, and together exercised effective
control of the new government. The inclusion of the moderate, former assimilationist leaders, Abbas and Ahmed Francis, stemmed from
a tactical choice made by Krim and his allies. Abbas, the most re-
nowned Algerian leader in European diplomatic circles, gave the
GPRA the prestige needed to win acceptability among Europeans,
especially French intellectuals, who might be influential in pressuring
the Paris government to cease hostilities in Algeria. Abbas' claim to
the premiership, therefore, did not indicate the moderate wing's control of the GPRA but rather showed that the process of leadership cooptation was continuing.

The third leadership division was composed of the imprisoned external leaders, the most prominent of whom was Ben Bella. His new
popularity resulted in large part from a hostile French press which
singled him out as the leader of the "rebel gang" in an effort to discredit the FLN among Muslims. French vilification had the opposite

effect because it ultimately projected him to the stature of national hero in Muslim society.

Increased divisions in the FLN's political leadership crystallized from a reshuffling of the GPRA in January 1960. Although the original cabinet's membership was modified only slightly, the changes reflected more accurately the loci of power within it. Boussouf controlled the cabinet's key post as minister of armaments and communications. Ben Tobbal retained direction of the interior, while Krim exchanged his former position as war minister to become vice-president and foreign affairs minister. This triumvirate constituted the effective leadership of the GPRA. Because they were suspected of assassinating Abane, their emergence to power indicated that the FLN would follow a decidedly military orientation. They were responsible for the appointment of Colonel Said Mohammedi of wilaya III (Kabylia) as the GPRA's fifth minister of state. He was regarded as a supporter of Ben Bella (who was named vice-president in absentia), and his selection was apparently made to give the GPRA an appearance of general leadership representation. Mohammedi replaced Lamine Debaghine, a regular CNRA member, with the result that the new cabinet comprised most of the major leaders involved in the FLN's crisis of leadership shortly before independence.

A more crucial division in the movement as a whole was not reflected in the GPRA's membership: the ALN general staff in Tunis had arrogated control of the external army from the GPRA. Colonel Houari Boumedienne gained control of the general staff in 1959 in the aftermath of an attempt by dissident colonels in Tunisia to overthrow the GPRA. He led the counterassault that blocked the attempted coup, and he emerged subsequently with influence over the entire external army (i.e., the ALN forces in Tunisia and Morocco).[16] Boumedienne had entered the war as deputy to Boussouf when the latter was commander of wilaya V. Now as a GPRA minister, Boussouf was most instrumental in repaying the GPRA's indebtedness to Boumedienne by appointing him as the ALN's chief of staff.[17] The general staff had benefited meanwhile from the ALN's involuntary exile to shape the guerrilla forces into professional, well-disciplined soldiers.[18] These troops were also well equipped because they acquired materiel that was intended for—but could not be delivered to—the guerrillas across the Meurice-Challe Line. The GPRA ministers knew of these developments but were helpless to prevent the government's

formal command of all military units from slipping into the real control of Boumedienne and the general staff.

While Boumedienne did not aspire to political leadership of the
GPRA, his intent to maintain control of the external army was clear
enough. To decide all military issues, the GPRA organized the Comité
interministériel de guerre in 1960; the triumvirate (Krim, Boussouf,
and Ben Tobbal) restricted the committee's membership to themselves but failed to have its authority accepted by the general staff. At
a third CNRA meeting that year, the GPRA tried to regain command
of all the armed forces but left with the ALN general staff still controlling the external army. Thus, by 1960, clear lines of conflict over
military leadership separated the GPRA from the ALN general staff.

Effective authority over the guerrillas in Algeria had shifted during
the same time to the control of the wilaya commanders. By design and
default, a number of these leaders began to establish their autonomy
from the GPRA by organizing guerrillas under their personal command. Cases in point were Slimane Dhiles in wilaya IV and Si Larbi in
wilaya V, who ruled their districts like private fiefdoms. The period
from 1958 to 1960 was one of intense battlefield activity that compelled all interior forces to concentrate on the war. Military exigencies
therefore facilitated the relegation of the GPRA's authority to the
wilayat. Having wrested their independence from the GPRA, the
wilaya chiefs gave no thought to surrendering it to the ALN general
staff.

The FLN political-military cells created after Soummam disappeared in the wake of the wilaya commanders' rise to autonomy.
There was not even a pretense of shared authority between FLN and
guerrilla operatives as control of the wilayat became blatantly mili-
taristic. The party organization never recovered from the internal disintegration of this period and, in fact, ceased to function as a cohesive
apparatus after 1958.

At least four divisions could then be perceived in the FLN's incipient leadership conflict. First of all, there was the political schism pit-
ting the GPRA triumvirate against Ben Bella and his supporters as
well as the Abbas moderates. Second, a major split had developed between the GPRA and the ALN general staff. Third, the wilaya separatists opposed control from all sides, particularly the GPRA and the
general staff. Finally, all FLN leaders, including the Islamists, were
divided on the question of ideology.

Despite their considerable differences, most FLN leaders agreed on the necessity of continued struggle. When de Gaulle declared France's readiness to concede independence to Algeria in June 1960, the issue of cease-fire negotiations was thrust upon the FLN leaders as the policy question *par excellence*.[19] But the GPRA did not significantly reduce its concentration on military strategies because its military chiefs had long since lost track of political objectives. Until the time when national independence was a proximate reality, the FLN leaders devoted little attention to issues of nation building, not to mention the reconstruction of the party movement.

Conflict in leadership naturally exacerbated the problem of FLN policy-making. Since political authority involved not only questions of personality but fundamental ideological differences as well, no consensus was possible on several substantive proposals. The ex-assimilationist group under Abbas continued to be suspected, though tolerated, by both the Krim and Ben Bella factions. Abbas' proposal for a nonrevolutionary regime in independent Algeria elicited no endorsement in either faction. Benkhedda apparently advanced certain general propositions for a socialist system,[20] but Krim and Boussouf diluted his policy-making influence in the GPRA. They rejected his proposal for a unitary political-military authority that would end the war and rule after independence. Benkhedda resigned when the GPRA was reconstituted in 1960.

Both Krim and Ben Bella espoused militant, revolutionary notions of social change. Yet, they did not make known the particularities of their views; with one man in active leadership and the other in prison, it could not be determined if their views were compatible. To be sure, the FLN leaders held different views of each other as well as of the political future of Algeria. But the problem of leadership attenuated their ideological notions, divesting them of independent force in the conduct of policy. This deficiency contributed to the impression that the Algerian leaders were merely engaged in a struggle for power.

The leadership's preoccupation with military issues and strategies plagued the FLN's political growth throughout the war. Although its administrative and rank-and-file structures were considerably improved by the implementation of resolutions from the Soummam and Cairo meetings, the party's institutional development was reduced in importance as military issues regained priority over the political after the Battle of Algiers. Inside Algeria, leadership of the fighting forces was now assumed by wilaya guerrilla commanders. The FLN, once vaunted as the agent of nationalist unity, disintegrated like an exploding atom.

The lack of a party program and ideology tended to intensify the process of disintegration. If political guidelines had been agreed upon, the FLN leaders could have conceivably transcended the personal divisiveness that precluded the consolidation of a unified party leadership. Equally important, they could have presented a domestic program to focus the expectations of their constituents. Ideology, therefore, would have served as a means of moderating dissension as well as a guide to organization.

The Evian Agreements

Negotiations between the GPRA and de Gaulle's government began in May 1961, but were abrogated when the two parties failed to agree on an agenda. Originally, de Gaulle offered three choices to the Algerian leaders: secession from France, complete integration into the French system, or an Algerian system federated to France. The GPRA leaders opted for secession and then proposed negotiations in two stages: the first to decide the date to proclaim Algerian independence, and the second to define future relations between France and Algeria. De Gaulle's main concern was to secure guarantees for the property and rights of French citizens residing in Algeria after independence. The Gaullist regime also maintained that the Algerian Sahara, where oil had been discovered,[21] was not an integral part of Algerian territory and therefore ought to remain under French sovereignty.

Antagonism mounted among FLN leaders over how the GPRA ought to handle the cease-fire negotiations. Boumedienne and the ALN general staff opposed all concessions to France, insisting that diplomacy should be restricted to the single issue of Algerian independence.[22] The GPRA, still directed by Krim and his allies, favored a more flexible approach and prepared to make compromises that would assure independence. In August 1961, the triumvirate selected Benkhedda as prime minister of the GPRA in order to take advantage of his generally recognized diplomatic skills and thus to strengthen their own position. The perspectives of the imprisoned exterior leaders remained unknown.

The CNRA authorized the GPRA to renew negotiations with France early in March 1962. An indeterminate number of the fifty-four-member body met secretly with Benkhedda, Krim, and Dahlab and approved the proposal for a cease-fire agreement, but did not specify the limitations the GPRA should respect in seeking it. However, they did enjoin the GPRA against making commitments on special guarantees for the protection of European residents in Algeria, and against granting rights to the Sahara where France had an interest in military, communications, and oil facilities. The Soummam Congress decided, it will be recalled, that such matters lay solely within the authority of the CNRA and could not be acted upon without that body's approval.

The GPRA succeeded in reaching a cease-fire agreement with the Guallist government in its negotiations at Evian (Switzerland) on March 18, 1962. Dahlab and Krim, chief among the GPRA negotiators, proceeded beyond the cease-fire question to advance other subjects for negotiation, including future Franco-Algerian economic cooperation and a referendum on independence. They finalized an agreement on these issues as well, but the GPRA leaders had manifestly exceeded their authority.

Both sides compromised previous positions in negotiating the general cease-fire settlement, which was entitled the Accords d'Evian. [23] France yielded to full negotiations with a body that lacked governmental status juridically and, as a result, won the right to maintain de jure sovereignty in Algeria during the interregnum between the settlement and the creation of a duly constituted Algerian government. The FLN leaders consented to the establishment of a Provisional Executive, or temporary government, composed of three European and nine Muslim Algerians who did not even belong to the FLN. The parties compromised elsewhere by adopting a series of "declarations of principles" on future economic and financial exchanges between France and Algeria, rights of French citizens in independent Algeria, and military concessions approving the French army's continued presence in the Sahara.

Krim, the GPRA vice-premier and foreign minister, signed the Evian agreements for the FLN. He and Benkhedda predominated at the Evian talks and, on their own initiative, made compromises that infringed directly upon the new nation's territorial sovereignty: viz., they granted France the right to maintain certain Saharan regions

over a five-year period for purposes of atomic testing; to occupy the
French naval base at Mers-El-Kebir for at least fifteen years (then re-
newable by mutual agreement); and finally, to retain control of
Saharan communications facilities that connected Algeria with the
trans-Saharan states of Africa. At no time did the GPRA leaders contact the CNRA to obtain approval of the negotiated agreements. This
omission later surfaced as one of the main sources of conflict at the
Tripoli Conference.

The tolls of revolution had weighed heavily on the Algerians since
1954, and the GPRA settlement at Evian seemed to indicate their
strong desire to prevent further losses by terminating the war. FLN
sources estimated in 1962 that a million or more Algerians had been
killed in the seven-year struggle. Scores of thousands survived as
wounded, maimed, or incapacitated casualties. Nearly three million
Algerians had been uprooted from their homes by the resettlement of
communities and the flight of refugees to the towns and cities. [24] In
contrast, official French sources placed total French losses (from 1956
to 1962) at 36,895 persons; [25] the vast majority of these were French
citizens of Muslim North African origin (i.e., the "harki"). FLN losses
had been borne almost completely by the internal forces, and this
reality evidently contributed to the GPRA's acquiescence in the Evian
compromises.

Ben Bella and the four external leaders were released from prison in
March 1962 following the signing of the Evian agreements. In prison,
Ben Bella had gained permission, as first vice-premier of the GPRA,
to confer on the negotiations with an emissary sent by Benkhedda.
Although Ben Bella favored more aggressive diplomacy than that
waged by the GPRA negotiators, he approved the final draft of the
Evian agreements. Thus, the GPRA leaders were shocked when he
openly repudiated the agreements a few weeks after his release. Ben
Bella condemned the Evian settlement as a sellout to France which, in
effect, nullified all the nationalist objectives and sacrifices of the war.
His disavowal set the stage for confrontation with the GPRA.

Boudiaf and Ait Ahmed, construing the repudiation as an attempt
to usurp power from the GPRA, dissociated themselves from Ben
Bella. The two other liberated leaders, Khider and Bitat, took Ben
Bella's position because they believed that he, as the most popular
among FLN leaders, had the best chance of mustering broad national

support and therefore of leading a consensus to govern independent Algeria. This interpretation is corroborated by the fact that Colonel Boumedienne, the GPRA defense chief, consulted Ben Bella as early as February 1962 on the formation of a new government. [26]

Benkhedda had alienated the ALN chief in September 1961 by ordering the abolition of the ALN general staff and its replacement with two separate staffs—one for the regular army stationed in Morocco and Tunisia, and another for the wilaya guerrillas in Algeria. The GPRA would directly control the proposed staffs. As noted earlier, the general staff operated independently of the GPRA, and by this time it "constituted a powerful force with control of its own budget and equipped with specalized services." [27] Benkhedda's action, therefore, exposed a desperate GPRA effort to regain command of the regular army.

When Boumedienne blocked the GPRA order, Benkhedda dismissed him. This action deepened the schism between the general staff and the GPRA, and virtually precluded Boumedienne's future support of the GPRA. In February 1962, he sent his emissary, Major Abdelazziz Bouteflika, to Ben Bella to start discussions on the Algerian government after independence. It then appeared that Boumedienne was sounding Ben Bella out on the possibility of overturning the incumbents. Boumedienne did not oppose Ben Bella's condemnation of the GPRA, which strengthened the belief that he supported Ben Bella.

The Tripoli Program

To resolve the differences, Ben Bella proposed to the GPRA that a CNRA conference be held in Tripoli prior to independence. He suggested three subjects as an agenda for the meeting: political reconversion and reorganization of the FLN; preparation for a transfer of power from the GPRA to a duly constituted government after independence; and the formulation of a party program. Benkhedda acknowledged the need to pursue these objectives but opposed the convening of a CNRA meeting. As he viewed it, such a meeting would amount to a trial of the GPRA because any of the proposed subjects would inevitably raise questions about Algeria's status as fixed by the Evian agreements.

During this conflict, the country was under the formal authority of the Provisional Executive, the caretaker government that the Evian negotiators created to rule in the interim between the cease-fire and independence. The Provisional Executive took no part in the GPRA's exchange with Ben Bella and worked mainly to prepare the referendum on self-determination (which the Evian agreements scheduled for July 1, 1962). The interregnum regime was headed by Abderrahmane Fares, a former Muslim member of the Algerian Assembly, who never declared his commitment to the FLN during the war. Like most FLN revolutionaries, the GPRA leaders distrusted this middle-class, pro-French moderate as well as the Europeans who belonged to the Provisional Executive. Accordingly, the GPRA systematically prevented it from functioning. This background explained why the Ben Bella group ignored the Provisional Executive and focused their opposition on the GPRA.

The Benbellists, a minority in the GPRA, appeared to constitute a majority in the CNRA,[28] strong enough in any case to convene the Tripoli meeting over the objections of the GPRA. The CNRA, both a party and a governmental organ, had created the GPRA and retained the power to change its composition. The possibility that Ben Bella would seek to undermine the bases of their authority compelled the GPRA leaders (Benkhedda, Krim, Dahlab, and Yazid) to retract their previous position and attend the meeting. For the first time since its organization, the CNRA assembled its full fifty-four-member constituency together at a single meeting. The GPRA leaders recognized that they were on the defensive and went to Tripoli in a last-ditch effort to defend their interests.

Two substantive issues concerned the FLN delegates who met at Tripoli on May 27, 1962. The first consisted of Ben Bella's two-part proposition that the FLN organize a Political Bureau to administer the country until a formal government could be established and designate candidates for a constituent national assembly after independence. The second mandated the adoption of a draft party platform presented under the title of the *Tripoli Program*. Of the two questions, the first drew immediate resistance from Benkhedda and his ministers because it demanded in effect that the Political Bureau supersede the GPRA.

Ben Bella introduced the motion for a Political Bureau with a list of six men to staff it: the four external leaders (i.e., Ait Ahmed, Ben Bella, Boudiaf, and Khider), Said Mohammedi, and Rabah Bitat, who was released from prison in the aftermath of the March decrees. Ait Ahmed and Boudiaf, undeclared as partisans of either side, were regarded as neutrals at that time. Mohammedi was the only GPRA minister known to be opposed to the GPRA leaders and their policies. The proposed party executive was obviously designed to establish Ben Bella's power, and Benkhedda, Boudiaf, and others walked out of the meeting in protest before a vote was taken.

Subsequently, Ben Bella retracted the original proposal and adopted a "unity list" carrying the names of Benkhedda, Krim, Boudiaf, Abbas, and his own for the Political Bureau. This slate represented a more balanced selection, split in a three-way division among the two GPRA leaders, the presumed neutrals, Ben Bella and Abbas. Abbas, incensed at the GPRA ministers who ousted him in 1961, had drawn closer to Ben Bella. For Benkhedda and Krim, the real question did not involve a decision of *who* should make up the Political Bureau but *whether* there should be such a body at all. They therefore spurned Ben Bella's proposal and reasserted the GPRA's claim to legitimacy.

The GPRA had to make a decisive response to the Ben Bella challenge if it hoped to endure. But the outcome of this struggle came to a rapid and dramatic conclusion in Ben Bella's favor before Benkhedda and the GPRA could move: Boumedienne, chief of the powerful external army, rallied to defend Ben Bella. The ALN chief denounced the GPRA's concessions to the French at Evian, then ordered his troops to arrest Benkhedda and the other GPRA ministers. Benkhedda and all the GPRA representatives fled the conference for their headquarters in Tunis. Confusion then reigned at Tripoli. The result was that no majority could be found to approve any issue, including the creation of a Political Bureau.

The draft for an FLN party program was the only concrete product of the Tripoli Conference. It had been prepared before the conference by a group of young militants seeking to formulate an FLN ideology and statement of goals. The Tripoli Program, as the party statement was called, attempted to recast the movement's aims in a political form and terminate past emphasis on military matters. It purported to be a guideline to future party objectives describing the political, social, and cultural bases of the postindependent political system.

The document articulated the social content of the nationalist movement as follows:

Since November 1, 1954, a new dimension has emerged in the previously static life of the Algerian community: the movement which is formed by the collective enlistment of the people in the nationalist struggle. . . .

Analysis of the social content of the fight for freedom underlines the fact that it is in general the peasants and workers who have been the active base of the movement and who have given it its essentially popular character. [Italics in the original] [29]

This statement embodied the first formal recognition of the peasant base of the revolutionary war. [30]

Continuation of the revolution by nonviolent means was a primary objective of independent Algeria, according to the Tripoli Program. In the future, the "war of weapons should be succeeded by ideological combat," and this struggle must be waged "through the deliberate construction of the nation within the framework of socialist principles." [31] This denoted what came to be known as "Algerian socialism" or the "socialist option." The sketchily phrased statement called for a vanguard composed of the "peasantry, the workers in general, the youth, and the revolutionary intellectuals" who represented the masses. [32] Leadership of the state and the FLN would henceforth be exercised exclusively by the Political Bureau.

The new economic system was to be based on the principles of socialist planning which, in practice, required centralized state control: "Economic planning and the control of the economy by the state, with the participation of the workers, are vital necessities. Only planning will make possible the accumulation of capital required for profitable industrialization and the elimination of waste and false costs." [33] A program of agrarian reform would be implemented through the creation of state-owned farms on land expropriated from the colons and through the "participation of the workers in the management and in the profits of such farms." [34] On the expropriated farms, the peasant farmers would organize "production cooperatives." Expropriating the plantations of dominant European landowners represented one of the platform's fundamental points. [35]

A special annex in the Tripoli Program emphasized that independence made imperative the conversion of the FLN movement into a political party. The formation of FLN staffs constituted the leaders' priority, requiring that the majority in all FLN organisms "consist of peasants, workers in general, the youth, and revolutionary intellectuals."[36] The program also advised the elimination of divergent ideologies and the FLN's establishment as a preponderant political party uniting Algeria's various socioeconomic groups. It did not demand that the political system be transformed into a one-party state.

The Tripoli Program instructed party leaders to determine policy guidelines and execute policies of the state. FLN leaders received priority in state institutions and especially in positions of leadership. Specifically, the FLN would ensure that "the chief of the government and the majority of the ministers are members of the party; the chief of the government is a member of the Political Bureau; the majority of the members of the Assemblies are party members."[37] In order not to be absorbed by the state, however, the FLN should remain physically distinct from the state or government. The Tripoli Program therefore prescribed that party officials below the highest levels shun governmental posts and devote their full energies to party work.

Mass organizations were designated to form the new FLN's organizational base. Social groups currently unorganized, such as peasants and nonuniversity youths, would be enrolled by the party and organized as national entities. Groups already organized, like the UGTA, would not be undermined in their specific areas of authority but would associate with the FLN according to their special interests. The program was careful to specify the party's relationship to the trade unionists:

> The party respects the autonomy of the unions, whose basic function is to defend the material and cultural interests of the workers. However, only the party, the vanguard of the popular masses, can assure the coordination of revolutionary forces within the country and fully utilize in an organic fashion the potentials and means inherent in the society.[38]

The FLN would be converted into a mass political party in which all national organizations participated, but over which party executives exercised ultimate authority.

Finally, with regard to the FLN's relationship to the army, the platform stated that Algeria's accession to independence required that a
part of the army return to civilian life and serve as FLN staff, while the
remainder should form the nucleus of the new national army. The
ALN would become a social service army assisting in the reconstruction of the country. This section recommended a reduction of the ALN
troops and (wilaya) guerrillas as well as the subordination of the entire
military command structure to the party. This interpretation seemed
to be corroborated by the program's instruction to politicize the army
by creating party cells within it.

The proposals and terminology of the Tripoli Program reflected the
ideological orientations of the men who wrote it. Its chief author was
Mohammed Harbi, a former UGEMA leader who joined the FLN
after 1954.[39] While a philosophy major in college, he embraced
Marxism-Leninism as an ideology and emerged during the anticolonial war as a leading revolutionary intellectual. Harbi participated in
the GPRA before March 1962 but aligned with Ben Bella sometime
later. He composed the main section of the document (chapter three
and the annex) with Mohammed Ben Yahia, another former student
leader supporting the GPRA who defected to Ben Bella. This section,
which outlined the FLN's perspectives on a dominant party-state,
suggested that the framers were inspired by the Soviet model. Two
shorter and less important chapters were formulated by Mostefa
Lacheraf and Ridha Malek: Lacheraf, a history professor and a moderate among FLN militants, had been arrested with the four FLN
leaders in 1956; Malek, a young Marxist intellectual, had maintained
neutrality in Ben Bella's conflict with the GPRA at Tripoli.

Given the conflict between the GPRA and the Political Bureau, any
attempt to reconstruct the party movement at Tripoli was foredoom-
ed. More fragmented than at any time since its formation, the FLN
existed as a shattered organization, all of whose elements—the
GPRA, Political Bureau, ALN, and wilaya guerrillas—now functioned relatively independent of each other. A party program and ideology
had at last been tentatively formulated, but the strife-torn FLN had
lost organizational control of its former civilian constituency, including workers and students.

The Political Bureau, in fact, constituted the FLN's only effective
unit after Tripoli. It acquired its power not from the party movement
but from the regular army. New political institutions were organized

after the Soummam Congress, but the leadership's preoccupation with military strategy destined them to a transient and ultimately unsuccessful existence. The absence of a party program, with a systematic statement of political objectives and ideology, facilitated the relegation of the FLN's political development to military goals and institutions.

The FLN did serve as a broad umbrella-like body associating the various elements fighting for independence, and this asset rendered it significant, notwithstanding its considerable weaknesses. It continued to act, in other words, as the aegis of national unity. In this respect, the party movement proved remarkably resilient through the resourcefulness of its military units and its mobile system of collective leadership. The French could frustrate the establishment of a stable leadership by eliminating particular leaders from the war zones, but they could not undermine the military resistance or prevent new leaders from stepping forward to fill the vacancies. On the other hand, the unity achieved by the FLN was limited to ousting the French. The formulation of a program of political and economic objectives for Algeria after independence, which might have minimized or eliminated the conflicts among FLN leaders, was left in abeyance. After 1958, politics and war became synonymous. To the extent that the FLN moderated dissension at all, it was in the military, not the political, arena.

Most importantly, the protracted intraleadership conflicts exacerbated the FLN's institutional weaknesses. These conflicts, which were based on both the political and personal interests of FLN leaders, frustrated the party's growth as a cohesive institution and finally precipitated its almost total dissolution at the very time the objective of independence had been won. At Tripoli, the wartime organization for political unity totally collapsed. The FLN, a triumphant anticolonial movement, had brought the country to independence after seven and a half years of arduous struggle only to face its gravest crisis.

4

Independence: The State-Building Priority

A genuine social revolution took place in Algeria between the outbreak of rebellion and the conclusion of the anticolonial war. Algeria became independent on July 5, 1962, following the Algerian people's massive approval of the referendum on self-determination. [1] Nearly nine-tenths of the 1,200,000 Europeans who once governed and exploited the country had fled to France, [2] both frightened by and vindictive at the demise of French Algeria. Out of the ruins of the colonial status quo emerged the new Algerian political system.

By the time of independence, the FLN was largely defunct as a result of the political and military fragmentation that had rended it during the war. Nonetheless, there was a strong possibility that the FLN could be redeveloped and converted into the preponderant political party recommended by the Tripoli Program. After all, Algeria possessed a significant group of political elites who had already demonstrated their organizational and technical skills in French political or trade union institutions as well as in the early development of the FLN. Through the continued legitimacy of the FLN, they could rightfully claim authority to rule. The war had mobilized all segments of the population and hence the time seemed propitious for coalescing them into a reorganized party constituency. Such advantages suggested a restoration of the party in the postindependent political system.

The transition from independence to the establishment of the independent system was not attended by the kind of proud celebrations and eager reconstruction that might have been expected after victory. Quite the contrary, Algeria reached independence to encounter a reality almost as grim as it had experienced in the preceding war: the country was in complete chaos and the prospect of new hostilities, this time among the Algerians themselves, loomed as a distinct probability when the Political Bureau and the ALN confronted the forces of the GPRA. The peace that freedom brings eluded the Algerians as the impending crisis thrust the new nation to the brink of civil war.

The chaos of the times was partly spawned by the exodus of the Europeans, who had heretofore maintained some semblance of law and order (at least in the cities). With them went the personnel of the civil bureaucracy and the economic managerial class whose hasty exit caused essential municipal services to grind to a halt. Meanwhile, more than two million Muslim men, women, and children whom the French army had detained in so-called regroupment centers since 1958 surged out of their quasi-concentration camps,[3] demanding governmental assistance in a period when no government existed. While some Algerians pleaded for food and shelter, others, on their own volition, took over businesses, luxurious villas, and apartments abandoned by the Europeans. In the countryside, peasants seized the vacated colon properties, especially the large plantation farms.

Wilaya commanders and their subchiefs intensified the collapse of law and order as they aggrandized themselves by "exacting taxes [from other Muslims] and occupying public and private buildings, acting in reality as autonomous units within autonomous units."[4] Independent of the FLN since about 1960, the wilaya separatists, such as Colonel Mohammed Chaabani in Biskra, asserted personal control of their military regions. They were able to succeed because the struggle between the Political Bureau and the GPRA prevented the establishment of a new national leadership. Nor, owing to the breakdown in communications since 1958 between the wilaya chiefs and the ALN general staff, was there a central military leadership. Individually and collectively, the wilaya commanders moved about unimpeded as they erected their personal fiefdoms.

Further aggravating the situation was the destruction left in the wake of a clandestine terrorist organization which die-hard Europeans formed by 1961 in the belief that if they could not continue to control Algeria, they could at least destroy it. Called the Organisation de l'armée secrète (OAS),[5] the French terrorists pursued a scorched-earth policy, demolishing buildings, factories, and communications networks with bombs or other incendiary devices. They also swelled Algerian war-related casualties by killing and maiming individuals wantonly. Long after independence, in fact, Algerians were occasionally the hapless victims of OAS excesses when they happened upon a booby trap or mine that lay undiscovered in their fields, offices, or homes.

Algeria's most acute problem at independence, however, was the crisis in FLN authority that pitted the GPRA against the Political Bureau. From an analysis of this crisis, there emerges a series of complex, often confusing, events that culminated in Ben Bella's accession to power and the birth of a regime that subordinated the institutionalization of a party system to the imposition of personal rule. Although Ben Bella did eventually seek to reconstruct a party system, he concentrated his initial efforts on consolidating his personal rule. His fateful alliance with Boumedienne, chief of the ALN, inaugurated this process by enabling Ben Bella to defeat the GPRA. Discussion of this violent episode in Algerian history is a necessary prelude to understanding the preponderant role that Ben Bella, in tandem with Boumedienne, played in deciding the FLN's development after independence.

Civil War: The Political Bureau Versus the GPRA

The Political Bureau was authorized at the Tripoli Conference to "assure the direction of the country, the reconversion of the FLN and the ALN, the construction of the country, and the preparation for a CNRA meeting to be held at the end of 1962,"[6] declared Ahmed Boumendjel, a spokesman for Ben Bella from the town of Tlemcen on July 22, 1962. The Ben Bella coalition, or the Tlemcen group as generally identified, thus revealed its intention to challenge the GPRA. The Tlemcen group was organized after the Tripoli Conference through Ben Bella's secret collaborations with key FLN and ALN leaders, including Mohammed Khider, Said Mohammedi, and Colonel Boumedienne; all had aligned behind Ben Bella in his quest to overthrow the GPRA. What confirmed the view that Ben Bella was struggling for leadership was the fact that the CNRA meeting at Tripoli did not ratify Ben Bella's Political Bureau nor authorize it to fulfill the objectives specified in the declaration. The Tripoli Program did contain a provision for a Political Bureau, and this indicated that Ben Bella and his followers had contrived their strategy well before Tripoli.

The Political Bureau, as finally assembled by Ben Bella in July 1962, consisted of five members, which was a remarkably small number for a group aspiring to national authority. Ben Bella held the top post as head of general administration and liaison with the Provisional Executive, the ostensible caretaker government. Hadj Ben Alla, an ALN colonel and one of the young soldiers close to Ben Bella, was responsible for military matters. Rabah Bitat, also a wilaya leader before his arrest in 1956, assisted the fifth member, Mohammed Khider, in the important task of planning the reconstruction of the FLN. Said Mohammedi, a member of the ALN general staff and a former wilaya commander, was appointed chief of educational affairs.

Mohammedi lacked professional qualifications for the post, and thus it could be inferred that Ben Bella selected him mainly because he was a Berber. This appointment blunted the accusation by Krim and other GPRA leaders that the Tlemcen group was hostile to Algeria's Berber minority. Mohammedi was also the least important member of the Political Bureau, but his inclusion counteracted the GPRA tactic for mobilizing Berbers against Ben Bella. The process of leadership cooptation, so prevalent during the war, resumed in the domestic crisis of independence.

Two other important FLN leaders, Mohammed Boudiaf and Hocine Ait Ahmed, were tendered membership in the Political Bureau. To Boudiaf, Ben Bella offered the Political Bureau's post of foreign affairs; he first accepted and then promptly vacated it, leaving the impression that he might join the GPRA. Ben Bella also made overtures to Ait Ahmed, but he declined, pending resolution of the leadership crisis.

In the aftermath of the Tripoli Conference, Benkhedda and the GPRA ministers transferred their headquarters from Tunis to Tizi Ouzou, capital of Kabylia, determined to retain governmental authority. Before the Political Bureau's declaration of July 22, Benkhedda had proposed a future CNRA meeting in the hope that it would uphold the GPRA and outvote Ben Bella. The GPRA prime minister also requested the Gaullist government to keep the Meurice-Challe Line activated in order to forestall the ALN's impending march on Algiers. Then, on June 30, 1962, he sought to reinforce the GPRA's position by firing Boumedienne, Major Slimane, and Major Ali Mendjeli from the ALN general staff.

This latter action proved to be the GPRA's fatal misstep. Although Benkhedda managed to have Major Slimane arrested, the entire GPRA strategy started to fall apart when Boumedienne ignored the dismissal order. Ben Bella, who remained a GPRA vice-premier nominally, took advantage of the incident to announce his resignation; he manipulated the dismissal to grand advantage by supporting the general staff's contention that the GPRA lacked the legal authority to dismiss them. After de Gaulle rejected Benkhedda's request early in July, ALN units in Tunisia and Morocco began to converge on Algiers.

In repudiating the GPRA, Ben Bella contended that Algeria's independence terminated the GPRA's legitimacy because the Provisional Executive had been created, and the GPRA leaders had "confiscated the revolution" by signing the Evian cease-fire agreement. [7] He identified selected provisions as the most odious; these included preferential rights to France in the development of Algerian oil fields, special citizenship status for the French remaining in Algeria, and the installation of French military bases on Algerian territory. He further dramatized his objections by publicizing Benkhedda's compromise settlement with the OAS which, according to Ben Bella, contravened an FLN injunction against recognizing the terrorist group. [8] In sum, he argued, these actions represented legal infractions that revoked the GPRA's right to existence.

The distribution of military and political forces weighed heavily against the GPRA. A small number of wilaya commanders answered Benkhedda's appeal for assistance, particularly Colonel Youssef Khatib who had quit his medical studies in wartime and eventually gained command of wilaya IV (Algiers). Khatib summoned perhaps 2,000 guerrillas to defend the GPRA. A guerrilla faction in wilaya II (Constantine) also stood with the beleaguered government. But the command structure among the guerrillas had deteriorated considerably since the cease-fire, and the schisms among the different wilaya separatists prevented them from operating as a unit.

The GPRA was reinforced temporarily by the emergence of a third protagonist, the "Tizi Ouzou group," as the Berber force from Kabylia was named. Krim had characterized the Political Bureau as enemies of his Berber people, and hastily marshaled the Tizi Ouzou batallion behind the GPRA in late July. Approximately a thousand troops followed the command of Colonel Mohand Ou El Hadj, a Berber, who had acted as the de facto governor of the region since March. Together with the two wilaya divisions, the GPRA could rely upon three military contingents.

Among the political elites, Benkhedda and the triumvirate (i.e., Krim, Boussouf, and Ben Tobbal) maintained the allegiance of GPRA ministers Yazid and Francis. However, few of the FLN leaders loyal to the GPRA had political acumen. Benkhedda and the triumvirate managed to hold the GPRA together after the Tripoli Conference, but they did not have the numbers, skills, and representativeness necessary for governing a complex society, especially one in the conditions of Algeria at independence. They held few solid alignments with the wilaya commanders who assumed practical direction of the country during the war, and they therefore could not generate enough coercive (military) power to compel the commanders' submission to GPRA directives.

Boudiaf yielded to the Political Bureau in early July, but he predicated his support on a ratification of the Political Bureau at a future CNRA meeting. He demanded also that the Tlemcen group collaborate with the GPRA in designating candidates for the proposed National Assembly. Boudiaf, realizing that Ben Bella had reneged on the agreement after the Tlemcen group's declaration of July 22, canceled his nominal membership in the Political Bureau and joined the Tizi Ouzou group. In aligning with the GPRA, he seemed to base his decision less on any personal or political commitment to the incumbent leadership than on a genuine determination to stop Boumedienne and the ALN from emerging as an integral force in politics. Earlier, he had insisted that "the army must not indulge in politics; it must return to [the] barracks."[9] Having endorsed the GPRA's dismissal of the ALN general staff, he took the next logical step.

The balance of power began to swing decisively on the side of the Political Bureau in August. This shift crystallized as a few activist factions in wilayat I, II, V, and VI rallied to Ben Bella. In the same period, Colonel Mohammedi of wilaya III (Kabylia) refuted Krim's allegation that the Political Bureau intended to suppress the Berber population, and this mitigated the initial hostility of Tizi Ouzou adherents. The most significant wilaya support came from Colonel

Chaabani in wilaya VI. His command post occupied a strategic route in southern Algeria which facilitated the movement of ALN regiments to the capital. Of the six wilayat, Chaabani's was the most abundantly supplied with exterior aid and consequently was the most amply equipped in materiel and heavy armaments.[10]

What ultimately determined the outcome of the crisis was Boumedienne's decision to unite the two divisions of the ALN behind Ben Bella. With a force of about 45,000 troops simultaneously converging upon Algiers from Tunisia and Morocco, he approached the scene with well-trained and well-armed batallions that the GPRA guerrillas could not successfully resist. Essentially, two factors explained Boumedienne's defense of the Tlemcen group: the GPRA's attempt to dismantle the general staff in 1961 and to expel the military chiefs in 1962; equally critical, Ben Bella's offer of control of the military establishment (to Boumedienne) in any government formed by the Political Bureau. Thus, a political and military alliance emerged with Ben Bella as the chief political leader and Boumedienne as the leader of the military forces.

The conclusion that the ALN's defense of the Political Bureau resulted in part from a forced choice has been corroborated by Boumedienne himself:

> [Early in 1962], we began contacts with the "five historic chiefs" detained in France. . . . We revealed to them the differences which placed us at loggerheads with the GPRA so as to make the situation clear and unequivocal to all. . . . We [later] resisted the GPRA's decision to oust us from the ALN general staff. This decision emanated from an authority which did not have the competence to take an initiative which the militants and the ALN rejected. It was then that Ben Bella came to inform us that he supported our position, and that he sided with us against [the GPRA].[11]

Why Boumedienne did not seek to govern the new regime without Ben Bella raises another question, which can be answered by noting the disadvantages arguing against such a course of action in 1962. Certainly, Boumedienne was not unconscious of the distrust with which the general Algerian population regarded the army. Nor could he have been unaware of his own limited popularity in the society at large; of all the Algerian leaders, Boumedienne ranked among the most obscure. He could not claim any particular distinction for action in the revolutionary war because of his involuntary withdrawal at the ALN general headquarters at Ghardimaou (Tunisia). Except for the GPRA leaders who ultimately denounced him, he did not enjoy the support of any of the principal FLN leaders until he joined the Ben Bella group. The *quid pro quo* arranged with Ben Bella constituted Boumedienne's most opportune alternative.

The fact that Boumedienne sent an emissary to confer with Ben Bella in February 1962 confirms the view that he entertained no hopes of leading a government himself. He was confident that any new government had to depend upon his army for the coercive force required to restore civil order, and consequently the government would depend on him for its very survival. Boumedienne saw the opportunity to obtain his maximal demands in another position, namely, as the number two leader in the new government. Logically, therefore, he aligned with the Political Bureau after Benkhedda attempted to oust the general staff.

The outbreak of civil war seemed imminent as the opposing military contingents mobilized for confrontation. To avoid this catastrophe, Ben Bella and Benkhedda relented, agreeing to a compromise that permitted the GPRA to maintain governmental authority until a national legislature could be elected. The GPRA, meanwhile, acquiesced in Ben Bella's demand that the Political Bureau nominate all candidates for the proposed National Assembly. This compromise merely postponed the violence because Colonel Khatib disregarded Benkhedda's order to stop fighting and, on August 2, arrayed his troops to block the Political Bureau's entry into Algiers. Thereupon, Ben Bella retreated to his Tlemcen stronghold to ready the ALN for a march upon the capital.

It was at this time that Mohammed Khider made a substantial contribution to Ben Bella's rise to power. As the veteran politician in Ben Bella's coalition, Khider retained a large, though unorganized, following in Algerian political and military circles. Like Ben Bella, he seemed ambitious and eager to exercise leadership in the new political system, but he planned to achieve this goal by converting the FLN into a mass political party that would control the entire governmental system. In the highly volatile events of the summer crisis, he contacted leaders of wilaya IV (Algiers) and negotiated an agreement with guerrillas to allow them temporary control of the Algiers' zone in exchange for a cessation of hostilities against the Political Bureau. Khider's intervention thus paved the way for Ben Bella's successful return to the capital.

The scene in Algiers presaged the defeat of the GPRA. Many guerrillas supporting the GPRA before Khider's negotiations informed Benkhedda that they could no longer protect his government. Colonel Khatib remained resolute in his opposition to the Political Bureau, but it appeared at this point that he acted more in his own interest (i.e., to maintain military control of wilaya IV) than to preserve the GPRA. Benkhedda's ministers began to flee the capital. Saad Dahlab, the foreign affairs minister, deserted his post for refuge abroad. After the flight of the GPRA's ministers, the GPRA guerrillas were left in the anomalous position of defending a virtually nonexistent government.

Between the two belligerents, the UGTA stood as the only national group capable of influencing the course of events. The trade union's membership was estimated at 300,000,[12] and its disciplined sections in Algeria's urban areas enabled it to affect the strategies of both adversaries. If it had chosen to intervene on the side of the GPRA, it might have compelled the Political Bureau and the wilaya militarists to negotiate a peaceful settlement. Arbitration between the antagonists was another UGTA possibility. But the UGTA leaders opted for neutrality and thereby dispelled the last possibility for a peaceful solution. With the GPRA in a state of dissolution, armed guerrilla bands started roaming and pillaging the capital, multiplying the chaos and disorder. When the ALN and wilaya batallions later exchanged gunfire in wilayat III, IV, and VI, independent Algeria foundered on the brink of civil war.

As the tragedy mounted in early August, Benkhedda capitulated, having witnessed the undermining of his government by the guerrillas who were supposedly defending it. He immediately surrendered the GPRA's control of internal affairs to the Political Bureau. The crisis abated as Boumedienne deployed ALN forces against the wilaya guerrillas, thus enabling the Political Bureau to make a second and decisive entry into Algiers. Ben Bella and his party then claimed the powers of the now defunct GPRA and, in the crisis-laden situation, began to restore order and government.

The triumphant arrival of Ben Bella and the Political Bureau in Algiers did not immediately banish the threat of civil war. The ALN battled guerrilla forces several days before the violence subsided. In the Algiers region, Khatib refused to relinquish control of the rudimentary form of administration he had assembled during the war. He also rejected the Political Bureau's demand that he dissolve his forces. This conflict, which one writer has aptly described as a case of "government centrism vs. regionalism,"[13] threatened to prolong the civil disorder.

It was the Algiers' masses who finally prevented the ultimate confrontation between the ALN and the guerrilla separatists. Thousands of Casbah dwellers interposed themselves between the antagonists, pleading for an end to the fighting once and for all. Boumedienne halted the ALN offensive when Khatib and his troops agreed to come to terms with the Political Bureau. The arbitration of the local populace, as manifested by their indignation toward both sides, marked the end of the FLN's tragic leadership struggle. No account has ever verified the number of fatalities resulting from the Political Bureau's victory, but they have been generally estimated at about three thousand.[14]

Thus, in the three-month period from June to August 1962, Algeria underwent the transition from colony to sovereignty, from revolutionary war to domestic crisis, climaxing in a struggle for power that produced a coup d'état after the revolution. The FLN group that led the struggle to destroy the old regime was itself overthrown by members of its own organization. Ben Bella justified the Political Bureau's coup by asserting that the GPRA, having been repudiated by the CNRA, had lost its mandate. The question remained open to debate in a legal sense. Realistically, it was not.

Victorious, the Political Bureau moved to consolidate its authority on a national scale. It controlled the government. It commanded the support of the regular army. It superintended the economic and material resources of the country. Notwithstanding some residual hostility of the wilaya separatists, this singular FLN body also seemed to be accepted as the official national authority by the general public. The Political Bureau's major advantage, however, consisted in its unique capacity to select candidates for the future national legislature. This prerogative qualified Ben Bella's group as the only de facto political authority in the country. The certainty that the elected candidates would in turn designate him to form a government forecast his installation as the paramount leader of the FLN and the state.

The cornerstone of the new political system was the symbiotic relationship between Ben Bella and Boumedienne. By combining their
political and military forces, they ascended to power. Just as the principle of collective rule became central to FLN organization after the
rebellion of 1954, the political-military alliance emerged as a principal element of politics after independence. Development of a party
system, therefore, could be advanced only to the extent permitted by
Ben Bella, subject to the military prerogatives claimed by Boumedienne. It was conceivable nevertheless that the FLN's military
success in wartime could be repeated politically under the new
regime.

The Imposition of Personal Rule

When the Political Bureau assumed control of Algeria in September 1962, it was clear that the establishment of the FLN as the national guide and authority of the new political system, as decided by the
new leaders at Tripoli, could not be achieved except through a massive commitment to party building. The deleterious effect of French
assaults on the FLN's wartime organization was compounded by the
Algerians themselves during the conflict at Tripoli and the subsequent struggle between Ben Bella and the GPRA. As a consequence,
the FLN survived at independence as a highly disorganized, fragmented movement whose adherents were separated into numerous
political and military factions. Against this background, the magni-
tude of the party-building task was self-evident.

One interpretation explaining why the FLN did not reach independence as a political party has been given by Mostefa Lacheraf, the
Algerian historian who was arrested with the internal leaders in 1956:

> The FLN ceased to exist as a "party" as conventionally under-
> stood after 1958. The political authority it represented and the
> national authority of which it was the sole agent, as leader of the
> nation in war, dissolved imperceptibly without serious organic
> differentiation. This authority . . . was later reduced to two poles
> limited to purely theoretical action; to two institutions, the
> GPRA and the CNRA, both having mitigated prerogatives
> which were often merely symbolic compared to the organized
> militants and the fighting men of the interior.[15]

In actuality, the FLN's institutional bases were reduced to the GPRA and the ALN as early as 1958. Wilaya separatists later increased the unsupervised decentralization of the FLN by establishing autonomous military units within their particular war zones. After the Political Bureau defeated the GPRA in 1962, the FLN's nominal representation shifted again, corresponding roughly to the Political Bureau and an indeterminate number of its followers and the ANP.

In membership, the Political Bureau was still composed of the five FLN leaders who were involved in its final organization during August 1962: that is, Ben Bella, Khider, Bitat, Ben Alla, and Mohammedi. Ben Bella, anticipating his election as Algeria's first president, designated Khider as the Political Bureau's secretary general, or party chief. It will be recalled that Ben Bella originally created the Political Bureau to function as a decision-making directorate of both the state and the party. Because the FLN organization was now largely nonexistent, the Political Bureau acted in fact only as an extragovernmental or informal state agency.

Boumedienne did not belong to the Political Bureau but occasionally shared with Ben Bella the major policy-making powers of the incipient political system. Boumedienne limited his activity mostly to matters involving the army, which he directed as his private domain. However, when Political Bureau decisions threatened the army's autonomy, Boumedienne's influence was usually decisive. It should be kept in mind, therefore, that Ben Bella's dominance over the state apparatus was always qualified by the position of Boumedienne.

It will be useful to identify certain structural criteria that apply theoretically to all mass political parties to determine the changes required to build the FLN into a mass political party as envisioned by the Tripoli Program. These can be stated as follows:

1. The party enjoys popular legitimacy, which is ordinarily a carryover from the role of the party or its leaders in the struggle against the *ancien régime*.
2. The party has a national leader, or a group of leaders, maintaining a monopoly of power, usually by control of the governmental bureaucracy and by exclusion of political competitors outside the party.
3. Procedures are established for the recruitment, selection, and training of party leaders.

4. The party maintains an organized constituency of all, or almost all, social and economic groups in order to implement party decisions and to gather information concerning the demands and interests of the various groups.
5. The party articulates an ideology and a program of political and economic objectives to promote the general welfare and engage the public in various aspects of the political process, such as voting, running for electoral office, canvassing, etc.
6. The party commands a mechanism for disciplining its members in accordance with particular decisions, policies, and doctrinal positions.
7. The party possesses a capability of financing its operations, usually through membership dues, donations, and governmental subsidies, or some combination of these sources.[16]

Except for the first, these criteria scarcely applied to the FLN at independence. As national leader, Ben Bella was seeking a monopoly of power through governmental control, but his personal interests clearly preceded the pursuit of party building. Indeed, the party as such did not exist. Thus, building a mass-party system demanded a monumental effort toward reconstructing the FLN. In assessing the FLN's development during the Ben Bella regime, specific elements of the above typology will be referred to in this and later chapters.

Faced with the enormity of rebuilding the party, Ben Bella chose instead to centralize political power in his own hands and to promote the development of the state or governmental apparatus. Purportedly, this would be the first step toward the political stability necessary for nurturing an institutionalized mass-party system. Practically and politically, of course, he could more easily fortify his authority over the state administration which he had already begun to control rather than over the FLN which offered only a potential for power. Yet, because Ben Bella expressed the goal of state building in the name of the FLN, the policies of the government were normally associated with Political Bureau decisions aimed at party building. The Political Bureau had supplanted the CNRA as the locus of executive authority prior to the formation of a duly constituted government. Because Ben Bella dominated it, the factor of personality became integrally related to the development of the new state institutions.

In late September 1962 the Political Bureau decided to proceed with the election of a Constituent National Assembly in order to legitimize the new political order. From the Evian agreements a plan was arranged for electing a national legislature to formulate a national constitution before the end of July 1962. While it possessed nominal authority, the Provisional Executive sought on three or four different occasions to conduct the election but was forced to postpone it each time because of the violence accompanying the Political Bureau-GPRA struggle. After the defeat of the GPRA, Khider postponed an election scheduled for September 2 because the Political Bureau "was not yet prepared to fully exercise its responsibilities."[17] This explanation meant in reality that the Political Bureau needed more time to revise the candidate list (drawn up by the Provisional Executive) in order to eliminate the names of its opponents in the GPRA and the wilayat. It was preordained that the National Assembly would be dominated by Ben Bella's partisans.

Ben Bella either selected or approved a majority of the list of 196 candidates. Generally, this majority consisted of those who were committed to him personally or politically as the paramount leader. As nominal FLN adherents, they could be described as the FLN representation. A minority of sixty other candidates, designated by Boumedienne, came from the Armée nationale populaire (ANP), as the regular army was renamed after independence. The soldiers were not required to relinquish their military status to serve in the legislature, and the FLN and ANP groups combined to form the legislature's dominant coalition.

Assured of a legislative majority, Ben Bella decided to nominate some of his recent opponents, seeking to create the impression of consensus among notable wartime leaders. They included wilaya separatists like Colonel Khatib and GPRA ministers Krim, Ben Tobbal, and Benkhedda. Though defeated, they remained too important politically to be excluded from the political arena. Ben Bella selected them for the National Assembly where their influence could be diluted and where "constructive" (parliamentary) opposition, as the Political Bureau termed it, would be tolerated. Ben Bella also placed nine women and sixteen Europeans on the list, a gesture that seemed to confirm his declared intention of welcoming all social elements into the system as active participants.[18]

Since most candidates were handpicked by Ben Bella, the significance of the Assembly election did not relate primarily to the candidates but rather to the scale of the electoral response. This index could be utilized to gauge public endorsement of the new leadership. As acceptance is a key element of legitimacy, the election served also to forecast the degree of popular support the regime might expect in the future.

The Political Bureau adopted the single-list system in presenting the list of candidates who represented Algeria's fifteen departments. This electoral procedure required the voter to register either an affirmative or negative vote for the candidates in his region. The voters could not nominate candidates themselves, and could indicate their opposition only by recording a negative vote or by abstaining from the election altogether. When the election booths opened on September 20, it was immediately evident that voter participation would be quite substantial and, despite sequels to the summer crisis in certain urban areas, the election proceeded in relative calm and order. What the final votes signified can be discussed after a perusal of Table 1, which shows voter responses to the candidate list and to the referendum authorizing the National Assembly to invest a government and frame a national constitution.

The table indicates that of the total of 6,504,033 registered voters, a majority of 5,303,661 voted for the Ben Bella-Boumedienne list. [19] Since this figure represented such an overwhelming majority, it tended to obscure the large number of abstentions. In Algiers, the abstentions probably stemmed from the GPRA's residual strength in certain quarters. Dissent aroused by the ANP's rout of the Tizi Ouzou group had not yet disappeared, and this evidently affected the voters' response in the Berber regions of Tizi Ouzou and Sétif.

The abstentions in Constantine were apparently caused by Boudiaf's intense opposition to the new regime. A resident of the area, he had already started to organize a clandestine movement, the Parti de la révolution socialiste (PRS), to challenge the regime through armed opposition. Boudiaf did not specify the political and programmatic goals of the PRS, but he did issue strong condemnations of Ben Bella on the night of the election by portraying him as an opportunistic politician pursuing his personal interests at the expense of the country.

Political unrest in the western regions of Oran and Tlemcen, fomented by King Hassan II of Morocco, caused the heavy abstentions there. The king, claiming Moroccan territorial rights to the

Table 1

ELECTORAL RESULTS FOR THE
CONSTITUENT NATIONAL ASSEMBLY AND THE REFERENDUM
SEPTEMBER 20, 1962

Département	Elections			Referendum	
	Registered	Voting	Abstentions (%)	Yes	No
Algiers	825,282	528,914	35.9	516,666	5,055
Batna	386,630	374,383	3.17	374,301	47
Bône	447,121	412,746	7.6	411,546	564
Constantine	771,363	662,149	14.16	658,408	789
La Saoura	103,449	89,080	13.89	88,041	319
Medea	505,588	454,911	10.03	452,883	573
Mostaganem	385,979	344,125	10.8	343,124	632
Oasis	286,494	263,011	8.20	262,259	65
Oran	517,850	416,665	19.54	408,443	5,455
Orléansville	387,851	323,085	16.7	—	—
Saida	138,208	117,606	13.02	117,370	168
Tiaret	196,098	174,538	11.00	174,136	277
Sétif	689,345	583,143	15.41	581,588	967
Tizi Ouzou	434,548	364,384	16.1	361,487	2,855
Tlemcen	231,239	194,069	16.00	193,273	569
TOTAL	6,504,033	5,303,661	18.46		

Sources: Le Monde, September 22, 1962, p. 4; and September 23-24, 1962, p. 2.

Saharan oil-rich areas of Tindouf and Colomb-Bechar, had an inter-
est in creating opposition to Ben Bella among the regions' residents.
Algeria's prospective socialist orientation encouraged Morocco's so-
cialist opposition, which threatened Hassan's conservative monarchy.
The king could readily influence the residents of western Algeria be-
cause many had received refuge in Morocco during the war. The
Oujda border passage remained accessible to both Algerians and
Moroccans, and the king's presence was continually felt there.

Significant abstentions in the other départements did not appear to
derive from voter opposition to the new leadership, but they indicated
that cleavages and dissidence persisted in these regions also. Still, the
election showed that a majority of voters in all départements accepted
the FLN-ANP ticket. Evidently, the Political Bureau did not falsify
the election because of the high rate of acknowledged abstentions.
The abstentions indicated generally that pockets of opposition con-

tinued and, hence, consensus-building as a means of monopolizing political legitimacy remained a task for the future.

In the National Assembly, Ait Ahmed emerged from the outset as the chief protagonist of the parliamentary opposition. Ben Bella had offered him a portfolio in the future government, but he declined to run for a legislative seat, expecting to act as an active critic of the regime. Ait Ahmed entered the Assembly without any past record of resistance to the Political Bureau. When he dissociated himself from Ben Bella in the summer crisis, he also kept his distance from Ben-khedda. Unlike Boudiaf, who first joined and later opposed the Political Bureau, he had not declared any specific objections to the new authority.

Three other deputies formed the core of the parliamentary opposition. They were Ahcene Mahiouz, a former wilaya commander; Boualem Oussedik, a politician who had held a minor FLN post in wartime; and Abdennour Ali Yahia, one of the UGTA's transient secretary generals during the war. Except for Ali Yahia, these deputies were relatively unknown in Algerian political circles. They sometimes acted in concert with Ait Ahmed, sometimes independently, and remained an insignificant minority in the history of the Assembly. Although it might have been expected that the former GPRA ministers would associate with the group, none in fact did. Benkhedda, who was defeated in the election, retired from politics and made no public statements except once, briefly in 1964 prior to the FLN congress.

The National Assembly convened on September 26, 1962, and immediately instructed Ben Bella to form a government. Of the 189 deputies present and voting, 141 voted in favor of his investiture. However, dissension ensued three days later when Ben Bella presented a list of cabinet appointees-designate. Not only were some of the nominees unknown to most deputies, but Ben Bella rushed the nominations through without allowing the deputies to debate or question his appointees. He simply outlined the current socioeconomic conditions of Algeria, and then he peremptorily requested a vote of confidence in the proposed government.[20]

Ait Ahmed attempted to sway parliamentary opinion by questioning the propriety of Ben Bella's action:

Numerous references were made to the Tripoli Program in Ben Bella's declaration, but I do not find in it any element proposing future policy perspectives. It contains only wishes, aspirations, and generalities. . . . It goes without saying that the prerogatives of this government must be defined clearly and that its powers will be exercised through this Assembly, the sole agent of national sovereignty. But I can only ascertain from Ben Bella's address that the mechanisms regulating authority between the Assembly and the government have not been formulated. [21]

While Ait Ahmed had made an accurate appraisal of Ben Bella's critical omissions on public policy and authority, the deputies were not deterred from approving the government. The tally of 158 affirmative votes, with 178 deputies present and voting, demonstrated Ben Bella's ability to marshal the Assembly in line with his decisions. The majority vote was a dramatic contrast to the total of nineteen abstentions and a single negative vote. [22] Ait Ahmed would later realize the rubber-stamp role of the Assembly.

The first duly constituted government of Algeria, like the National Assembly, was formed with the Ben Bella-Boumedienne alliance controlling the political system. It was composed of political and military personnel, some ministers performing strictly political functions, and others serving as quasi-proxies for the army. Ben Bella assumed major responsibility for appointing them, and so the cabinet mainly consisted of his personal or ideological allies. [23] Mohammed Nekkache, minister of public health, who was originally associated with Boumedienne, believed Ben Bella shared his radical socialist orientation and had aligned with him after independence. A Marxist like Ouzegane, Nekkache had rallied to Ben Bella when he announced his intention to "algerianize" (i.e., nationalize) the national economy. Mohammed Khobzi, the minister of commerce, was a wealthy Mozabite merchant (and Colonel Chaabani's patron), who supported Ben Bella in the summer crisis. [24] Bitat (the deputy premier) and Mohammedi (the minister of war veterans and victims) had helped Ben Bella to establish the Political Bureau. Other ministers like Boumendjel (reconstruction and public works) and Bachir Boumaza (labor and social affairs) could also be characterized primarily as adherents of the FLN and allies of Ben Bella. By staffing the government with a majority of his own supporters, Ben Bella asserted his authority as supreme political leader.

Besides Boumedienne, the ANP representation included four newcomers to political leadership: Abdelazziz Bouteflika, minister of youth and sports, who belonged to the ANP general staff and had distinguished himself as an ALN major in wartime; Ahmed Medeghri, minister of the interior, who had commanded ALN divisions at Oujda and Tlemcen; Laroussi Khalifa, minister of industrialization and energy, who had assisted Boussouf in the GPRA but sided with Boumedienne during the Political Bureau-GPRA struggle; and Moussa Hassani, minister of telecommunications, who was a former ALN captain. All of these men owed their appointments to Boumedienne, the new regime's minister of national defense.

Ben Bella's government included few of the FLN's major wartime leaders. Here the FLN's leadership turnover was revealed, and it underscored the extensive realignment of political and military forces after independence. Ben Bella and Bitat were the only "historic chiefs" who reached the postindependent power structure. [25] Except for Francis and Madani, none of the GPRA's final leaders participated in it. The decline of the former leaders resulted in an almost complete change in executive leadership, all in about seven years and all within the same political movement.

By 1962, a younger generation of political and military militants, newly arrived to authority, had replaced the deposed leaders. Mohammed Khemisti and Bouteflika typified the newcomers. Born in Marnia (Ben Bella's birthplace) in 1930, Khemisti embarked in nationalist politics as a UGEMA secretary while he was studying medicine at the University of Montpellier in the mid-1950s. He was arrested in 1957 for student agitation in France, and he later joined the FLN, aligning himself with Ben Bella following his release in March 1962. Khemisti participated as a Ben Bella partisan in the Provisional Executive before independence and thereby assured his prominence in the new leadership. Bouteflika, borne in 1935 at Oujda (Morocco), abandoned lycée studies to support the revolutionary struggle. Unlike Khemisti, he entered the regular army as the route to leadership mobility, beginning as an assistant to a wilaya IV unit and rising eventually to command the ALN headquarters at Oujda. Khemisti received his promotion through Ben Bella while Bouteflika earned his promotion through his close relationship with Boumedienne. Leadership mobility therefore was inextricably bound to alliance with either Ben Bella or Boumedienne. This pattern became a constant in the socialization of political elites in the history of the Ben Bella regime.

Another significant development resulting from the formalization of the government was a further convolution of authority between the state and the Political Bureau. Since all members of the Political Bureau, except Mohammed Khider and Hadj Ben Alla, held positions in the government, the question inevitably arises as to who made governmental policy and who decided FLN policy. Further clarity is required to distinguish the Political Bureau from the Council of Ministers, the state executive composed of all cabinet ministers.

As a practical matter, there was merely a vague distinction between the government and the Political Bureau because Ben Bella acted as the primary decision-maker of both bodies. The Political Bureau continued to function as an informal state agency exercising consultative and advisory powers. The Council of Ministers had more members, but it could not otherwise be differentiated from the Political Bureau. Functionally, the state and FLN executives corresponded to each other. State and FLN instrumentalities were fused in the Political Bureau, with the result that a superimposition of executive roles and functions blurred their separate identities.

As pointed out earlier, Ben Bella intended to solidify his control over the government and the legislature. This ambition explained why he selected Ben Alla, his anchor man in the Assembly, to become vice-president of that body. Abbas, the Assembly president, had sided with the Tlemcen group in the summer crisis, but the moderate leader exhibited no firm loyalty to Ben Bella. Ben Bella distrusted Abbas' pro-Western ideological orientation and, to thwart this influence, had Ben Alla seated next to him. Boumedienne worked exclusively to retain independent control of the army and wanted civilian leaders to defer to him on military matters. He had also manifested some interest in broader political leverage as evidenced by his selection of ministers to the government and deputies to the Assembly.

The personality factor was featured again when Ben Bella restructured the state administration. Algeria still existed under the civil administrative system created by the Europeans in the colonial period. In descending order, this hierarchy of authority consisted of 15 départements, 100 *arrondissements* (districts), and 1,590 communes (townships).[26] A *préfet*, a *sous-préfet*, and a mayor presided over each of these divisions, respectively. When Ben Bella reorganized the administration in late 1962, he left the département and arrondissement networks intact, but compressed the communes into 630 units (later increased to 675) and placed them under the control of newly created bodies called the *délégations spéciales*. [27] Each delegation, whose membership fluctuated from town to town, wielded considerable local influence by exercising control of budgets and law enforcement. Administratively responsible to the Ministry of the Interior, the new agencies were required to submit their proposals and decisions for approval to the presidency. The government first announced that the delegations would be chosen through municipal elections, but Ben Bella appointed or approved all of them.

The government appointed former soldiers to head several prefectures and subprefectures, which established the army's participation in civil administration. The Ministry of the Interior published statistics revealing that ALN officers governed seven of the prefectures which were reconstructed by 1963; former *internés* (soldiers imprisoned by the French in wartime) controlled two prefectures; and former FLN officials headed six. [28] The eighty-three subprefectures then functioning consisted of twenty-five soldiers, thirteen internés, thirty-five former FLN officials, and ten militants or current FLN adherents.

The system of local control operated inefficiently in certain areas. Corruption was uncovered in January 1963, when members of the Aumale and Tounin delegations were arrested for embezzling public funds. Malfeasance of this sort often caused the government to dissolve entire delegations, with the result that some local administrations existed on a sporadic basis.

In Constantine and the Sahara, wilayism prevailed as strong guerrilla commanders forced the new institutions to surrender their authority. Si Larbi, a wilaya II commander who seized political and military control of Constantine during the war, kept the local administration entirely under his authority. [29] Similarly, Colonel Chaabani, commander of the Saharan territories of wilaya VI in the war, maintained his region as a personal preserve. The government coexisted with these local autocrats shortly after independence because Ben Bella was indebted to Chaabani for his military support in the summer crisis, and Si Larbi remained Boumedienne's loyal lieutenant. Wilaya control, however, nullified the effect of Ben Bella's administrative reorganization in the two regions.

The delegation system proved dysfunctional in certain areas, but it succeeded generally in establishing the regime's local control. Despite its weaknesses, the administration maintained the only organized civil institutions and established the state's authority and visibility in the country. The administration became an instrument of personal rule because it functioned mainly as the policy-implementing arm of Ben Bella's leadership. Lacking institutional autonomy, the administration, like the government and National Assembly, reflected the prevalence of personal rule.

It has already been observed that the Assembly included a military faction of about sixty deputies. As partisans of the government, they strengthened the FLN (Ben Bella) majority in the legislature. The combination of ANP administrative and legislative representatives allowed what might be called a military bloc to emerge in the political system. This development was a logical consequence of the political-military alliance. The Assembly's army faction concentrated its attention on budgetary benefits for the ANP, while the soldiers in the administration received their orders directly from the government. Like Boumedienne, the soldiers in politics generally referred to the politicians under Ben Bella on issues that did not affect the army.

The basic features of the new political system were solidified by mid-1963. In one year Ben Bella had constructed a legislature, a government, and civil bureaucracy that conformed to his personal preferences. When Ben Bella annexed the post of foreign affairs to the presidency following the death of Khemisti in April,[30] he augmented his governmental authority. Boumedienne remained a cooperative ally since Ben Bella did not interfere in army matters. The new state institutions developed precisely as they did because of Ben Bella's decision in 1962 to centralize political power in accord with his personal prerogatives.

In view of this analysis on state building, tentative conclusions can now be offered regarding the criteria for the development of the FLN as a mass party. The election results affirmed the popular legitimacy of the FLN. Ben Bella, as the supreme national leader, had made significant strides toward a monopoly of political power through the new state administration which he structured and also controlled. His decisions, made in the name of the FLN, tended to make it something more than a symbol of authority, and the various FLN adherents at the sublevels of the state apparatus represented the potential cadres for a widely diffused party organization. The Political Bureau assumed the role of party executive and, being largely indistinguishable from the government, enhanced the possibility for developing the party into an authoritative institution.

The FLN satisfied hardly any of the other criteria for a mass party (identified above). The party system the Political Bureau claimed to represent was largely nonexistent; membership in the party executive was determined by Ben Bella's personal selection, not through a regularized process of recruitment, training, and promotion. The Tripoli Program elaborated a party ideology and program, but it was too general as a systematic guideline for specific actions. And although the Political Bureau could avail itself of the coercive backing of Boumedienne's army, the FLN leaders were totally dependent on a nonparty institution to enforce party decisions. The financial capability of the FLN was uncertain, but it could be assumed that the government as well as nongovernmental institutions, groups, and individuals affiliating with the FLN would respond to this need. [31]

The monopoly of political power that Ben Bella was in the process of acquiring constituted, in his view, a prerequisite to the rebuilding of the FLN. Instead of building the party from the base upwards, he decided to organize it from the top downwards. What resulted was a centralized political system that enabled him to determine local leadership and governmental priorities on a personal basis. The progressive expansion of governmental control led to the creation of new state agencies that were subsumed under the various ministries already in existence. The Ministries of Agriculture and Labor, for instance, set up special bureaus for agrarian reform and trade union affairs in order to entrench the government's authority in their respective domains. As political organization increased at the state level, Ben Bella's decision-making powers spiraled in conformity with his state-building formula.

5
Personal Rule and the FLN

The process of party development under the Ben Bella regime provoked a resurgence of many problems that the FLN leaders had failed to resolve at the Soummam Valley Congress. The Political Bureau's victory over the GPRA terminated the struggle between internal and external leaders but, as will be discussed in this chapter, the problem of intraleadership conflict prevailed within the Political Bureau itself. By now, civilian government was firmly established over military rule. Consequently, political issues had taken precedence over military concerns, but political and military operatives became intertwined once again through the political-military alliance. This phenomenon was illustrated most vividly by the FLN-ANP coalition in the National Assembly. The alliance finally closed the question of collegial leadership, but at the cost of institutionalizing Ben Bella's personal rule.

Also critical to the FLN's postindependent development were the problems of a party ideology and a definition of the party's relationship to such mass groups as the trade unionists. The Tripoli Program represented a considerable theoretical advance from the ideological lacuna inherited from Soummam; it did not, however, constitute a *Weltanschauung* capable of inducing action consequences. The party's orientation toward mass groups was clarified somewhat by the Tripoli Program, but they had been largely autonomous of the FLN since 1958. All these problems had remained unresolved since Soummam and now resurfaced, though in diminished form, to bedevil the FLN's growth after independence.

Ben Bella sought to formalize his emerging monopoly of power through a national constitution. In the name of the FLN, he had already established a new state system and started the process of eliminating and coopting his political opposition. Since his personal rule was built around the new administrative edifice he constructed, the government and the National Assembly also required a formalized status. The role and powers of the FLN now demanded definitive elaboration because the political system itself was ostensibly centered on the party. The constitution Ben Bella introduced in 1963 completed all these requirements. It also formally integrated the army into the political system.

Serious efforts were being made toward party building while Ben Bella concentrated on consolidating the state system and formalizing his control over it. It was not Ben Bella but Mohammed Khider who, as secretary general of the FLN, initiated this formidable undertaking. Ben Bella, who approached party development cautiously, had resisted the call for a party congress to overhaul the FLN's institutional deficiencies, but he granted Khider a relatively free hand in rebuilding the atrophied party movement. To expedite the elimination of political opposition to the FLN, Ben Bella also authorized the use of ANP troops. But at the point where Ben Bella perceived Khider's partial success as a threat to his personal rule, he forced Khider out of office and thus prolonged the delay in party building.

What becomes clear from an analysis of these events is a complex web of politics that involved a fundamental contradiction between Ben Bella's personal rule and the institutionalization of a mass-party system. Khider, who had leadership ambitions of his own, made considerable progress in revitalizing the FLN through new party institutions and a reorganization of its constituency; procedures were also formulated for the recruitment and selection of party leaders. [1] But the dynamic of conflict persisted between Khider's efforts and the priorities of Ben Bella's personal power. The outcome, as will be shown, produced a retrenchment of the latter at the expense of party reconversion.

Legitimizing Personal Rule: The Constitution of 1963

Algerian voters mandated the National Assembly to draft a constitution by approving the constitutional referendum of September 20,

1962. This task was supposed to be completed, and the draft constitution submitted for ratification by the electorate, before the legislature's one-year constituent status expired. Ben Bella encouraged the deputies in this effort when they invested him to form his government: "Concerning the constitution, your Assembly is sovereign. You will give the country a constitution which, in your estimation, responds to the people's aspirations. As to its content, as well as the modalities of its adoption and application, the government will remain in rigorous neutrality."[2] Accordingly, the president of the Assembly, Ferhat Abbas, organized a Special Constitutional Commission to fulfill the legislature's mandate. Two drafts were introduced to the Assembly as early as April 1963; one had been prepared by Abbas, and another by a group of deputies which included Boualem Oussedik, a member of the government's parliamentary opposition. Thus, the deputies were astounded when the Political Bureau announced on July 30 that a group of FLN adherents, not the Assembly, would meet the next day to approve the "official" draft constitution that Ben Bella and FLN leaders had formulated.[3]

Abbas reacted strongly against this preemptive tactic and, in protest, announced his immediate resignation as Assembly president. In his judgment, the "presidential regime and personal power" had made a travesty of the law:

> The government has submitted a draft constitution to the so-called cadres of the party, which in fact does not yet exist, without informing the Assembly. To go further and have such a fundamental text, which falls in the essential jurisdiction of the deputies, approved by [FLN] militants not only creates confusion but also violates the law.[4]

Ben Bella and the government, however, had already contravened one law (i.e., the Assembly's mandate), so it was no surprise that the next step, approving what in fact was Ben Bella's draft, was taken. If Abbas intended to dissuade the deputies from supporting Ben Bella, he promoted the opposite result; for Ben Bella directed the FLN-ALN parliamentary coalition to elect his ally, Ben Alla, as the new Assembly president. The deputies had not been able to make substantive decisions independently of the government since the legislature's creation, though a few like Ait Ahmed had tried. Now with a member of the Political Bureau as its chief officer, the Assembly was fully relegated to a rubber-stamp role.

Labeled the "official draft from the conference of FLN leaders," the Ben Bella constitution was presented to the Assembly for debate on August 24 by five progovernment deputies. They included Mohammed Benmahjoub, an FLN adherent close to Ben Bella; Ali Mendjeli, a soldier who supported Boumedienne in the Assembly by chairing its national defense committee; and Belkacem Cherif, another Boumedienne supporter and a soldier. Ait Ahmed did not attend the debate, but other opposition members attempted to contest the constitution's proposals for party control of all state machinery. Since the Political Bureau already controlled the state, it followed that such sections, once ratified, would merely legitimize the status quo.

Ali Yahia, a prominent member of the opposition, and two other deputies introduced an amendment requesting precise definitions of the party's composition, functions, and organization. The amendment was clearly designed to expose the fiction of the party-state sections because the demanded definitions were bound to show that the FLN did not possess the requisites to qualify as a genuine party. Zohra Driff, a deputy and wife of Rabah Bitat, emphasized the point: "We cannot hand over all power to a party which, among other things, does not yet have its structures organized."[5] Other deputies introduced amendments to maintain the Assembly's (nominal) legislative powers, but none was adopted.

When the debate ended on August 28, the 170 deputies present and voting approved the original Ben Bella draft by a vote of 139 in favor, 23 against, and 8 abstentions. The National Assembly sanctioned, in the caustic assessment of one opposition member, a "constitutional regime of the government by the party. . . . *The party is everything.*"[6]

The Political Bureau conducted a preratification campaign to solicit public support for the new constitution. An intensive program—involving discussions, explanations, and a defense of various constitutional provisions—was devised to shape public opinion. Campaign methods included public speeches, mass rallies, and direct personal contacts with large family or communal heads. The constitutional ratification was deliberately publicized as an opportunity to endorse the Ben Bella regime, and voters tended to equate their views on the document with their orientation toward the government. They appeared to regard the constitution as a related part of the social and economic order in which they, as citizens who voted for Ben Bella's chosen candidates in 1962, had a vested interest.

The turnout at the polls on September 8, 1963, was considerable. A total of 5,122,854 Algerians, out of 6,314,451 registered voters, cast ballots. Compared to the 1962 Assembly election, the number of voters decreased by 200,000 (from 6,504,033 to 6,314,451) because of a drop in registrations.[7] The results from all thirteen départements are tabulated in Table 2.

The large number of abstentions in Algiers (219,773) and Constantine (133,642) was clearly related to political unrest. After its formation in the fall of 1962, Boudiaf's underground opposition, the PRS, attracted a small force of discontented trade unionists, intellectuals, and college students to carry on his underground resistance to "personal power."[8] The movement never acquired significant member-

Table 2

POPULAR RATIFICATION OF THE REFERENDUM
FOR THE ALGERIAN CONSTITUTION
SEPTEMBER 8, 1963

Département	Electorate		Ballots		
	Registered	Voting	Yes	No	Abstentions
Algiers	747,879	528,106	516,457	11,649	219,773
Bône	477,391	432,283	431,328	678	45,108
Constantine	772,434	638,792	632,726	6,066	133,642
La Saoura	103,650	93,923	93,615	137	9,627
Mostaganem	385,865	348,204	343,088	1,304	37,661
Oasis	305,511	278,329	277,660	485	27,182
Oran	421,443	404,400	400,780	1,565	17,043
Orléansville	399,489	360,411	359,742	526	39,078
Saida	124,887	109,201	107,720	1,281	15,686
Tiaret	189,150	173,393	172,693	586	15,757
Tizi Ouzou	427,480	205,825	167,817	36,711	221,655
Tlemcen	139,101	125,687	123,427	179	13,414
Batna*					
Medea*					
Sétif*					
TOTAL	6,314,451	5,122,854	5,016,692	95,175	

*No data available.
Source: Le Peuple, September 10, 1963.

ship or organizational structure, and Ben Bella had it banished in the summer of 1963. While the PRS existed, it succeeded in fomenting substantial opposition to the regime in Algiers and Constantine.

The most numerous abstentions were recorded in the Tizi Ouzou département (viz., 221,655), revealing the significant protest there. Violent opposition surfaced in the Berber heartland during June 1963 when Ait Ahmed, convinced that parliamentary opposition would not influence governmental policy, quit the Assembly to organize a clandestine movement, the Front des forces socialistes (FFS). Through armed struggle, he aimed to overthrow the Ben Bella regime, which he considered corrupt, and then to institute a policy of "humane socialism."[9] The FFS had as few as 150 members at first, but it began to pose a serious challenge in late September when Colonel Mohand Ou El Hadj, the former wilaya commander who led the Tizi Ouzou battalion at independence, rallied to the insurgent movement. Like Ait Ahmed, he was a Berber. He commanded some 3,000 ANP troops and was evidently prepared to employ them against the regime. Neutrality was impossible between the FFS and the government, the colonel concluded, because "those who really fought the [revolutionary war] are going hungry."[10] He accused the government of awarding job priority to political newcomers, whose essential qualifications were loyalty to Ben Bella, and to soldiers who had made up the external forces of Boumedienne's army. Although the FFS did not call for open warfare at that time, its appeal in Kabylia must have caused many Berbers to abstain from the election.

Since the government publicized the decline in voter registration as well as the high rate of abstentions in sensitive areas, it can be assumed that it did not rig the election. In number, the voting population that ratified the constitution closely corresponded to that which approved the National Assembly in 1962.[11] It could be surmised therefore that popular support for the regime remained fairly high despite significant protest.

The new constitution formalized a state system in which national authority was exercised by a powerful presidency. As Borella pointed out in his study, the president became more than an executor of Assembly decisions, and the principle of the separation of powers did not obtain in the document.[12] Article 47, for example, enabled the president to form his government without parliamentary investiture, while requiring that at least two-thirds of his ministers be deputies.[13] Article 54 empowered him to appoint all civil and military positions. Under Article 48, the president alone defined, directed, and conducted the government's foreign and domestic policy "in conformity with the will of the people as formulated by the party and expressed by the National Assembly." While Article 52 authorized him to assure the execution of the laws, Article 53 permitted him to exercise statutory power.

Article 28 stated that the Assembly "voted laws and controlled governmental action," but the president exercised direct lawmaking powers under certain conditions. For a "limited period," according to Article 58, he could enact laws through such powers as the Assembly delegated to him upon his request. After expiration of the delegated authority, he simply had to "submit" the enacted measures to the deputies for ratification. The bias toward presidential power was reinforced by Article 59 which enabled the president to take "exceptional measures" for protecting the nation's independence and institutions in case of "imminent danger," a condition that he alone determined.

In the face of the broad powers of the president, the Assembly retained a single check. It could invoke presidential responsibility (under Article 55) by a motion of censure signed by at least one-third of the deputies. In addition to the restriction (under Article 56) that an absolute majority was necessary for the motion, censure compelled an automatic dissolution of the Assembly itself. Ben Bella's coalition predominated in the Assembly; hence, this legislative constraint appeared as a mere chimera. It is worth noting in this context that the deputies defeated an opposition member's amendment that would have limited the president's tenure to two five-year terms. As Article 39 fixed his tenure at five years without further time limitations, it intimated that Ben Bella intended to hold office for an indefinite future.

Significantly, Article 34 identified the National Assembly president as the second-ranking official in the state. This provision meant that Ben Bella, using Ben Alla as an intermediary, could now legally impose governmental decisions on the legislature. Considering that Ben Alla already acted as a Political Bureau executive and as the Assembly president, the new (third) role further confirmed Ben Bella's attempt to interlock state and party operations to better control both. As if more proof was needed, Article 36 authorized the chief executive and the deputies to initiate legislation. This provision, in practice, enabled

Ben Bella and his immediate followers to make the laws. The constitution thus legitimized an arrangement between the state and the party whereby the government's decision-making powers substituted for the legislature's and the party's too. It went beyond a mere codification of the status quo, so far as Ben Bella's formal powers were concerned, and elevated presidential authority to an unprecedented degree.

The Ben Bella constitution contained no provision for collegial rule. Personal rule had replaced collective leadership as the basis of political organization, and the main intent of the constitution was to ratify the president's exclusive authority. The Draconian provisions for the presidency fulfilled this purpose.

Although Article 43 made the president supreme commander of the armed forces, Ben Bella's alliance with Boumedienne necessarily attenuated formal presidential prerogatives. Nevertheless, the state's political institutions could be considered under the control of one man so long as he maintained the army leader's support. Collegial rule had collapsed as a force in Algerian politics at the Tripoli Conference, and the new constitution discarded it once and for all.

Predictably, the political-military alliance was reflected among the constitution's provisions. For instance, Article 8 permitted the army to act in the making of economic and social policies as well as to engage in political activities. Indeed, military participation was so central to the constitution that the preamble also carried this provision. Article 8 and the preamble circumscribed the army's role "within the framework of the party," but it is instructive to note that Ben Bella's original draft authorizing the FLN to "control the ANP's action" did not appear in the constitution,[14] a deletion that responded unmistakably to Boumedienne's intervention. The army's right to political participation was established unconditionally.

All military questions rested exclusively with the Higher Council of Defense, according to Article 68. Its composition, as fixed by Article 67, consisted of seven members: the president (Ben Bella) and two of his appointees; the ministers of defense (Boumedienne), the interior (Medeghri), and foreign affairs (Ben Bella); and the chairman of the National Assembly's defense committee (Mendjeli). Ben Bella could also decide military policy, and Article 45 authorized him to preside over the council. The functions of the council, like its composition, were supposed to introduce civilian influence into Boumedienne's domain. This provisional encroachment may explain why the council apparently did not come into existence.[15]

Ben Bella authored the constitution, of course, but the substantial prerogatives it conceded to the army were attributable to Boumedienne. Did the constitution thereby bring into question the stability of the Ben Bella-Boumedienne alliance?

At the time of the constitutional election, no evidence could be adduced to show that Boumedienne maneuvered to usurp governmental authority. While it remained obvious that the ANP posed a danger to Ben Bella's leadership, general opinion agreed that Boumedienne did not seek political control. No serious disagreement occurred between the two leaders, except for Ben Bella's attempt to supervise the army through the FLN (as indicated by his constitutional proposal discussed above). Boumedienne was cognizant of the public's distrust of military leaders and probably recognized the difficulty of governing without the political and moral consensus that Ben Bella, a "historic chief" and a national hero, brought to the regime. Moreover, he had already obtained his maximal demands by controlling the ANP and influencing governmental policy. "Army organization," Halpern notes, "may make it peculiarly difficult for [military chiefs] to succeed in politics unless they are uncommonly blessed with charisma, political skill, or incompetent opponents."[16] Boumedienne possessed none of these qualities, and Ben Bella's competency was not seriously in question. The political-military alliance reflected mutual dependence and hence mutual need.

Creation of the One-Party System

The new constitution subordinated all governmental institutions to the party and, by Article 23, the FLN was declared the only legitimate political party in Algeria. Theoretically, the party was to predominate over the presidency and the National Assembly. Article 27, acknowledging that sovereignty rested in the people, authorized the FLN to designate the deputies who exercised it through legislation. Article 23 and Article 26 made the FLN responsible for defining national policy, inspiring the state's policies, and controlling the activities of both the National Assembly and the government. As noted in Article 48, the president executed policies in accordance with "the will of the people as formulated by the party." The preamble left the powers of the party open-ended, stating that the FLN supervised the activity of *all* other institutions described in the constitution.

Taken together, the constitution's prerogatives for the FLN formalized the authoritative capacity necessary for the evolution of a strong party. Although a definitive statement of the FLN's ideology and program was yet to be made, the legal or formal bases for the implementation of party decisions were now established.

The new constitution accomplished what Ben Bella intended. That is, it further legitimized and consolidated his regime's right to power, endowing it with what Apter calls "moral validity."[17] Soldiers were assimilated into the system as guarantors of Ben Bella's personal rule. Insofar as Ben Bella's personal interests were concerned, the constitution succeeded most by centralizing governmental power in the presidency. Instead of differentiating the existing state structures, the constitution fused them even more. Its direct effect on the political system was the formalization of nearly absolute legal authority in the presidency.

Although the constitution enhanced the legitimacy of the FLN and provided a formal structure for FLN leaders to monopolize political power, there emerged also the specter of undue military influence over the FLN in the constitutional provisions for the ANP. This development did not appear to impede party building because Boumedienne assisted the process by providing an enforcement capability that the FLN could not generate from within its own organization. At the same time, the possibility existed that the party would outgrow its dependence on the army.

It will be recalled that the Tripoli Program proposed that after independence the FLN should be developed into a mass political party that would prevail over the entire political system. FLN leaders were expected to control the government at all levels and also to implement policies that emanated from the party system. The constitution furthered this objective by establishing de jure the single-party system. Henceforth, FLN organization could be promoted without competition from other (legal) political organizations. But the pervasive powers that the constitution conferred òn Ben Bella determined that party development could not be separated from his personal leadership. Party development also depended upon the political-military alliance because Ben Bella's ability to enforce political decisions was ultimately tied to the coercive support provided by Boumedienne and the ANP. For the FLN's future development, therefore, the critical question was whether Ben Bella's personal goals coincided with the growth of a fully institutionalized party system.

Party Development and Personal Interests

The FLN organization was in shambles when Khider undertook the process of party building in late 1962. For the most part, the FLN had lost control of its organized, dues-paying constituency in wartime, and no new recruitment procedures had been established. Then Ben Bella's chief political partner, Khider, declined government membership to accept the strategic position as secretary general of the Political Bureau. He considered a cohesive national party organization essential to consolidating the political system; he advocated not simply the party's preponderance but its complete monopoly over public affairs. Ben Bella concurred in this principle as the Political Bureau's official guideline on party conversion. As the main FLN strategist, Khider planned to reify the principle by converting the FLN into a forceful political structure devoid of military dependence.

In the development of the FLN's leadership, Khider advocated a mass political party that would draw its leaders from all popular constituent groups. Ben Bella, on the other hand, favored an elite mass party that would admit only a vanguard of highly politicized party leaders to effective party participation. The distinction between a mass party and an elite mass party represented a difference in degree, not in kind; as explained later, this distinction served mainly to mask a power struggle between Khider and Ben Bella.

With Khider its principal advocate, the FLN appeared to have strong leadership at the top. After all, he was the most influential leader in Algeria after Ben Bella and Boumedienne. There were also three Political Bureau members who represented the FLN in the government: Ben Bella, deputy premier Bitat, and minister of war veterans Mohammedi. Hadj Ben Alla, then vice-president of the National Assembly, served as party liaison in legislative affairs. Boumedienne, a nominal FLN adherent, did not belong to the Political Bureau but participated in governmental policy-making when party matters concerned the army. Boumedienne was not on the Political Bureau because of its members' decision to develop the FLN with a personality independent of the military.

While the FLN remained an impotent force in politics, its representatives frequently conducted policy as though it were a full-fledged
party. The handling of a labor bill at the first regular session of the
National Assembly illustrates the point. On the request of UGTA
leaders, Abdennour Ali Yahia (a former UGTA secretary general)
joined other deputies sympathetic to the trade union in introducing a
bill that proposed a consultative function for the UGTA in the Assembly's working committees. Ait Ahmed argued that the bill guaranteed
trade union participation in policy-making and labor unity in the
building of Algerian socialism.[18] Ben Bella, however, fearing that
such a prerogative might allow the UGTA to influence governmental
policy, instructed the coalition of FLN-ANP deputies to oppose the
bill. Ahmed Kaid, a deputy who spoke for the Political Bureau, com-
municated the official line: "The party must take precedence over the
government and the parliament, and all national organizations must
follow party channels. . . . The last word must be given to the party and
to the party alone."[19] The majority coalition subsequently defeated
the bill. Notwithstanding the FLN's illusory character, its adherents
did not hesitate to defend their actions in its name.

Viewed in substantive terms, the "party" at that time referred to
Khider's headquarters, to the Political Bureau's membership, and to
the innumerable loosely associated individuals whose informal and
intermittent involvements with the FLN gave it potentiality. Ben Bella
lent his personal prestige to the FLN, declaring it to be the new arena
for the aggregation of all mass social and economic groups. When
Boumedienne eliminated the wilaya guerrillas from the army, he
urged them to join the FLN as civilians. The FLN occupied the nominal center of Algerian politics after independence, and this strategic
position endowed it with singular symbolic value. It appeared significant not because it exerted organizational force in politics but
because influential leaders spoke and acted in its name.

As to the redevelopment of party institutions, Ben Bella and Khider
decided in July 1962 that a CNRA meeting should be held before the
end of the year in order to reconstruct the FLN and formulate a party
program. This agreement was one of the terms of Khider's support in
the summer crisis. But the Ben Bella-Boumedienne alliance had since
supplanted the CNRA as a national party executive, and Ben Bella
now argued that the earlier decision was null and void. Khider dis-
agreed, proposing that a party congress be substituted for the CNRA

meeting in order to accomplish the same purpose. The two leaders' positions thus involved substantial differences on the priority of party building.

Bourgès, a Frenchman who served as an advisor to Ben Bella, has explained that the ostensible procedural differences carried personal overtones:

> Ben Bella, seconded by Hadj Ben Alla, believed it difficult if not impossible to undertake the simultaneous construction of a solid state system and a revolutionary party right after independence. . . . Structuring the state and preparing for the development of institutions envisioned in the Tripoli Program were the important tasks he thought should be realized, even before contemplating a party congress. In any event, the congress would primarily benefit Khider because it would bring together numerous militants who lacked a common ideology and served merely as tools for personal maneuver. [20]

Khider yielded to Ben Bella and dropped the plan for a party congress, but eventually persuaded Ben Bella of the necessity of beginning early to develop the FLN. Ben Bella's acceptance (or toleration) of immediate party building could be interpreted in terms of the personal debt he owed Khider. That is, Khider's adroit negotiations with the opposing wilaya leaders in the summer of 1962 were largely responsible for Ben Bella's return to Algiers, and thus his triumph over the GPRA.

Ben Bella did not interfere with Khider's efforts because he usually fixed his attention on foreign policy whenever he turned from state building. He aspired to promote socialist Algeria (and himself) as leader of the revolutionary forces in the Third World. This ambition was affirmed by his trip to Cuba in October 1962 and to the Addis Ababa meeting of the Organization of African Unity in May 1963, and by his regular presidential receptions for such prestigious leaders as Nasser (in May 1963) and Chou En-lai (in December 1963). [21] Ben Bella's goal was to align himself diplomatically and ideologically with these leaders. But this focus on foreign policy did not distract him from promoting his major domestic goal, namely, institutionalizing the bases of his personal power.

Ben Bella's neglect of party affairs did not facilitate Khider's task, but it left Khider in the advantageous position of being able to operate more or less independently. This freedom by default would have serious consequences not only for party development but also for the relationship between the two men.

Establishing FLN supremacy started as a drive by the Political Bureau to suppress all political movements or groups resisting it. More precisely, it involved Ben Bella's decision to eliminate all organized opposition to his leadership and, as a secondary effect, to eliminate group competition to the FLN. FLN affairs also concerned Boumedienne—directly through the use of the ANP for the FLN's coercive power and indirectly by encouraging the guerrillas whom he expelled from the army to join the FLN. Thus, in different ways, party development involved Khider, Ben Bella, and Boumedienne.

One group the Political Bureau decided to eliminate upon independence was the PCA. Ben Bella harbored deep hostility toward Algerian communists because they seemed to oppose his rise to power. The PCA also objected to his insistence on Arab-Islamic culture as the normative roots of Algerian socialism, with the peasant masses as its social basis. In the summer crisis, the communists kept their distance from Ben Bella and Khider, whom they distrusted; later, the PCA refused to approve the Political Bureau and the Tripoli Program. The PCA instructed its adherents to vote for the Political Bureau list in the National Assembly election, but condemned the "anti-democratic method of designating candidates." [22] As Marxists, they were conditioned to view society in terms of class struggle; they regarded the peasantry as a *lumpenproletariat* and urban workers as the truly progressive, revolutionary social group. The fact that ANP soldiers were largely of peasant origin, and anticommunist as well, reinforced their conviction that the peasants constituted reactionary elements. As internationalists and atheists, the communists rejected Ben Bella's insistence on an Arab-Islamic identity.

The Political Bureau's opposition to the communists was heightened by their demand for party autonomy after independence. To dramatize his opposition, Ben Bella condemned the PCA in a public address on November 4, 1962: "The PCA's action, inspired only by demagogy, does not accord with the country's interest. We will not allow the communists to propagate negative and pessimistic positions, especially since they did so little to bring about our [national] liberation." [23] The communists did not know it at the time, but this was their last warning to accept cooptation into the FLN (i.e., direction from the Political Bureau) or to be outlawed in the political system.

The PCA remained influential among urban labor and intellectual groups after independence, particularly in Oran and Algiers, although its organizational structure was almost devastated by the war and subsequent European emigration. The residue of PCA adherents, or individuals who called themselves communists, approximated 10,000. [24] Rather than party cadres or organizational strength, PCA influence consisted in its virtual monopoly of Algeria's newspaper media. This control represented significant influence because the government had not yet established a television network and had just begun to expand its radio broadcasting facilities.

The communists published the country's largest selling newspaper, *Alger républicain*, which sold 30,000 copies daily after it resumed circulation in July 1962. [25] When the FLN-operated *La Dépêche d'Algérie* folded in 1962 because of fiscal mismanagement, the PCA paper's circulation rose to 70,000 copies daily. The official FLN organ, *El Moujahid*, was the main source of public information during the war, but it sharply declined in circulation and public interest after independence. The Political Bureau established another party newspaper, *Le Peuple*, in August 1962, and, despite substantial governmental subsidies, its daily circulation never exceeded 3,000 copies. [26] The small core of communists penetrated the political and ideological consciousness of the urban Algerian public to a much greater extent than their membership might indicate.

Besides controlling the most widely read newspaper, the communists published two other journals: *Révolution africaine*, a weekly written in magazine format, and *El Hourriya*, a weekly newspaper. Jacques Vergès, a lawyer and French communist, founded *Révolution africaine* after independence, and it soon became the herald of the pro-Peking line in Africa. The communist papers, especially *Alger républicain*, were of better journalistic quality and tended to be less propagandistic in reporting events than the FLN papers. They appealed to articulate elements such as university students, trade unionists, intellectuals, and some bureaucrats, as shown by the high distribution of the communist publications. The successful communist papers often criticized the regime's policy positions. The Political Bureau became increasingly concerned that such criticisms might stimulate public opposition.

Very soon after independence, the government suppressed the PCA and contained its publications. *El Hourriya* was seized on November 23, 1962. Mohammed Hadj Hamou, minister of information, announced six days later that the government had banned the PCA. Given the Tripoli Program's prescription for a party system, he said, "there is no room for a communist party in present-day Algeria." [27] Ben Bella transferred the editorship of *Révolution africaine* to his confidant and political advisor, Mohammed Harbi, having compelled Vergès to leave the country. A Marxist, Harbi maintained the journal's socialist orientation, but he made it decidedly more nationalistic, substituting a bias toward the Political Bureau for the pro-Peking line. The regime permitted *Alger républicain* to continue but required its communist editors to stop criticizing the FLN and public leaders.

As to future relations between the communists and the FLN, the Political Bureau upheld the standard applied to the PCA during the war: communists could participate in politics only on the condition that they join the FLN as individuals. This prerequisite had the desired effect of crushing them as a separate group in the political system. Many communists with French citizenship subsequently embarked for France, while others subordinated themselves to their Muslim ideological counterparts like Harbi, serving as executive assistants, aides, and the like.

The Political Bureau next focused its attack upon the PRS. It will be recalled that the movement was organized by Mohammed Boudiaf, one of the FLN's "historic chiefs," after his abrupt withdrawal from the Political Bureau during the summer crisis of that year. Boudiaf's militant opposition to Ben Bella, so soon after independence, indicated deep-seated personal and ideological differences between the two leaders. The socialism Ben Bella promoted, he believed, merely benefited the privileged minority of governmental bureaucrats at the expense of the masses, and was a camouflage to preserve the "personal power" already in place. [28] Boudiaf opposed Ben Bella on tactical grounds also; the incorporation of the army into governmental authority triggered this opposition. The Political Bureau had not yet secured firm control of the political system, and it may be presumed that Boudiaf entertained hopes of ascending to power himself.

The anti-Ben Bella leaflets the PRS distributed in Algiers in September 1962 were widely read by students and trade unionists. Whatever the merits of his case, Boudiaf never mustered more than a small faction of less than a hundred activists. The ANP suppressed the movement after a few months, and in June 1963, Boudiaf was intercepted and placed under arrest. As with the PCA, the Political Bureau justified the destruction of the PRS as a prerequisite for establishing a one-party political system, although the constitution mandating such a system was yet to be written.

The government's suppression of the PCA and the PRS signalled, less than a year after independence, that Algeria would soon have a one-party political system. The FLN, not yet decreed the sole legitimate political organization, existed as the only de facto party movement. Official pronouncements on the FLN's status indicated that Political Bureau leaders already considered it the single legitimate party. Party development then approximated the trend that Wallerstein discovered in other African nations where "the choice has not been between one-party and multi-party states: it has been between one-party states and either anarchy or military regimes or various combinations of the two." [29] The FLN, initially the dominant party movement that once tolerated the existence of other political groups, was fast emerging as the exclusive political organization.

While the government suppressed the political opposition, Khider concentrated on developing the FLN. According to his plan, the FLN was to be converted into a mass party, or a single organism encompassing all the major national groups. It required diverse groups like trade unionists, students, peasants, women, and even soldiers to coalesce into a unified structure. The Political Bureau was supposed to function as the decision-making center of state and party policies, the mass base as a supplier of demands, questions, and issues. A mass-party system, he insisted, was essential to the viability of the political system itself.

In late 1962, Khider began to restructure the FLN's organizational framework to systematize party organization. It then consisted of the remnants of the FLN-ALN structures that were created at Soummam. A political commissariat survived in most of the wartime wilayat. The commissariat was established originally to maintain the primacy of political over military issues, but events after Soummam stimulated a steady deterioration of the FLN's political organisms, with the result that guerrilla commanders took effective control of the commissariats by the time of independence. Khider restaffed the pre-existing structures with selected FLN adherents and former guerrillas. Boumedienne supported this effort by banishing the guerrillas from military service. In time, Khider completely demilitarized the FLN's composition by integrating the guerrillas as civilians into a strictly political structure.

Many guerrillas entered the ANP to become professional soldiers, but a majority of the estimated 75,000 guerrillas attempted to maintain dual status as wilaya separatists and nominal FLN adherents after independence. Bitat, Khider's political assistant, directed the major operations in regrouping the former guerrillas into the party organization. They were required to surrender their military status and to subordinate themselves as civilians to a centralized party structure controlled by the Political Bureau; if they resisted, they were ousted from party association altogether. Khider and Bitat toured the countryside and urban areas regularly, building FLN federations and exhorting the guerrillas to chose between the military uniform and a party membership card. During this period, Boumedienne also rooted out most of the wilaya overlords from their wartime strongholds, including Si Larbi of Constantine. The ANP's monopoly over military functions thus promoted party development by circumscribing the range of participation available to individuals who, in the absence of ANP hegemony, might not have accepted the FLN as the center of authority.

In Algiers, an embryonic party base already existed. Its leadership was largely provided by Harbi and his Marxist colleague, Abdelazziz Zerdani, whom Ben Bella appointed editor of *Le Peuple*. Called the FLN's Fédération du Grand Alger, it contained perhaps a thousand adherents. Despite its small size, the federation had enlisted some of the most militant, politicized elements of the urban population—workers, university students, and intellectuals. Harbi and Zerdani set the tone for the federation's socialist orientation, drawing their ideas partly from the Tripoli Program but mainly from their own understanding of Marxism-Leninism. Significantly, they weeded out most wilaya IV guerrillas before Khider took direct command of the federation in November 1962. Here Khider found a solid base on which to proceed with his plan of party development.

After setting up the FLN federations, Khider expanded the FLN's popular or mass basis by incorporating national organizations into the burgeoning party structure. New civilian institutions had to be created since the UGTA was the only major organized group at the time of independence. He initiated this aspect of party building by organizing the Union nationale des femmes algériennes (UNFA) in November 1962. The Algerian population then totaled 10,450,000 inhabitants, and women outnumbered men by a million.[30] Undoubtedly, Bourguiba's success in strengthening his regime's popular base by bringing Tunisian women into active political participation suggested this strategy to FLN leaders.[31]

Seventy-five UNFA delegates met with party leaders in Algiers (January 20-21, 1963) and approved a program that called for the general education of women as well as their entrance into effective national participation. Article 10 specified that their "educational activities will conform to the political directives of the FLN, controller of the feminist movement."[32] The UNFA contained about 200 members and could boast ten female deputies who belonged to the National Assembly. However, the inertia of Algeria's patriarchal order predetermined that women would not evolve as a dominant force in politics, despite the substantial support they rendered during the war. In organizing the UNFA, the Political Bureau simply pointed the direction for the integration of women into the political system. The veil still symbolized the main lifestyle of the female population.[33]

Khider recognized the need to engage significant national groups in the FLN's constituency, and in early 1963 he led in establishing party control over the UGTA (as will be examined in the next chapter). Because the national constitution was not yet ratified, Khider rationalized the FLN's cooptation of the national organizations through various provisions of the Tripoli Program. He interpreted the Tripoli Program as a mandate for a unitary concept of state and party; unity in totality, rather than in diversity, was the organizational guideline. The Tripoli Program did not define a systematic ideology and statement of goals, but its rudimentary and vague tenets permitted facile rationalizations for any action FLN leaders took. The very nonspecificity of the document enabled the leaders to transcend it.

The FLN's separate identity in the political system was taking shape as Khider engineered its fiscal autonomy from the state. To enlarge the FLN treasury, he assumed control of existing funds the FFFLN had collected during the war.[34] The funds of other groups like the AGTA were also appropriated. Later, he introduced the payment of party dues as a requirement for FLN membership. This innovation failed to raise expected revenues because payment schedules depended on the individual's ability to pay, a provision exempting many from payment altogether. Nevertheless, the FLN treasury possessed perhaps as much as 50 million NF ($10 million) in early 1963. The government subsidized many FLN expenditures, such as newspaper publications, and these contributions augmented the party's financial resources.

The plan for party building initiated in late August 1962 had produced definite results by April 1963. In about eight months, Khider managed to transform an inert party embryo into an organism with seemingly functional characteristics. The FLN exhibited the beginnings of structural form, an identifiable, albeit incohesive, membership, and a developing financial capability. It then became plausible to view the Political Bureau as a party executive, superintending a party structure, and not simply as an autocracy representing itself.

The Political Bureau headed the new pyramidal hierarchy of the FLN. Its subordinate organs consisted of federations at the prefectoral level, *dairas* (cantons) at the subprefectoral level, and *kasmas* (communes) at the local or village level. The cells, the structure's base, constituted the smallest party units, each grouping ten party adherents. To the basic skeletal framework must be added the national organizations like the UNFA which were subordinated to the Political Bureau. Khider and Bitat succeeded in organizing 17 federations, 109 dairas, and 1,112 kasmas.[35] The leaders of the principal organs (the federations) were appointed by Khider personally. FLN membership fluctuated widely but party leaders variously claimed 200,000 to 300,000 adherents.

Diagrammatically, the party structure would appear as shown in Figure 2. It is necessary to bear in mind that this diagram depicts a nascent mass-party system. It maintained no records of dues-paying members, no criteria determining the exact qualifications for formal membership, no defined pattern of recruitment, and no coercive or disciplinary authority regulating the conduct of members and the jurisdictional limits between the various components of the hierarchy.

Figure 2. The FLN Party Structure, 1963

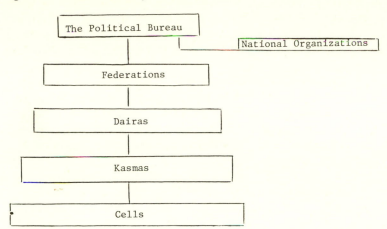

In remote rural regions, the party had no form of representation at all. Khider had simply finalized a blueprint for an organization that was not fully operationalized.

Moreover, the much used term *FLN militant* could at best be defined as an Algerian who participated in the war of liberation and who had since embraced the regime's "socialist revolutionary option." The FLN did employ paid party officials, who received monthly remunerations of 1,000 DA (or about $200), [36] but they inadequately performed their assignments of integrating local and regional units into the overall party structure. Their failures often resulted from incompetence, poor organizational preparation, and sometimes corruption. The government ordered the arrest of several party officials in late 1962 and 1963 for embezzlement, but Ben Bella postponed acting on Khider's demand for a purge of corrupt party officials. In all party operations, the scarcity of competent and experienced cadres added to the FLN's basic structural weaknesses.

The FLN was also wanting as a conveyor of demands and policy suggestions from constituents at the base to leaders at the apex. In practice, the Political Bureau (i.e., the government) imposed its decisions and policies on the entire network as though it were a monolith. It was evident nonetheless that Khider significantly advanced his plan for party development. Before he could consummate it, however, the process was suspended as a result of a conflict between him and Ben

Bella which arose ostensibly over Ben Bella's objection to the mass-party concept. Instead of mass-party organization, Ben Bella advocated a tightly organized body of party elites working under the direct tutelage of the Political Bureau. He met with party officials at El-Riath (near Algiers) on April 4, 1963, to expound on his position:

> There are some problems between [Khider and me], but we shall solve them in order to have the party that we proposed to create, an avant-garde party which distinguishes between militant and sympathizer, between militant and adherent, so that we can encompass all the Algerian people into a single unit as before.
>
> Upon independence, we had to establish a context. This context, for us, carries the name of socialism. That is why we had to find another framework for the party.... We demand a party of militants who will be the best whatever they happen to be: by "best" I mean he who is the most dynamic, who has the greatest loyalty, who sets an example, who somehow has no other interest than the party. . . .
>
> [For our new party organization] 100-150,000 militants should be sufficient. [37]

Thus, Ben Bella insisted on limiting the FLN to an elite vanguard of political militants who represented and made decisions for the masses without their direct participation.

Disagreement over the type of party organization constituted a genuine issue, but the fundamental conflict between Ben Bella and Khider emanated from a personal struggle for power. The secretary general, advocating the principle of party hegemony over the government, was seeking to impose his authority over the state through party control. If he could build a party strong enough to dominate the state, it followed that he, as party chief, would control the entire system. Khider's personal ambitions were exposed on April 3, 1963, when he assembled about 250 of his FLN allies to draft a national constitution. As Ben Bella would do later, Khider bypassed the National Assembly and drew up a document to assure the FLN's ascendancy over the government.

Ben Bella, who was touring the country at the time, reacted angrily on learning of Khider's maneuvers in the capital. Infuriated that Khider had drafted a constitution without consulting other members of the Political Bureau, he quickly summoned Ben Alla, Mohammedi, and other influential partisans to thwart this move. Rumors spread in Algiers that Khider's ouster from the party was imminent. What exactions Ben Bella imposed on the party chief remains unknown, but Khider retreated on April 9, announcing the withdrawal of his draft because the Political Bureau had not approved it.

To settle their conflict, Khider proposed that a plenary FLN congress be convened promptly. He repeated his earlier observation that such a meeting had already been ordered by the CNRA in its last session before independence. Since Khider reorganized the party and was personally closer to a larger number of party stalwarts than other FLN leaders, he anticipated a certain endorsement of his position by the party congress. But there was no chance that Ben Bella would submit to such a test, especially not before the ratification of his own constitution. It came as no surprise, therefore, that he mobilized his partisans on the Political Bureau to veto Khider's proposal.

Equally pertinent to Khider's decline was his earlier attempt to demote Boumedienne from governmental leadership. Khider had long pressured Ben Bella to relegate the ANP chief to a less prominent status, and this tended to deepen their dispute over the type of party organization. He argued that Algeria's major foreign policy interests were limited to the Maghrib, whereas Ben Bella and Boumedienne maintained that they lay principally with the Arab socialist republics, particularly with the United Arab Republic. To Ben Bella, at least, Nasser represented the leadership of the Arab world, and Egypt the main propagator of Arab socialism. In reaffirmation of the political-military alliance, Ben Bella insisted that the government needed Boumedienne and the army for viability and control. In Ben Bella's view, the objection to Boumedienne was simply Khider's attempt to sunder the alliance and facilitate his own drive to power through the FLN.

Ben Bella, the Political Bureau's most powerful member, soon reduced Khider's functions as secretary general, depriving him of any effective role, practically if not officially. Khider, cognizant that his position was undermined, announced his resignation on April 17, 1963. He disclosed various reasons for this decision, without acknowledging that he quit under duress:

> After the FLN leaders' meeting of April 4-6, 1963. . . , I informed party members and the public that I would maintain membership in the Political Bureau but was resigning as secretary general because of fundamental divergences in viewpoints relative to the preparation and convening of a national FLN congress before the present Assembly's mandate expires.[38]

Ben Bella designated himself the new FLN secretary general on the same day Khider resigned. This usurpation of party leadership, endorsed primarily by Ben Alla and Mohammedi, led directly to a more definitive entrenchment of Ben Bella's personal power in the political system. The party became subservient to the Political Bureau, the Political Bureau to the state, and Ben Bella was now the paramount chief of all three.

Following Khider's resignation, whatever competition Ben Bella might have encountered from opposing political leaders seemed to disappear. The penalties he imposed on Khider and Abbas were indicative of the treatment future opponents could expect: Khider was permitted to remain in the FLN but was reduced to powerlessness; Abbas was voted out of the party in reprisal for his condemnation of Ben Bella's draft constitution. The delegation of authority, like the right to dissent, was contained effectively by Ben Bella's authoritarian leadership. At the zenith of political power, he brooked no rivals and stymied the development of any institution that might challenge his leadership.

Party development thus gave way to Ben Bella's personal rule. Instead of differentiating party and state institutions, he simply subsumed the FLN under governmental control. Ben Bella himself later admitted the need to differentiate the organization of public structures: "A clear definition in the relations between the state and the party, between the party and the national organizations is indispensable. [But] I must say that there still reigns too much confusion in this domain, and it prevents the government's measures from being fully effective."[39] Evidently, he did not perceive that the confusion resulted from his own actions. Either he had to permit the development of an independent party, and therefore delegate the necessary power to its leaders, or settle for the subservient and impotent party structure that his actions produced. As the FLN's secretary general, he later resumed party development as a means of lessening his dependency on the army. But, as will be shown, he made the choice for a successful outcome of party development too late.

Where personal rule is a factor in party development, personality is likely to play a critical role, tending to counteract positive means adopted for party development. Halpern has isolated the function of personality in his study of Middle Eastern political parties:

> The important distinction in the *character* of parties is whether they remain centered upon individuals or crystallize instead around an ideology, that is, whether party life is moving from a conflict of cliques to a conflict of orientations. The important distinction in the *function* of parties is whether they mean to secure the supremacy of a single individual, interest, region or class, or whether they mean to initiate all individuals for the first time in the modern age into a common political culture. [40] [Italics in the original.]

For the balance of this study, this distinction should be borne in mind because it was integrally related to the attempt to convert the FLN into a mass party under Ben Bella's leadership.

6

Trade Unionism Versus Party Integration

The Algerian trade union organization, the UGTA, was the one powerful civilian institution to emerge from the war of independence. In contrast to the wartorn FLN, the UGTA maintained well-organized, cohesive cadres, and was excelled only by the ANP in terms of institutional force. The trade union's organizers and leaders were among Algeria's most competent and ideologically sophisticated elites. With 500 syndicates, the UGTA represented 250,000 urban workers,[1] all of whom were in skilled or semiskilled occupations. These considerable assets stimulated the Political Bureau to focus on the UGTA in the first phase of its "politics of cohesion," or the integration of diverse socioeconomic groups into the FLN.

Very early, however, the trade unionists resisted party integration on both political and ideological grounds. The UGTA leaders temporarily favored the GPRA during the summer crisis of 1962 but later adopted a position of neutrality. They adhered to this position even after Ben Bella's victory. The "socialist option" of the Ben Bella regime also put the UGTA at odds with the Political Bureau. Though not communists, the trade union leaders constituted the extreme left of Algeria's political constellations,[2] and their radicalism far surpassed the socialist goals Ben Bella claimed to propagate. The UGTA leaders were nurtured by the doctrine of syndicalism during their affiliation with the CGT, the labor arm of the French Communist party, and this doctrine had inculcated in them the indispensability of trade union autonomy. From the beginning, the UGTA was at loggerheads with the Political Bureau.

Mohammed Khider shaped the Political Bureau's strategy toward the UGTA after he assumed the role of FLN secretary general. While he remained in office, Khider tried to accelerate the process of building a mass-party system by unifying the UGTA with the FLN. Because of his own political ambitions, Khider also endeavored to control the UGTA via the party, thus solidifying the basis of his authority. He succeeded in both objectives in early 1963 by forcibly coopting the trade union into the FLN. Ben Bella, who assisted Khider, became the ultimate beneficiary following Khider's expulsion from party leadership. The pursuit of personal power passed like a thread through these events, and the outcome, as will be seen, resulted in a power shift that augured ill for the future of party development.

Syndicalism: Doctrinal Background of the UGTA

The general features of the UGTA at the time of independence suggested that it was already a viable institution in the new political system. The trade union had a capable and relatively united leadership. Almost all labor leaders belonged to the indigenous working class, so that few could be described as outsiders to industrial labor. They had learned the principles and practices of modern trade unionism during their participation in the CGT from 1944 to 1956. Prior to independence, the UGTA formulated the fundamentals of its program dealing with agrarian reform and worker self-management. Unlike FLN leaders, the UGTA leadership had given early attention to the programmatic interests of its rank and file.

A cardinal aspect of the leadership's ideological orientation involved indoctrination in the syndicalist tradition of the CGT. The doctrine of syndicalism, or "revolutionary syndicalism" as it was sometimes called, regarded political neutrality as the correct trade union stance in any political system.[3] In emphasizing the necessity of class struggle, syndicalism demanded that workers promote their objectives through their own independent confrontations against the state. As the means to labor's ends, this doctrine proposed direct action, a strategy that might range from economic pressure in its simplest manifestation to the general strike at its highest stage. Syndicalism thus required trade union practices that excluded participation with political parties or parliamentary bodies. The theory and practice of syndicalism never fully coincided under the CGT, but it was the ideological school that molded the Algerian trade unionists, and thereby predetermined their policies toward the Ben Bella regime and the FLN.

Syndicalist influence on the Algerian trade union leaders was deducible from their backgrounds. The UGTA's first secretary general, Aissat Idir, born in 1919, entered primary school in the Berber village of Djemaa-Saharidja and continued at a school in Tizi Ouzou.[4] He enrolled for secondary studies at the Ecole Normale in Bouzereah, but he soon quit as a result of family financial pressures that obliged him to support his extended family. He then secured a job at the Maison Blanche, the Algiers' airport, emerging as chief of its administrative and claims control in 1944. In this capacity he joined the CGT. As an MTLD nationalist, he sought the creation of a Muslim trade union executive inside the CGT during 1947; the CGT rejected his plan but he remained a member of the organization until the FLN ordered Muslim workers in 1956 to break with the French trade unions and organize the UGTA. Although he led the new Muslim labor organization into affiliation with the FLN during the anticolonial war, all of his notions on trade unionism derived from the French syndicalist background.

Rabah Djermane, of the same generation as Idir, was also introduced to trade unionism through the CGT. He had no secondary education and grew to maturity as a dock worker in Algiers. As a minor official in the CGT's port and dock federation in 1949, he recruited other Muslim workers for the syndicate and eventually became its secretary. At a CGT convention, he was outspoken in discussions supporting independence for a number of African countries, including Algeria. After the FLN rebellion, he gave up membership in the MTLD to join the revolutionaries. As Aissat Idir's close assistant, he helped to develop the UGTA, and became the titular and doctrinal head of the organization after Aissat Idir's death in 1959. In contrast to his predecessor, he was not an imaginative leader and owed his reputation to long and intimate association with Idir.

The older generation of UGTA leaders—including Taher Gaid, Ali Remli, Attalah Benaissa, and Majid Ali Yahia—can be placed more or less accurately in the doctrinal context of the trade unionists discussed above. They all originated from poor families, embraced the syndicalist doctrine, and entered the nationalist movement as trade unionists. Nothing in their backgrounds prepared them for any ideological orientation other than the syndicalist principles of the CGT, the largest trade union organization in France. Only a minority of the old leadership held membership in the FO or the CFTC,[5] rival organizations of the CGT; those who did, like Safi Boudissa of the CFTC, generally resided in France.

A new generation of labor militants reached the forefront of labor activity by independence. During the war, there was a succession of seven national secretariats as a result of dissolution, exile, or retreat into clandestine activity. The repression by the French army before the cease-fire agreement, and later the OAS terrorism, necessitated these turnovers in the trade union executive. Although Aissat Idir and Djermane remained the recognized leaders, other militants occasionally presided over the UGTA. Each new secretariat thus formed brought new and younger men to the front ranks of the organization's leadership. Significantly, the new men were often better educated and more ideologically committed to socialism, as opposed to syndicalism, than their elders. Nevertheless, the new leaders adhered to the syndicalist principle of trade union autonomy.

Boualem Bourouiba typified the group of young, militant trade unionists. Born in Algiers around 1925, he enlisted early as a nationalist in the PPA and later in the MTLD. He participated in the CGT's railway federation and arrived in 1948 as its principal secretary. Upon the formation of the UGTA, he assumed command of its railway federation. Bourouiba differed from the older leadership in his ideological orientation, for he had superimposed on the syndicalist background a new body of Marxist-Leninist ideas.[6] This philosophical system also formed the trade union concepts of Mustapha Lassel, Raymoun Dekkar, and Mohammed Flissi, members of Bourouiba's generation. Lassel was a university-educated intellectual turned trade unionist, a singular distinction among Muslim trade unionists; Dekkar, a laborer, ascended through the ranks of the CGT's post-telephone-telegraph federation in Algiers; and Flissi, a labor organizer, had served in one of the UGTA's wartime secretariats. Another of Bourouiba's colleagues, Amar Ouzegane, had been a member of the PCA.

The doctrinal differences, however, did not appear to cause dissension in the UGTA leadership. The younger leaders espoused more radical notions than their elders, but all agreed on the necessity of unity and autonomy in the working-class movement. Though a minority in the general leadership, the radical group emerged as the

UGTA's intellectual vanguard. It was the young radicals who formulated the UGTA's program on agrarian reform and autogestion, which predated Ben Bella's historic March decrees by about six months.[7]

A common denominator among the trade union leaders was the fact that they had all been "Westernized," or schooled in the rudiments of French education. All of them francophones, their education in trade union theory and practice derived from the French system. The notions on which they acted seemed more applicable to a technically advanced society than to industrially underdeveloped Algeria. As in other new states of Africa, the ideological choices of Algeria's trade unionists were inherited from the colonial past.[8]

Another important factor was that the labor leaders originated from the major cities either by birth or resettlement. Algiers and Oran comprised the main centers in which Muslims joined the CGT, or one of its rivals, as dockers, communications operators, tramway conductors, hospital attendants, and public utility specialists. The Algerian trade unionists could be considered urbanites by definition because these trades developed primarily in urban areas.

From a sociological standpoint, it would be inaccurate to characterize the UGTA leaders as members of the Muslim middle class, although, as urban laborers engaged in more or less skilled occupations, they certainly ranked high above the peasantry in the country's social hierarchy. They formed a class beneath the liberal, technical, and bureaucratic professionals (i.e., the middle class) who constituted the minority of lycée and university graduates after independence. The trade unionists earned 120,000 to 250,000 AF monthly, as contrasted to office workers whose salaries began at 300,000 AF or 350,000 AF.[9] Halpern's concept of "the new middle class" would be amiss if applied to Algerian trade unionists.[10] A more accurate description would be what Frantz Fanon has called "an intellectual elite engaged in trade."[11] For, if lacking in formal education, they had received wide experience in trade unionism as theory and practice.

Apart from its leadership, the UGTA stood out from other national organizations in 1962 by the unity it demonstrated between leaders and followers. Labor unity stemmed from two different sources, the main one being the CGT organizational heritage. The Algerians duplicated the French example organizationally by centralizing the executive hierarchy of the UGTA to its rank and file. The concentration of workers, as a result of urbanization, facilitated close communications and ties between leaders and followers. During the war, they organized syndicates and federations rapidly by adapting the French-designed structures to coincide with nationalist activity. Building new sections was obviated by existing French trade unions in instances where the Algerians simply ousted the Europeans and restaffed the old syndicates with their own members. The wave of strikes the UGTA set off in 1956 and 1957 attested to its control over the rank and file.

Labor's resistance to colonialism produced a second source of unity. Immediately after the UGTA's creation, its leaders began to organize the general body of Muslim trade unionists behind the war effort, though the FLN directed their actions. As a nationalist initiative, Algerian unionization confirmed an aspect of trade union development that Meynaud and Salah-Bey discovered in their classic study of African trade unionism:

> Trade-union unity has been introduced in Africa not as an end but as a means. While imperialism prevailed, it became necessary to oppose it with a powerful and unified force in its own image. Unionization was thus a "strategic imperative," a fundamental step toward the realization of every trade union's objectives on a national level. [12]

Resistance to the colonial onslaught in wartime deepened the cohesiveness among the trade unionists and thus contributed to the UGTA's organizational consolidation *prior* to independence.

Competent leadership and stable organization enabled the UGTA to survive the Political Bureau-GPRA crisis in the summer of 1962. Both Ben Bella and Benkhedda solicited the UGTA's support in their respective bids for power, and it seemed inevitable that the trade union would be drawn into the struggle. The trade unionists initially evinced some preference for the GPRA but soon retracted it without explanation. Neither faction risked taking the trade unionists' support for granted. This concern catapulated the UGTA into the thick of the conflict.

As the crisis intensified, the UGTA leaders rebuffed the belligerents by proclaiming trade union neutrality, then proposing to mediate between them to resolve the conflict peacefully. As early as May 13, the trade union leaders sought to conciliate the opposing groups, according to *L 'Ouvrier algérien*, the UGTA journal: "Different resolutions were addressed to the [GPRA], the wilaya chiefs, and the Provisional Executive demanding a constructive and immediate policy in the supreme interest of the country and for the realization of the objectives of the revolution."[13] The labor leaders issued another resolution on June 17, imploring the GPRA to take the initiative in restoring public order. The appeals for unity were to no avail at this time because the Political Bureau-GPRA struggle had already thrust the country to the point of civil war.

To further clarify labor's position, the trade unionists established a new executive body called the National Provisional Bureau. It included veteran leaders Djermane, Bourouiba, Majid Ali Yahia, and Attalah Benaissa. When civil war became all but a reality, these leaders went before the Algiers populace to declare unequivocally their indignation toward Ben Bella and Benkhedda: "They are speaking in the name of the people, but they wish to ignore what the people are saying. Let the [opposing] chiefs descend from their pedestals and listen to the words of the crowd. . . . Algerian workers, do not forget that you are the most important force in this country!"[14] As Ben Bella's group prepared to march on Algiers, the UGTA leaders upheld a position that clearly dissociated the labor force from his faction and even questioned his personal integrity. It was a unique position, and one that fixed Ben Bella's later opposition to the trade union leaders.

The immediate explanation as to why the UGTA refused to align with either the GPRA or the Political Bureau related to the strength the trade union commanded. In leadership, numbers, and resources, the UGTA could afford to resist both opponents with impunity. Djermane and his colleagures had been prepared for firm leadership by the French labor movement; and they had demonstrated their capacity to organize and control their rank and file in wartime. Besides its regular membership in Algeria, the UGTA also maintained close liaison with its affiliate in France, the Association générale des travailleurs algériens (AGTA), which superseded the FFFLN in November 1962. Algerian workers in France subsidized the UGTA monthly through the AGTA; with dues-paying members in Algeria and France, the UGTA became financially independent.[15] Except for the ALN's external units, the UGTA constituted the only national group that was fully organized. While the ravages of war rended party and government alike, the urban labor core retained unbroken links with its leadership.

Political neutrality was only one of the UGTA's potential responses. Alignment with the Tlemcen group was a possibility. This move would have helped concentrate the balance of power more firmly on the side of Ben Bella, and the trade union, like the army, could have expected a dominant role in the new political system. As another alternative, the UGTA could have supported the fledgling GPRA, following the CGT's example toward the Popular Front in 1936.[16] Supposing Ben-khedda triumphed, the trade unionists could have awaited similar rewards. Or the UGTA could have attempted to gain control of the state, a position that would have elevated the doctrine of syndicalism to its supreme expression.

When the UGTA leaders opted for neutrality, they were also responding to the isolation the FLN had imposed on them during the war. Notwithstanding the FLN initiative in the creation of the UGTA, no labor leader after Aissat Idir was appointed to the FLN's decision-making agencies, the CNRA and the GPRA. FLN leaders relegated the UGTA to a secondary role of "representing Algerian nationalism in foreign labor movements, preparing militants, and regulating social affairs."[17] Isolated from the centers of power, trade union leaders became estranged from FLN leaders in general.

Pushing the UGTA into the background forced it back on its own resources. After 1958, it operated as another discrete element among the nationalist units. This development gave labor leaders the time and presence on the scene of struggle to organize their cadres into a relatively cohesive entity. Yet, for more than three years, they were ignored by the FLN's decision-making bodies, and they did not participate in the Tripoli meeting where the Ben Bella-Benkhedda conflict deepened. On independence, therefore, the UGTA "had no interest in supporting this or that leader, all appearing equally opposed to cede one iota of their decision-making power to the workers."[18] As Benkhedda and the Krim group had held executive power longest, the trade unionists decided against supporting the GPRA.

It also appeared that the UGTA was largely unaware of the actual power Ben Bella commanded. The outcome of the Political Bureau-GPRA struggle remained uncertain until June 1962 when Colonel Boumedienne aligned the ALN's external units behind the Tlemcen group. The crisis itself did not climax until Benkhedda and the GPRA surrendered at the beginning of July. Thus, even if the UGTA leaders wished to endorse Ben Bella out of self-interest, they had no assurance that he would in fact be the new governmental leader until as late as July 3, just two days after the ratification of the referendum on independence. As the UGTA later explained: "The absence of a national authority, the overlapping of local authorities undermined the energies of all and even called into question the prestige of the chiefs of the revolution. . . .Solicited from all quarters, the UGTA could not take sides with opposing men and groups without endangering its indispensable autonomy."[19] Instead of resolving the dilemma, the labor leaders decided to make no decision between the Political Bureau and the GPRA.

As was unknown at the time, an additional source of trade union neutrality involved disagreements among the UGTA leaders themselves. The young radicals, led by Bourouiba and Lassel, coupled their insistence on autonomy with a demand for a general socialist policy that advocated the workers' command of the entire state apparatus. To say that they sought to preempt power from the GPRA or the Political Bureau would exaggerate the case, but they did aspire to social and economic authority as an independent group, regardless of which faction triumphed. The older leadership under Djermane, unattuned ideologically to this more extreme doctrine, settled the issue for the time being by rejecting the radicals' demands.

Finally, overriding all the events of the summer crisis was the general chaos of the times. No central authority existed. National and local administrations ceased functioning after the exodus of French bureaucrats. The enforcement of law and order had reached a standstill. Opportunists among the wilaya chiefs, like Colonel Khatib in the autonomous zone of Algiers, busily parcelled out their own little fiefs, adding to the general disintegration. Above all, the prospect of civil war rose ominously as armed battle commenced between the ALN troops and wilaya guerrillas defending the GPRA. Events moved so rapidly that it became impossible to measure the exact state of affairs at any given moment. In such universal confusion, the UGTA's policy of *attentisme* seemed eminently wise.

Trade Union Autonomy and the Political Bureau

After the Political Bureau established itself in Algiers during August 1962 the UGTA leaders promptly notified the new authority that "the Algerian workers as a whole and the UGTA in particular . . . expect a program which will not be an enumeration of slogans, but a detailed list of concrete tasks and proposals that will be implemented." [20] Subsequently, they often reminded the government of its responsibility to the programmatic interests of labor while insisting on the maintenance of trade union autonomy.

The official basis for UGTA autonomy had been foretold in the Tripoli Program. It charged the FLN inter alia with the "coordination of revolutionary forces," but instructed party leaders to "respect the autonomy of the trade union for its basic function is to defend the worker's material and cultural interests." [21] However, the UGTA's neutrality in the summer crisis placed it in a very delicate position vis-à-vis the new regime; trade union leaders who had recently refused to support Ben Bella now had to deal with him on his terms.

Ben Bella's opposition to UGTA neutrality was first confirmed in a press interview he gave shortly after defeating the GPRA:

> We have criticized the UGTA for evident reasons. . . . Its ruling members do not reflect our realities, which explains why they were inclined to adopt negative positions—such as the talk about "neutralism"—during the crisis. As a labor organization wishing to represent one of the country's most conscious elements, the UGTA had no right to ignore the current debate. By adopting a position of neutrality, the UGTA favored those in office, the GPRA. [22]

Labor neutrality, in Ben Bella's assessment, ceded political advantage to Benkhedda not as an inadvertent but as a calculated action by the UGTA leadership. Ben Bella argued that their position had nothing to do with "national unity" (as the UGTA leaders declared). Instead, it really concerned "authority born out of the conflicts among a central power, the Political Bureau, and wilaya IV." [23] These were already serious charges, and he elaborated the indictment by associating the labor leaders with the anarchic activities of the wilaya chiefs. By remaining silent, the trade unionists "adopted an attitude contrary to working-class interests" and thus "played one of the most negative roles in Algeria since independence." [24]

To recuperate lost prestige and advantage, UGTA leaders sought to justify their neutrality as much to the regime as to their constituents. They emphasized in an editorial:

The UGTA is wrongly classified among the opposition. . . .It is time to put some order in the ideas of those who have made hasty conclusions. . . .The trade union has no intention whatsoever *at the present time* of opposing a power we ardently wished for and which has barely come to the fore.[25] [Emphasis added]

They reaffirmed their endorsement of the regime but, significantly, did not indicate readiness to agree with it at all times. On the contrary, they implied that they might oppose it under certain conditions and refused to yield on their insistence for autonomy in the management of labor affairs.

Later, the trade unionists cooperated with the regime by taking an active part in *Opération labours*, a campaign Ben Bella initiated in September 1962 to attract volunteers to till and harvest the vast agricultural crops abandoned by the colons. The produce of some 2,700,000 hectares of arable land was then at stake.[26] The UGTA leaders, declaring that they were prepared "to play an important role in the building of socialist Algeria,"[27] summoned their members to the farms and helped to save the crops.

The labor leaders also endorsed the FLN-ANP candidates during the National Assembly elections. Upon the formation of Ben Bella's government, they informed him that workers would assist it in the country's reconstruction "on the basis of the Tripoli Program."[28] They did not mention their discontent over labor's gross underrepresentation in the legislature, which, among its 196 deputies, contained only two trade unionists, Taher Gaid and Abdennour Ali Yahia. At this time, Ali Yahia was not an official UGTA representative because Djermane had expelled him from leadership during the turnover after independence. In a real sense, only one labor leader (Gaid) actually belonged to the National Assembly.

As UGTA leaders struggled to strengthen their position, Khider launched what eventually became the Political Bureau's strategy to subordinate the trade union to the party. He had already begun to convert the FLN into a mass party, a process that he initiated in 1962 by organizing the UNFA. This FLN component, as explained before, was incapable of producing a substantial membership or a well-articulated structure for the party; as a consequence, the UGTA became his prime target. At first, the Political Bureau engaged in obstructionism against the labor organization. In October, for example, party agents prohibited a UGTA national secretary from contacting local labor leaders—notably in Bône, Constantine, and Ain-Temouchent. Although the party remained weak and dysfunctional in its basic structure, Khider demonstrated that it could be a force to contend with.

Khider and the Political Bureau held a meeting with the labor leaders on October 19, 1962, to demand that they relinquish trade union autonomy and accept integration into the FLN. The UGTA leaders countered by insisting that autonomy was absolutely necessary for them to play an effective role in "the construction of socialism." [29] They also raised the topic of FLN pressures against laborites in the three cities mentioned above. These measures, they complained, were not conducive to working-class unity and certainly did not improve the workers' image of the regime. As an alternative to integration, they proposed a horizontal arrangement between the UGTA and the FLN in which policy consultations occurred at the executive levels of both organizations. Despite the Political Bureau's objections, the trade unionists' preference prevailed at the meeting's end.

Khider's disagreement with the arrangement was evident when the FLN renewed its strategy of obstructionism late in October. For instance, a special edition of the UGTA's newspaper was seized under mysterious conditions by the General Information Service of the Algiers prefecture. (Khider apparently wished to prevent further publication of the UGTA's claim to autonomy and influence.) The journal did not circulate again until UGTA leaders protested to the Algiers prefect and the Ministry of Justice. In the interior, at Aumale, a UGTA newspaper correspondent was summarily arrested without evident cause.

Intensifying its opposition to trade union autonomy, the Political Bureau attempted to divide the whole trade union movement. Through the creation of "party unions," Khider aimed to infiltrate the labor ranks with FLN units in every area of the country (except in Algiers and Oran where the UGTA was especially well entrenched). He approached the UGTA local at Kolea in November, urging its 2,000 members to disaffiliate themselves from the UGTA and unite with the party sections. [30] This strategy backfired immediately as the -Kolea local rejected the FLN proposal and asserted its loyalty to the UGTA. Not one of the UGTA affiliates separated from the UGTA, and the "party unions" failed to emerge. Though a confirmation of the UGTA's institutional strength, this episode exposed the Political Bureau's authoritarian approach to party integration.

The trade union leaders affirmed publicly that "there has never been any difference between the party and the UGTA,"[31] while privately they grew apprehensive about the Political Bureau's increasing opposition. Radicals pressured the government to nationalize European-held properties and put them under worker control, hoping to reinforce the UGTA's position by controlling the nationalized properties and the workers employed on them. Meanwhile, Djermane and the older labor leaders, though still committed to UGTA autonomy, softened their resistance to party integration, being clearly intimidated by the Political Bureau's show of power.

Representing the UGTA, Djermane and national secretaries Bourouiba and Gaid contacted the Political Bureau on December 20, 1962, to press for a resolution of the conflict. Except for Rabah Bitat, Political Bureau conferees are not known, but it can be assumed that Khider, Ben Bella, and probably Boumaza also attended the secret meeting. Djermane informed the rank and file the next day that party leaders concurred in the UGTA's demand for autonomy. This seemed corroborated by a joint statement in which the two parties decided that:

1. The workers will elect their leaders in closed meetings.
2. The workers will designate their representatives to the different labor committees on commerce, management, and cooperatives (in the government).
3. The trade union syndicates (local, regional, and provincial unions and federations) will receive their orders directly from the UGTA secretariat.
4. The FLN will constantly respect the UGTA's autonomy.
5. The FLN will not tolerate any act that undermines the trade unionists' freedom of action and expression.
6. The UGTA will coordinate its internal and external activities, positions, and general orientation with the FLN through periodic contacts.
7. The commission preparing the first UGTA Congress will be enlarged.[32]

The Political Bureau acceded to the UGTA's primary demand, trade union autonomy, and acknowledged the UGTA's control of its rank and file by consenting to the broad prerogatives dealing with elections, representation, programs, and leadership. These concessions suggested that the FLN remained powerless to impose its authority over the UGTA, while the agreement to protect the trade unionists' freedom of action amounted to an admission that Khider's obstructionist strategy had failed.

On paper, the FLN-UGTA agreement represented a definitive victory for the labor leaders. The Political Bureau extracted only two important concessions from the labor leaders: the first involved the ambiguous provision that the UGTA coordinate its activities and policy with the FLN; the other concerned the ostensibly routine enlargement of a preparatory commission for a future UGTA convention. The impact of these provisions on trade union autonomy was not discernible at the time, but they eventually proved to be the Achilles' heel of independent trade unionism during the Ben Bella regime.

The UGTA victory could be explained by its organizational strength, and conversely, by the fragility of the political system and the party. The trade union's system of centralized authority enabled the leaders to make all significant decisions alone. At no time in the immediate postindependence period did the leaders reach their decisions by soliciting the rank and file; the latter had been conditioned both by wartime necessities and by French syndicalism to obey the leaders. Ben Bella and Khider did not wish to further aggravate relations with the UGTA because its leaders were essential to winning control of the organization as a whole. Capturing the UGTA leadership, in other words, was a precondition of controlling the organized labor force itself.

The contingencies under which the regime operated reinforced labor's bargaining power vis-à-vis the Political Bureau. In his quest for personal power, Ben Bella had alienated the labor leaders by excluding them from substantive participation in the new political system. While party organization constituted Khider's political priority, Ben Bella deferred provoking a show of force with the UGTA before consolidating the bases of his regime. Although the government had designated the FLN as the agent for coalescing different national organizations into a single-party structure, it appeared that the UGTA would continue as a forceful, independent organization advancing labor's interests according to the decisions of its leaders.

The First UGTA Congress

Heralded as the "convention of independence," the first national UGTA congress met in Algiers, January 17-20, 1963. Trade union radicals like Bourouiba and Lassel, anticipating a showdown between the UGTA and the Political Bureau, planned to consummate their struggle for autonomy and nationalization by controlling the convention's proceedings. The Political Bureau had not expanded on its position beyond the November 19 agreement, and the radicals entered the meeting with great confidence and optimism.

In attendance at the congress were approximately 365 trade union delegates representing the UGTA's federations and locals throughout the country. The UGTA had invited sixty-two foreign observers as guests, including Soviet-bloc laborites and Western groups like the ICFTU. Khider, slated as the Political Bureau's official spokesman, was then traveling abroad; Ben Bella and Boumaza represented the party in his absence. Although Khider's failure to attend the opening sessions did not then strike observers as significant, everyone would witness the import of his return.

In his inaugural address, Ben Bella indicated the FLN's current position toward the trade unionists:

> We have formulated a program which has become the charter of every Algerian militant. In this program, the fundamental option is a single form of political thought. . . . The activity of all national organizations, and particularly that of the trade-union movement, must be situated within this framework. . . . It is fitting that the trade-union movement and the working classes . . . have complete managerial autonomy. . . . [But] the party elaborates and controls the country's political thought. We take for granted that the judge of our action is the party. [33]

Ben Bella conceded to managerial autonomy while serving notice that the imperative of "singular political thought" prohibited any ideological views contrary to the Political Bureau's. The speech was aimed at the young radicals who were pressing the government to undertake the nationalization it had been promising since October 1962. The "formulated" program referred to the Tripoli Program which, incidently, did contain a provision supporting the single "political thought" formula, [34] but Ben Bella introduced the notion that the FLN was the ultimate authority of the mass organizations.

Ben Bella escalated his criticisms of the trade unionists by warning them against the practice of *ouvrièrisme*, or trade union corporatism.

As this practice pertained essentially to demands for higher and higher wages, he argued:

> The workers should not continue making high wage demands because they risk becoming a privileged class of citizens: the fallah earns no more than 20,000 francs annually. Today's spectacle will be more convincing when 80 percent of those present are fallahin, when the fallahin are organized into agrarian trade unions. [35]

On the surface, Ben Bella's criticisms merely reflected the general knowledge that the vast body of Algerian workers, peasant and low-paid, did not participate in the UGTA. Related to this distinction were the workers' syndicalist background and their privileged material status relative to the peasantry. On another level, Ben Bella contended that the unorganized rural peasants ought to take priority over urban workers in national labor affairs. In implying that the UGTA limited its interests to the material welfare of its members, he also obliquely criticized the organization's constituency, deeming it unrepresentative of labor in the changed ("socialist") conditions of independent Algeria.

To silence the protagonists of rapid nationalizations, Ben Bella retorted that he had already nationalized 100 vacated properties which the trade unionists had failed to operate competently. [36] He suggested that these domains constituted the areas in which the radicals should concern themselves. He did not seem to grasp the key aspect of the radicals' demands: that nationalization was not an end in itself but simply the first step toward worker *control* of the economy. As managers of the nationalized properties, they intended to fortify the trade union's hold on the entire urban sector.

The next day the UGTA radicals presented the *Rapport d'orientation*, a fifteen-page labor program composed by Bourouiba, Flissi, Lassel, and Rachid Ben Attig. It reviewed Algeria's current economic and social problems at length and proposed general solutions to them; for the most part, the program merely reiterated items adumbrated in the Tripoli Program. Its new and significant contents described economic socialization and the UGTA's role in a single trade union society.

Concerning economic policy, the report underscored the need for urgent and extensive nationalization: "The vacated and abandoned properties offer us the opportunity to escape the constraints of private capital and to realize a socialized sector. The abandoned businesses, the restaurants, and department stores, like the farms and large agricultural domains must be placed under labor management." [37] The radicals demanded a total "algerianization" of the economy and concomitant UGTA control of it. Their insistence on state ownership anticipated the March decrees, which Ben Bella proclaimed two months afterwards as the regime's basic policy on agrarian labor. The radicals noted elsewhere that, although the national railway system and the metropolitan bus company were nationalized, the railway system needed "coordination" while the bus company lacked guidelines for occupational promotion. [38] They also described Ben Bella's nationalization policy as dilatory, and they rejected his appeals for moderation.

The radicals advanced definite and unconditional positions regarding the role of trade unionism. The labor movement had to maintain its unitary order; a plurality or even a duality of trade union organizations could not be tolerated. Hence, rural workers should become integrated into the UGTA and should not be organized as a special group as Ben Bella had recommended. The UGTA did not seek primarily to increase its constituents' wages but to "oversee and direct production plans in the socialized industries." [39] The trade unionists, asserting their right to decision-making authority in economic policy, outlined a clear dichotomy between the UGTA and the FLN: the UGTA acted as the exclusive and permanent representative of a single social group (i.e., the workers), while the FLN merely represented multiple national elements in a transitional period.

Failure to appreciate the distinction between the two organizations, the report stated, had caused "certain party officials—who had nothing to do with trade unionism and were probably motivated by personal interests—to seek domination of the UGTA and its affiliates. . . . In some cases, they went so far as to create party cells in the trade union. But instead of promoting trade-union activity, the party cells attempted to destroy it." [40] The radicals thus admonished the Political Bureau for its earlier attempts to disrupt the labor organization and demanded that party leaders desist from such activity in the future.

No sooner was the report delivered than it came under attack by certain FLN partisans. Mohamed Tahar Chafai, one of three new members who joined the congress's Preparatory Committee as a result of the November 19 agreement, rose to declare: "It is the FLN which created the UGTA. And it is the same party which has permitted the trade union to represent Algerian workers throughout the world." [41] Notwithstanding the antagonistic line the Political Bureau and its agents took, the incumbents maintained the support of UGTA delegates. Delegate sympathies were partly evidenced by the resounding applause with which they approved the *Rapport d'orientation*. When the delegates turned to the election of the convention's steering committee, they reaffirmed their support of the incumbents. A proposal requiring members to pay regular fixed dues was also approved, thus assuring the solvency of the UGTA's treasury. With such backing, the radicals approached their goal of establishing the UGTA as a largely autonomous force in the political system.

Developments took a decidedly different course when Khider returned to Algiers on January 19, one day before the convention closed. On the night of January 19-20, he instigated the strategy that enabled the Political Bureau to usurp control of the labor organization by defeating its incumbent leadership.

Several changes in format struck the eye when the convention resumed on the third day. New guards restricted entry to the halls of assembly. Newly arrived representatives of the FLN's Fédération du Grand Alger prohibited the incumbents from regaining their seats at the rostrum. The dais where they had presided was occupied by a new group of trade unionists and FLN agents. Unknown individuals declaring themselves new "delegates" had appropriated the seats of regular UGTA delegates. [42] The newcomers questioned the validity of the convention's proceedings and the legitimacy of the regular delegates' representation.

Then Ben Bella and Boumaza entered in the company of Djermane and some of his cohorts. They heightened the mystery by suddenly leaving the hall without identifying the new persons or explaining their presence. Shortly afterwards, Boumaza and Djermane returned and canceled the morning's program in order to allow Ben Bella and Boumaza time to negotiate future FLN-UGTA relations privately. Two of the radical trade unionists, Ben Attig and Dekkar, attempted to protest the Political Bureau's intervention but were barred from addressing the convention. Thereafter, Boumaza and Djermane joined Ben Bella, presumably to begin the negotiations.

Developments became further complicated as the delegates split into so-called majority and minority factions. Those supporting the Political Bureau called themselves the "majority," a status instantly obtained by the FLN agents or new "delegates,"[43] although in fact the regular delegates, who opposed the Political Bureau, were in the majority. The leader of the FLN agents, Cheikh Benghazi from the UGTA local in Sidi-Bel-Abbes, inveighed against the incumbents in defense of the Political Bureau:

> Some who have appeared at this rostrum have insulted no one. But others, having lost their case before the majority, have gone so far as to insult a party militant. . . . We invite these same people to come here and condemn such elements as the PRS. Let them declare themselves militants of the FLN. Let them say here and now that they support the Political Bureau of the FLN. [44]

Obviously seeking to implicate the incumbents with the political opposition, Benghazi directed his harangue at the radicals in order to discredit them in the labor movement. Like Chafai, he was one of the new members with whom the Political Bureau stacked the convention's enlarged preparatory committee (after the November 19 agreement).

The Political Bureau dealt the fatal blow in the afternoon session when it ushered in a gang of 2,000 individuals who declared themselves "representatives of the people."[45] Literally invading the hall, they consisted of vagrants whom Khider had rounded up that morning to serve as additional "delegates" to the convention. They performed their task well, brandishing party banners, seizing the seats of legitimate delegates, and shouting down everyone who expressed views favorable to the incumbents. Then, after the incumbents were ejected from the convention floor, the Political Bureau introduced its own candidates for the new UGTA leadership. The ICFTU and other foreign delegations protested this spectacle by walking out.

Announcing the leadership turnover, Ben Bella declared that Rabah Djermane, the new UGTA secretary general, would be assisted by a secretariat including:

1. Mohammed Flissi, secretary of press and publications
2. Cheikh Benghazi, secretary of organization

3. Mohamed Tahar Chafai, secretary of finance
4. Safi Boudissa, secretary at large

Not a single member of the previous leadership succeeded to the new UGTA executive. Ben Bella and Khider handpicked the new leaders, thus confirming that personal power would circumscribe the development of the trade union as it had the National Assembly and the government. The "politics of cohesion" was exposed plainly as the politics of governmental force. Thus, it came as no surprise when the convention (i.e., some official delegates together with Khider's band) approved the new secretariat by acclamation the next day. So ended the election of trade union leaders at the UGTA's first national convention.

Given the new leaders' ideological and personal leanings, the capitulation of all except Flissi could be readily understood. Benghazi, for instance, had been a leader of the Messalist MNA, an organizer of the antinationalist USTA, and did not even join the UGTA until 1958. This background of opposition to the nationalist movement did not win him favor with the incumbent radicals. Thus, he fell easily to the Political Bureau's overtures designed to discredit the radicals; he profited by raising his public image through the respectability of membership on the UGTA executive. Djermane, a pliant personality not accustomed to resisting superior authority, yielded to Ben Bella and Boumaza during the private negotiations. He was the obvious choice for secretary general because his prestige in the labor movement, which derived from his close association with Aissat Idir, ostensibly legitimized the new leadership.

Khider seemed most responsible for drawing the others to the Political Bureau's position. To men like Chafai, the offer of leadership sufficed. They appeared to be motivated by personal interest and did not have profound ideological commitments. Flissi's conversion, however, was more problematic. The radicals denounced him as an opportunist, but he had previously conducted himself as a principled leader, staunchly advocating their demands for autonomy and nationalization. It was conceivable, as Favret surmises, that some radical trade unionists who feared the creation of "party unions" (a real possibility had the Political Bureau failed in its strategy) preferred any alternative that would not split the UGTA.[46] If the organization maintained its unity, under any condition, the radical leaders might be able to recapture it whole in the future. In any case, Flissi betrayed his old allies in capitulating to the Political Bureau.

The UGTA was not absorbed as a willing institution. On the contrary, the ultimatums directed at its former leaders, and the intimidation of UGTA delegates by *agents provocateurs*, compelled the UGTA's entry into the FLN on the Political Bureau's terms. The institutional resources of the UGTA were still intact, but this coercive method alienated the new UGTA leaders from the rank and file. In the political system, meanwhile, the FLN's cooptation of the UGTA produced a critical alteration in the preexisting balance of power. The triangular pattern of 1962 involving the party, the army, and the trade union was now transformed into a bipolar arrangement between the party and the army. Ben Bella, of course, advocated centralized political power as a means of reinforcing his regime's authority; the coincidental strengthening of the ANP's position was probably not his intention.

Why the Political Bureau refused to allow an autonomous trade union movement is a question that warrants consideration. During wartime, and now after independence, FLN leaders established a leadership style of neutralizing organized political opposition. Thus, competition from groups like the PCA and the PRS was contained. The UGTA, under the radicals' leadership, presented another target on the Political Bureau's list of politically competitive organizations.[47] The Political Bureau's opposition could also be attributed to Ben Bella's resentment of the UGTA for refusing to support him in the power struggle of summer 1962. Although the radical leaders (then in the UGTA provisional executive) did not resist the Political Bureau, they leaned toward Benkhedda, who in their estimation represented the more liberal tendency at the time.[48]

Ideological differences were also involved in the coup. For Ben Bella, the rural masses, the peasantry, formed the focal point of Algerian socialism. He chose this option to counter the radicals' policy favoring urban workers (that is, their constituents) and to foster governmental policies oriented toward the countryside. The radicals emphasized the importance of class consciousness and trade union autonomy consistent with their French syndicalist background, whereas Ben Bella contended that the rural peasantry ought to control the urban workers and not the reverse. Khider endorsed this position because he saw his own benefit in the Political Bureau's control of both groups.

The coup responded to Khider's scheme for refurbishing the institutional structure of the FLN. Trained leaders, an organized constituency, structural bases, and internal disciplinary mechanisms accrued to the party as a result of the forced incorporation of the trade union. The Political Bureau also gained access to the UGTA's treasury and its press and propaganda machinery; by controlling the labor leaders, the party could more directly influence the rank and file. After the cooptation of the UGTA, party development began to take concrete form. But it crystallized firmly around individuals, not ideology.

Ultimately, it was the priority of Ben Bella's personal rule which, as the independent variable, decided the subjugation of the UGTA. Just as he had already eliminated his political competitors because they threatened his leadership, he also refused to permit any institution with a capacity to exert independent influence in the political system to wield authority over national groups. Already ensconced as supreme leader of the state apparatus, Ben Bella now sought to disseminate his power among popular groups. Whether he would succeed remained to be seen. After he demoted Khider from leadership of the Political Bureau, however, Ben Bella acquired undisputed sway over the party organization.

In hindsight, it is clear that the ideological positions of the radical trade union leaders precluded a voluntary merger between the UGTA and a mass-party system, i.e., supposing such a system existed. The French syndicalist background of the UGTA certainly militated against such a possibility. This, however, was a moot question because the apparent "conflict of ideologies" between Ben Bella and the radicals was not an ideological conflict at all. The radicals held a developed, systematic ideology, whereas Ben Bella's views were described by vague, amorphous concepts that appeared to be based more on personal interest than on fundamental notions of social change. The real conflict involved power relationships. Ben Bella simply exploited ideology to accelerate the pace of his drive to control the political system.

At the end of the convention, Khider declared that this "historic congress" paved the way for the future FLN congress. [49] The old issues dividing the Political Bureau and the UGTA—autonomy, nationalization, ideology, etc.—were resolved. The FLN's authority had been imposed on the trade union, and the time was opportune for integrating other mass groups into the party structure. Bitat, speaking later for the Political Bureau, stated candidly that the UGTA "has become, under the aegis of the FLN, one of *its* national organizations."[50] FLN absorption of the independent labor movement, he said, was necessitated by the one-party system. This status did not become formalized until the constitution of 1963 but, clearly, Political Bureau leaders had begun to act as if it already were. The conclusion of the UGTA convention marked a watershed in the trade union's relations with the Political Bureau and anticipated the strategy of party building that soon affected other mass organizations.

7

Autogestion: The Peasant Base

Once the Political Bureau decided to convert the FLN into a mass party, party leaders necessarily turned their attention to organizing the peasantry because a genuine popular base was impossible without peasant participation. Algeria remained about two-thirds rural as late as 1963. Its largest body of workers was composed of the *fallahin*, or peasant farmers, who numbered roughly 1,250,000 persons in 1963.[1] To introduce the rural peasantry into party organization, the Political Bureau adopted the worker self-management system, which was known popularly as *autogestion.* The Political Bureau, however, did not attempt to affiliate peasants directly within the formal structure of the party. Instead, the FLN leadership relied on newly created governmental agencies to organize the rural autogestion system, which was to act as the party-related framework for mobilizing the peasants into a mass FLN constituency.

Organizing the fallahin on a mass scale was unprecedented. In the colonial period, metropolitan trade unions like the CGT never attempted to organize farmers, believing it impossible to unionize an "amorphous sub-proletariat."[2] Although the French colons transformed most peasants into wage laborers, many peasants continued to farm family or communal plots of land while the nomads and semi-nomads labored mainly as seasonal workers. Following independence, the UGTA leaders also recognized the inherent difficulty of organizing peasants: unionization required an extensive system of communications that did not exist in the Algerian countryside, much of it mountainous terrain and desert.[3]

The new system of autogestion was established in both rural and urban areas, but it represented an essentially rural phenomenon because the Algerian population in 1963 totaled only 3,450,000 urban residents, as compared to approximately 7,000,000 rural inhabitants.[4] Ideologically, autogestion constituted the most original feature of socialism under the Ben Bella regime; politically, it expanded the FLN's presence in the countryside. But the worker self-management system was plagued from the outset by the foibles of its own administration, the enduring influence of traditional society, and the authoritarian prerogatives of Ben Bella's personal rule. In the outcome, autogestion foundered as an instrument for organizing the peasants into a mass-party constituency.

Origins of Autogestion

Autogestion had its beginnings in historical accident. The Europeans fleeing from Algeria in 1962 abandoned almost all their plantations and urban business firms. In the cities, they vacated residential units, restaurants, factories, and other commercial enterprises. In the countryside, they deserted as many as 2,700,000 hectares of the country's prime farmlands.[5] Gradually, peasant farmers who once worked as salaried employees on the farms began to occupy them like settlers. In the absence of all governmental authority, the rules and regulations required for an orderly administration of the abandoned properties were never defined.

Wilaya guerrillas compounded the disarray in the countryside by laying personal claim to several of the abandoned farms. Major Si Larbi of wilaya II (Constantine), for example, usurped at least a dozen farms on which he employed his guerrilla troops to manage the harvesting of the crops. In the environs of Algiers, guerrillas of wilaya IV divided Cheliff Valley farms among their troops. Colonel Chaabani of wilaya VI appropriated farms in the Bou-Saada region and date-palm plantations near Biskra; then he proceeded to "rent" them to his cronies.[6] The absence of any national leadership at the time enabled the wilaya separatists to assert themselves as the new patrons of agrarian society.

The UGTA was an exception, between the peasants and the guerrillas, in the handling of the abandoned colon properties. Then under the leadership of the radicals, the UGTA requested authority from

the Provisional Executive on June 20 to reopen the factories and to
regulate the farms. Radicals like Lassel and Bourouiba, noting the
Provisional Executive's inability to govern, sent their members to several farms to organize and operate them. By August 1962, the UGTA
succeeded in administering forty-three farms near Boufarik and
Orléansville, employing nearly 2,300 farmworkers.[7] About 500,000
DA ($100,000) were invested in the Boufarik operation for farm ma-
terials and equipment.[8] Using pressure and money, the UGTA induced wilaya IV guerrillas to transfer Cheliff Valley farms to trade-
union administration.

Of all the disparate interests involved on the vacated farms in summer 1962, the UGTA alone provided tentative guidelines for a systematic organization of the farms and the workers on them. The radical trade unionists advocated worker management of the abandoned
properties and had begun to organize them accordingly before the
Political Bureau sacked the GPRA. This UGTA initiative was short-
lived, however, for Ben Bella preempted the trade unionists by
announcing in his inaugural address to the National Assembly (on
September 28, 1962) the appointment of a special governmental commission to formulate an official self-management program. Thereafter, the subject of autogestion became the exclusive domain of the
government, the Political Bureau, and the FLN.

The government recognized, de facto, the unauthorized occupations in two decrees issued on October 22 and November 25. Ben Bella
acknowledged that these measures involved "merely the ratification
of the status-quo which the working masses . . . created throughout
the country."[9] He formalized the status of the *bien vacants*, or abandoned properties, in the famous March decrees, promulgated on
March 18, 1963. The laws, approved by the National Assembly, dis-
allowed all future appeal against the legality of properties seized
before March 22; before that time, the government said, the Europeans could return to Algeria for repossession of or compensation for
their former properties.

Ben Bella later clarified the March decrees and the future status of
the vacated properties in a radio and television address:

> All enterprises, whether concerned in industry, commerce,
> crafts, finance or mining, all agricultural and forestry con-
> cerns, all premises, buildings or parts of buildings which were

subject, by 22nd March, to Vacancy Decisions are, and will remain, once and for all, "vacant properties;" and as such, their management lies finally, once and for all with the Algerian workers.

Henceforward we will speak [no] more of "vacant properties" but of enterprises and concerns under self-management.[10]

The Tripoli Program's revolutionary principle, that responsibility for all property belonged to those who gave it value through their labor, was thereby translated into formal policy.

As defined by the March decrees, autogestion required the creation of an agricultural system in which the workers, a workers' managerial body, and the state operated a given farm or urban enterprise conjointly. The worker components of the pyramidal system were established at three levels: in ascending order, they formed (1) a workers' general assembly, (2) a workers' council, and (3) a self-management committee. The workers' general assembly, composed of the regular laborers in a given enterprise, constituted the organizational base of autogestion. By secret ballot, the general assembly elected the workers' council, a body that included at least two-thirds of the workers in a given enterprise. The council served a three-year term and selected three to eleven of its members to direct the self-management committee, which was the workers' central decision-making body. Altogether the components of the self-management system were supposed to enable all peasants in it to participate in formulating farm policy.

Procedurally, power in an enterprise was anchored in the self-management committee. This committee had the right to determine wage rates, work or development programs, the sharing of profits, the recruitment of seasonal workers, and the means of marketing produce and services. Each year it designated one of its members as president, who in turn represented the enterprise in external relations and before the law.

A professional technician (called the state director) controlled the economic and financial operations of the enterprise. He possessed broad decision-making prerogatives, including the right to oppose any management or development plans that conflicted with the government's national economic plan for reconstruction and development. The director was an automatic member of the self-management committee and voted in its deliberations. Under specified conditions, he could veto measures proposed by the committee.

The director was subject to dismissal either because of incompetence or a show of nonrecognition by the Communal Council for the Animation of Self-Management. A public service group, the council facilitated the organization of the self-management system in given areas. It was composed of the presidents of the workers' self-management committees, FLN representatives, leaders of the UGTA and the ANP, and heads of the prefectures. It collaborated with the self-management committee and could dismiss the state director on an appeal from a majority of the workers on an enterprise. The dismissal process was initiated by a charge of "obvious incompetence" submitted by the committee's president.[11] The director's authority, though substantial, was not absolute.

The March decrees reflected certain situational determinants existing in Algeria upon independence and the ideological orientations of the special governmental commission that formulated the autogestion program. The decrees responded to a situation that predated the Ben Bella regime, i.e., the peasants' occupation of the vacated farms. The government was not willing to expel the peasants from the farms because the force required amidst the turbulent events of summer 1962 was too prohibitive and because Ben Bella needed peasant support to develop a rural constituency.

Five highly intellectual ideologues staffed the special commission Ben Bella appointed to draft the decrees. Michel Raptis, a French Trotskyist who once presided over the Fourth International, conceived a major portion of the autogestion policy. As was true of some other European leftists, he started working for the FLN in wartime and stayed on after independence at Ben Bella's invitation. Raptis was assisted by two other foreign intellectuals: Luftallah Solliman, an exiled Egyptian Trotskyist closely associated with Zerdani; and Mohammed Tahiri, a Moroccan land reform expert and a Trotskyist sympathizer. Abdelkader Maachou, director of the newly created Office of Biens Vacants, and Mohammed Harbi were the only Algerians involved in the formulation of autogestion.

Harbi, who served as Ben Bella's political advisor, represented the regime among the formulators of the March decrees. Without governmental portfolio, he surpassed most Algerian political elites in shaping the ideological contours of governmental policy. He enjoyed this unique prerogative because Ben Bella engaged him as an ideological proxy, as it were, in an attempt to compensate for his own paucity of knowledge on socialism and ideology generally. Intellectually gifted, Harbi brought to a regime nearly devoid of intellectual elites a developed synthesis of the Marxist and Marxist-derivative theories that tinged the doctrinal concepts of autogestion.

The concept for a worker self-management system was borrowed in general terms from the land reform program of Yugoslavia.[12] Harbi and the other framers of Algerian autogestion adapted the foreign model to the particular socioeconomic conditions of Algerian society. Since the country was nearly two-thirds peasant and rural in 1962, Algerian self-management focused on socializing the peasant majority through this modern socialist framework. Harbi had also been influenced by the theories of Fanon, and he shared Fanon's principle that peasants constituted the only revolutionary group in colonial society.[13] In the editions of *Révolution africaine*, the official FLN journal which he edited, Harbi propagated his socialist notions and in the process extended his influence to articulate segments of Algerian society. Although the Fanonist dictum could easily be contradicted by an empirical examination of twentieth-century peasant uprisings, in Algeria and elsewhere,[14] Harbi enthroned this principle as the basic rationale for the government's economic policy generally, the March decrees specifically.

Nationalization of foreign-owned properties was another key guideline of the March decrees, and Ben Bella inaugurated the establishment of the rural self-management system by acting on it. In 1963, the government sequestered most of the 22,000 farm units from the 2,700,000 hectares of abandoned lands, and organized about 15,000 self-management committees to regulate them.[15] These reforms reached about 600,000 permanent workers and a comparable number of semipermanent or seasonal workers. In the countryside, the active masculine population (fifteen to fifty-five years old) totaled approximately 1,600,000 workers in 1963.[16] At one time or another, about two-thirds of the rural population, as either permanent or semipermanent workers, participated in the self-management system.

To sustain the system financially, the government invested 803,000,000 DA as expenditures on agriculture in 1963.[17] Thereafter the level of government financing declined steadily, but the initial huge outlays indicated the regime's serious commitment to the rural self-management system. In terms of economic development, Algeria was rather compelled to concentrate on labor-intensive methods because the exploitation of the Saharan oil fields remained at a rudimentary level, and consequently a capital-intensive approach was not yet conceivable. Agriculture, in the short run at least, appeared to be the keystone of Algerian development.

The nationalizations did not involve most of the communal farmlands that peasants owned in the colonial period. Such lands constituted the bulk of agrarian property, or about 7,130,000 hectares; [18] but this property consisted largely of the country's least fertile, most mountainous terrain. Soil productivity in these areas was extremely low, and the government, like the colons earlier, deemed these properties unworthy of particular concern. Consequently the nationalizations were limited to the rich fields vacated by the Europeans.

If autogestion did not affect all rural inhabitants, the socialist sector in urban areas, by contrast, attracted many workers into organized occupational activity. There the appeal of autogestion was especially compelling because of the country's serious unemployment problem. High unemployment, underemployment, and disguised unemployment affected the entire urban labor force in 1963. [19] For every four employed workers (1,280,000), there were three either underemployed (550,000) or unemployed (370,000). [20] The *Revue du plan* listed an additional 50,000 persons in such occupations as artisanry and domestic service as being fully employed, but it would be more accurate to include them among the underemployed because of the relative irregularity and unproductivity of such work.

The figures cited above pertain to the urban working class exclusively. No data exist to reveal rural unemployment, but the government asserted that unemployment was scarcely a problem in the agricultural sector: "Underemployment can be said to affect the totality of the rural population, exceeding the number of full-time jobs provided by agriculture; but unemployment, strictly speaking, does not exist in this category of the population." [21] While this interpretation could be challenged, it is important to note that farm labor often comprised entire family and communal units. Furthermore, it can be taken for granted that many rural inhabitants who survived would have starved in a wage economy because employed workers supported their relatives in accordance with the traditional practice of mutual assistance among Muslim extended families. In other words, a kind of built-in social security system prevailed in agrarian society.

Despite high unemployment, the urban workers represented a privileged group compared to the peasantry. Urban workers made up the core of the skilled, semiskilled, and largely literate segment of the overall labor population. With the establishment of the agrarian self-management system, many of these workers found employment in occupations related to rural development and thus became the sole beneficiaries of new employment arising from the nationalized urban enterprises.

The immediate economic policies of the government did little to alter the predominantly urban character of employment. Budgetary outlays for new jobs in 1962 and 1963 further inclined the employment disequilibrium toward urban workers. Amin, analyzing 1963 accounting statistics, discovered that during this period approximately 450,000 jobs were created outside of agriculture. [22] These comprised 180,000 industrial occupations, small-scale business trades, and bureaucratic positions in the socialist (urban) sector; 150,000 civil service bureaucrats; and 120,000 military positions. New merchants and handicraft artisans also entered the labor market, perhaps as many as 180,000 altogether. [23] But since many in this group held occupations of dubious productivity—such as street lemonade vendors, shoeblacks, and peddlers of various sorts—the term *merchant* must here be weighed with discretion. For those gainfully employed, the above figures represented the emergence of new occupational groups that benefited much more from the nationalization than the less advantageous urban residents or the peasantry.

The importance of autogestion to rural economic development stemmed from the fact that the agricultural sector contributed about 75 percent of Algeria's nonmanufactured products and more than 60 percent of its total exports. [24] On the country's commercial balance, agriculture generated considerably more revenue than its factors of production might indicate. This was exemplified by the cereal and vegetable harvest of 1963 which showed a marked increase over previous colon returns. [25] To improve the efficiency of the system, the government organized 350 farms into 185 administrative units of 2,000 to 2,050 hectares each; the result was an increase in the volume and variety of crops as well as in the number of workers employed. [26] The

Ben Bella regime accurately perceived autogestion as the crucible determining the success or failure of Algerian socialism.

In an effort to galvanize agrarian development, Ben Bella established the Office national de la réforme agraire (ONRA) in March 1963. Its basic function was to supervise the self-management committees on the state-owned farms; it also provided other important services, such as financial and technical assistance. The Coopératives de commercialisation de la réforme agraire (CCRA), a subsidiary of the ONRA also created in 1963, increased ONRA responsibilities, including the provision of seeds, cash, and tractors. For the marketing of agricultural products, the government had already established two other agencies: the Office national de commercialisation (ONACO) and the Coopératives régionales agricoles (CORA). Whereas ONACO assisted in the marketing of produce for export, mainly to France, CORA was responsible for sales and marketing of produce on the domestic market. In less than a year's time, there emerged a giant new bureaucracy to oversee governmental policy toward the rural self-management committees.

Bureaucracy and Peasant Society

From the beginning, the political and ideological dispositions of ONRA bureaucrats were at odds with the socialistic goals of autogestion, especially the goals of peasant participation and self-management. Individuals who had worked in the colonial administration, Frenchmen included, comprised a majority of the ONRA personnel; as a group, these bureaucrats maintained ideological biases and practices that seemed more suitable to middle-class than to socialist values. Half of the senior administrators consisted of former political and administrative chiefs of the FLN and the GPRA, but most of them had gained little previous experience in national administration.[27] A majority of the secondary bureaucrats responsible for routine decisions and execution descended from the colonial administration. Meanwhile, most of the lower level bureaucrats, among those recently employed, were followers of FLN leaders and acquired their employment as a reward for personal loyalty rather than political orientation. In the absence of a compelling FLN ideology, the ONRA bureaucrats were motivated by Ben Bella's personal orders or, conversely, remained entrenched in the procedural and ideological methods of their French predecessors. Thus, a salient contradiction arose between the socialistic goals of agrarian autogestion and the personnel entrusted with administering it.

At the governmental level, the initial subterfuge against the implementation of the March decrees was caused as much by Ben Bella as by Ahmed Ali Mahsas, the first director of the ONRA. Mahsas, who supported Ben Bella's insistence on state control as the regime's political priority, strongly resisted peasant management of the state-owned farms in the belief that it would dilute governmental authority in the countryside and produce an autonomous decentralized system. To preclude this eventuality, he took control of the farms' financing and marketing mechanisms late in March 1963, and in the process violated a provision of the March decrees that reserved this prerogative for the self-management committees. The next month Ben Bella transgressed the March decrees in a presidential order that established the ONRA as Algeria's exclusive agency for granting farm loans and credits; in practice, this regulation restricted the future money flow to the ONRA. These reversals occurred less than a month after the promulgation of the March decrees and clearly exposed Ben Bella's intention to replace worker self-management with governmental control.

The gap between the goals of rural autogestion and Ben Bella's personal priorities widened even more during the Congress of the Fallahin (peasant farmers' convention), which met in Algiers, October 25-27, 1963. The convention was attended by 2,500 to 3,000 farmworkers, including all the presidents of the self-management committees together with worker delegates (each delegate representing a hundred workers). [28] Evidently, Ben Bella summoned this meeting primarily to mobilize popular support for the regime because it was then threatened by the FFS uprising in Kabylia and the border war with Morocco. Not only did the meeting lack an agenda, but the farmworker delegates did not even receive the main report for discussion until after the convention began. With respect to the government's priorities, Ben Bella issued a warning to the farmworkers: "In the course of the year to come, the Algerians who have until now been very privileged in the division of the national income will have to make important sacrifices for their less well served brothers. The workers in the agricultural sector [of autogestion] will not see their standard of living improve very rapidly." [29] Instead of defining a policy, Ben Bella portrayed the workers on the state-managed farms as a privileged group in an attempt to win the support of the peasant and unemployed masses. What made his appeal for economic austerity on the state farms more ironic was the glaring governmental extravagance exemplified by the ONRA.

The convention delegates responded to Ben Bella's appeal with a plethora of complaints, including the government's unfulfilled promise to supply essential farm machinery, irregular salary payments, and inadequate financial and technical assistance. They expressed fierce objections to the state-appointed director, the ONRA representative on the farms, who was accused of undermining the application of worker self-management. For permitting this subterfuge to occur, the delegates singled out Mahsas, whom Ben Bella had promoted to head the Ministry of Agriculture (when the second cabinet was formed in September 1963). The delegates then voted a number of resolutions favorable to agrarian autogestion, as for instance a 30-percent increase in the minimum wage which raised it to 8 DA or $1.60, daily. [30] But the ONRA was indifferent to most of these resolutions; after the convention, the ONRA bureaucrats either did not implement the resolutions or did so partially and halfheartedly.

The official obstruction of agrarian autogestion necessarily engendered an adverse impact on peasant society where the state-managed farms existed. When Gallagher surveyed the farms in 1964, he discovered many failures of autogestion, but still concluded that "rural inertia has been destroyed, hopelessly static patterns have been broken, with every expectation that this is irreversible." [31] This assessment was premature; it did not take into account the system's considerable weaknesses that emerged independently of governmental intervention. These weaknesses concerned countervailing customs, traditions, and behavior endemic to peasant society.

A major complication arose from the peasant farmers' inability to understand and assimilate the French text of the March decrees. The Arabic version of autogestion lent itself to misinterpretation. In Arabic, the term *autogestion* corresponds to the idea of free management or autonomous administration. Consequently, many fallahin did not regard themselves as members of a cooperative but as individual proprietors who earned other income from the state coincidentally. This misinterpretation engendered complacency among the peasants because their expectation to receive the same monthly salary, regardless of the regularity of their labor, was unfulfilled.

Ben Bella sought to overcome this tendency by introducing a daily salary advance of 7 DA that was supposed to be deducted from the annual profits of the cooperative's produce. The peasants, however, ignorant of the distinctions between gross and net profits, claimed the advances as the salary itself. The March decrees required that a cooperative's annual revenue be distributed equitably among the workers, the state, and farm investments. The peasants' proclivity for salary preferences undermined the acceptability of this fiscal arrangement. It was finally destroyed by the government's failure to share farm profits.

Autogestion was also vitiated by the fallahin's psychological reaction. The self-management system responded to a modern technological concept of agrarian reform and therefore disrupted the inveterate forces of traditionalism in peasant society. As Hagen discovered in his analysis of peasant behavior: "Just as it does not occur to the peasant that he can influence any of a wide range of phenomena of the physical world that are of great emotional importance to him, so it does not occur to him that the social structure is amenable to change."[32] The peasants continued to revere the traditional elders, the leaders of dominant extended families or religious functionaries, with the result that these functionaries emerged as quasi-communal chiefs on many of the self-managed farms. For instance, in the formation of a self-management committee, the March decrees prescribed that the peasants on a given cooperative congregate and, after deliberation, elect the committee. However, elections were meaningless on farms where the traditional leaders maintained authority. Management on such farms was claimed naturally by the peasant elites, who conducted themselves as if they represented the system against the state-appointed director. In the end, the reformist ideal of the March decrees, collectivity of the producers, was negated by the prevalence of tradition in rural society.

In his study on autogestion, Jean-Francois Kahn found that the peasants often considered the director a troublesome intruder.[33] The peasants, freshly projected into a directing role through the self-management committee, viewed him as a contradiction of autogestion—that is to say, of "autonomous administration." Because the director held special authority in the committee, they resisted what they considered alien control. Because he was a technician who ordinarily had been sent from the city, they shared little primordial affinity with him.

A conflict at the Roux farms in the Orani region illustrates the tension between the peasants and the director. When the director attempted to expel the committee's president by charging him with the theft of farm properties, the president's co-workers countered the director and forced him to retract the charge. The president retained his position.

Technical incompetence, combined with a scarcity of trained directors, further eroded rural self-management. By the end of 1963, there were 450 state-owned enterprises, but a mere twenty-five directors had been employed to regulate them.[34] Because of low wages, the government generally failed to keep skilled mechanics and technicians in its employ. Algerian engineers and other technical professionals preferred employment in private business, which offered them salaries far superior to governmental wages.[35] Consequently, the majority of the self-management committees and farms functioned without a director. On these farms the peasants continued to work more or less according to traditional farm practices, ignoring the government's plan for coordinated agricultural production.

Closely related to the system's local administrative deficiency was a scarcity of machinery and equipment. Most of the tractors, harvesters, and like equipment in Algeria before independence were destroyed by the OAS. Ben Bella tried to remedy the situation by obtaining equipment from the USSR and Yugoslavia. However, the new machines and equipment soon fell into disrepair as a result of peasant ignorance and lack of maintenance. Algerian agriculture probably should have been labor intensive in any case, but governmental policy attempted to make it capital intensive and in the process maximized the self-management system's dependence on foreign assistance.

The ANP's participation on a number of farms constituted another source of weakness in the self-management system. In Blida, for example, the army administered plantation outlets known as the Boudissa farms. They had been originally directed by Safi Boudissa, a wealthy Muslim farmer who curried favor with the Political Bureau and thereby rose to membership in the UGTA secretariat during the shakeup of January 1963. Productivity and efficiency increased on the farms under army direction. Encouraged by its success, the ANP sought to extend what Daniel Guérin termed the policy of "militarized agriculture." [36] The soldiers reserved priority on the self-management committees for army veterans, while supervising the fallahin as wage earners with no participation in management. The notion of cooperative farming was corroded rapidly on farms where the army acted as manager.

The March decrees provided for trade union participation in autogestion. The UGTA attempted to continue the farm cooperatives it started in summer 1962, but it soon encountered formidable opposition from the peasants who distrusted the trade unionists' urban mentality and orientation. The urban background of the trade unionists also made it difficult for them to communicate with the fallah in his own language and value symbols. Ben Bella accentuated the UGTA difficulties by circumscribing the trade unionists' activity on state farms to prevent the UGTA from infringing competitively on his authority. These obstacles accounted for the trade unionists' failure to make significant inroads into the agrarian sector.

Insofar as the party was concerned, the FLN's formal involvement in agrarian autogestion compromised the workers' decision-making functions as defined by the March decrees. [37] The Political Bureau began to impose party agents on several self-management committees in late 1963, seeking to obliterate traditionalist influence and supplant it with a loyal, rural party constituency. Certain normal labor privileges, such as the right to strike and arbitration, were rejected in favor of unilateral state action in the determination of wage schedules and profit-sharing. As a result, the self-management system gravitated toward the local components of the FLN—viz., the federations, dairas, and kasmas—which had been neither popularly based nor popularly elected.

Meanwhile, the bureaucratization of the peasant labor force through the ONRA stymied or completely prevented the development of autogestion's grass-roots organisms. For example, the two main participatory bodies of the rural self-management system, the workers' general assembly and the workers' council, met very infrequently in the country as in the city. [38] The March decrees also recommended the establishment of communal councils to assist the peasants in organizing and maintaining the farm cooperatives, but few were ever

created. The proposals for regional councils, which the fallahin convention approved in 1963, never left the ONRA drafting boards.

In his terse class analysis of autogestion, Clegg has argued that the
new bureaucratic elites, firmly entrenched in the state and the party,
were the major forces behind the failure of worker self-management.[39] Far from promoting the consolidation of the self-management system, the ONRA bureaucrats emasculated it by ensconcing its
formal powers under state control:

> In the absence of any real theory on what relations between the
> enterprise and the [center] should be, the superstructure was
> pieced together in an *ad hoc* fashion. Each successive stage in
> this process placed the [self-management committees] more
> firmly under central control until the administration came to
> control every essential aspect of economic activity of the [com-
> mittees], rendering the concept of autogestion derisory.[40]

The socialistic transformation promised by autogestion represented a
political threat to these bureaucrats, and as administrators of the system they undermined it. Thus, the March decrees, which laid the
foundation for Algerian socialism, were turned into a victory for the
new middle class.

The ONRA did ameliorate urban unemployment somewhat by hir-
ing more functionaries, but this simply accelerated the transfer of
decision-making prerogatives from the self-management committees
to the central administration. Isolated from the various administrative structures, the peasant farmers reverted to traditional forms of
farm organization, leadership, and production as they found it increasingly easy to escape central control. This result satisfied Ben
Bella's desire for more direct control of the system's organizational
framework, but it inadvertently enabled the peasants to resume traditional farm practices at the local level. As a result of these developments, both popular participation and agricultural productivity
declined.

Failure of Autogestion

Ben Bella recognized the general weaknesses of the agrarian system
as early as 1963. At the fallahin convention, he freely acknowledged
the obstacles caused by governmental intervention or inaction:

> Difficulties have arisen in the concrete application of the March
> decrees . . . , and in the development of socialist labor relations
> in the countryside. . . . We have ascertained that the administra-
> tion of the self-management system is mal-adapted to the coun-
> try's new socialist structures. . . . We know now that agricultural
> credit is mal-distributed, that materials are not often placed at
> the producer's disposition, that crop commercialization is
> faulty, and that the workers' remuneration relative to their pro-
> duction is irregular. [41]

Earlier he admitted that the Political Bureau imposed party personnel on the self-management committees. [42] Yet, it was not until a year
later that he began to seek a redress of the system's deficiencies, particularly those resulting from ONRA excesses.

The government launched this effort in December 1964 by organizing the Fédération nationale des travailleurs de la terre (FNTT), an
organization designed to draw the fallahin on the self-managed farms
into the UGTA. Ben Bella hoped that this innovation would also bring
the trade unionists into closer association with the party. The FNTT
added about 220,000 permanent farmworkers to the trade union's
ranks, [43] satisfying the radical trade unionists' demand for a role in
the rural sector. Ben Bella thus reversed the Political Bureau's previous policy that prohibited the UGTA from participating in the agrarian system.

Ben Bella provided additional evidence that the Political Bureau
had changed its policy toward the trade unionists at an FNTT convention in Algiers on December 25, 1964. His plan was almost foiled when
a conflict developed between the 500 FNTT delegates and an indeterminate number of representatives from the ONRA. The minister of
agriculture, Ali Mahsas, objected to UGTA control of the self-management system, suspecting that the trade unionists would coerce
ONRA policy-makers through job slowdowns and strikes. To extract
concessions from private industry, the trade union radicals had applied the strike weapon about a hundred times in 1963 and thirty
times in the first half of 1964. [44] As the ONRA was responsible for
managing the agrarian sector, Mahsas aimed to preclude such actions
against his ministry by stacking the FNTT's executive committee with
an ONRA majority. Anticipating the maneuver, Bourouiba and other

radicals approved a motion that barred ONRA representatives from sitting on the committee. The ONRA nominees then summarily resigned from the ministerial agency in order to qualify as "workers" in the election.[45] Ramdane Bouchebouba, the ONRA representative who conducted the convention, emerged as the FNTT's secretary general.

The radicals denounced the ONRA subterfuge at once and associated it with the Political Bureau's usurpation of the UGTA in 1963. In an effort to dissociate himself from the conflict, Ben Bella rebuked Mahsas publicly:

> Relations between members of the self-management committees and officials of the Ministry of Agriculture are not harmonious. Some of the latter have exceeded their powers. This is one of our shortcomings and we must correct it.
>
> The fallah must no longer be considered an object and must be given a position of responsibility. He should be the initiator of action. We must permit the workers and the peasants to assume such prerogatives.[46]

This statement tended to improve Ben Bella's standing with the trade unionists, but the ONRA's action clearly penalized him in his attempt to project the Political Bureau as a defender of the UGTA in particular, the peasants in general.

Weighed against the UGTA's success in agriculture was the continuing colonial structure in trade relations between Algeria and France. During the colonial era, Algeria's exports to France, and those controlled by French interests, amounted to 80 percent of the mineral raw materials and agricultural produce, consisting of wine, fruits, and vegetables.[47] This structure caused permanent instability in the domestic economy because internal trade was far less remunerative, and therefore less important, than trade between Algeria and the métropole. Ben Bella destroyed foreign ownership of the modern agricultural sector when he nationalized the colon plantations in 1963, but the structure of trade prevailed. Accordingly, the new agrarian system also depended on French importation of Algerian products.

Under Mahsas, the Ministry of Agriculture promised to diversify the agrarian system by converting land used for the production of colonial staples to new products like wheat and corn. Algeria needed the new crops not only to gain an independent capacity to feed the domestic population, but also to resolve the structural trade pattern. However, the process of crop diversification necessitated a protracted process in which land had to be fertilized and left fallow (for as long as six to eight years) before seeding the new products. [48] In the interim, the economy was bound to sink disastrously because existing staples like wine were not produced and sold. Little wonder, then, that Ben Bella did not initiate this economically essential, but prohibitive, process.

Urban autogestion was also afflicted by the giant multinational firms, such as Michelin, Durafour, and Berliet, which remained under French ownership. This reality prevailed despite the March decrees and the Charter of Algiers, which enjoined the government to nationalize *all* foreign-owned properties. Ben Bella had exclaimed in 1963:"We have begun and we will not finish until the day when all the means of production are placed in the hands of the workers."[49] He followed this affirmation by nationalizing the important glassmaking complex Verreries de l'Afrique du nord and the Acilor metallurgical ensemble. However, this socialist gesture was largely symbolic. It concealed his lack of intent regarding the multinationals because they still provided the bulk of Algeria's industrial and manufacturing commerce. Underscoring Ben Bella's fear of losing the trade and investments of the giant foreign capitalists was the fact that urban nationalization was limited mainly to middle-level, relatively unimportant companies in meat produce, semolina, brick masonry, food, and furniture. The multinationals, like sacred cows, were never touched.[50]

Meanwhile, the state-appointed director emerged as the supreme agent on the few worker self-management committees that did function in the cities. Instead of simply representing the government in the committee's decision-making functions, the director imposed governmental policy in ways that exceeded his authority (as defined by the March decrees) and thus nullified the possibility of effective worker management. Expressly prohibited were the workers' right to strike and the practice of managerial syndicalism (i.e., trade union control independent of the FLN and the state). By 1965, the prerogatives of Ben Bella's personal rule had contributed, more or less decisively, to the demise of autogestion in the cities as in the countryside.

This background lay behind Ben Bella's decision to entrust the development of the FNTT to the trade unionists. So far he had failed to mobilize the peasantry into a rural party constituency. His own popularity had also fallen in the hinterland because of the farms' declining productivity, together with the deficiencies of the rural self-management system itself. There was no doubt that his was a highly opportunistic decision, but at least here finally was an official recognition that rural and urban development should be coordinated by the workers themselves.

Notwithstanding Ben Bella's belated turn to the trade unionists, all chance had been lost for resuscitating agrarian autogestion from its accumulated failures by 1965. The system probably would have achieved some success if it had been placed under UGTA direction in the first place. The workers were more knowledgeable and capable on labor problems generally than either the politicians or the bureaucrats, and this advantage seemed to qualify them to take the lead in developing the system. This chance too was lost when the Political Bureau overturned the UGTA leadership in 1963.

In retrospect, it can also be seen that some of the deficiencies of the self-management system were not attributable to Ben Bella and would have prevailed regardless of who the actuators of the system were. The deep-rooted traditions of peasant society and culture repelled even the most enlightened advances which were alien to the hinterland. Tradition was an inherent obstacle to organizing the peasants into a technical, highly specialized system. Since the system was bound to be directed by urban elites, conflict between modernization and traditionalism was inevitable.

Ben Bella rationalized the failure of autogestion by accusing "counterrevolutionaries," such as the FFS, of disrupting the system. If the regime's organized opposition posed a threat to general political stability, there was never a corresponding impact on rural society. Disruption occurred, to be sure, but by and large it derived from the tactics and intervention of the government. Ben Bella's rhetoric simply glossed over his failure to prepare the peasantry via autogestion for participation in an institutionalized mass-party system.

Peasant mobilization did develop in fact, but, as discussed, it
tended to be ambiguous, ill-directed, and promoted haphazardly.
Never an organized force before, the peasants were suddenly projected into national politics by the March decrees, though only to be
transformed into a disenchanted clientele of the state. Ben Bella
spoke in the name of the country's majority, the peasants, but he did
not accord them meaningful participation either in the decisions
affecting the self-managed farms or in the administrative network
established to coordinate them. Ultimately, he distorted the autogestion system in a deliberate attempt to fashion it into an appendage of
personal rule.

The "School of Socialism": Youth and Students

Ben Bella's relative failure in building a party constituency among the peasantry was compensated to some extent by the Political Bureau's extraordinary success in organizing youths into the Jeunesse du FLN (JFLN), as the party's youth section was called. The JFLN succeeded in gathering a broad national spectrum of nonstudent youth in the cities and in the countryside. The JFLN youths readily accepted integration into the FLN and became some of Ben Bella's most enthusiastic supporters. Even after his downfall, they comprised "some of the few who . . . still talked openly of his time in power as the golden age."[1]

In contrast, the Political Bureau encountered major obstacles in absorbing UGEMA, the university student organization, into the party. Though small in numbers compared to the JFLN, the student movement represented an influential political group in Algerian society, and a few students had even played prominent roles in the war for independence. Unlike the JFLN, however, the UGEMA insisted on organizational autonomy from the FLN.

The Political Bureau's special interest in youths and students emanated from a 1963 survey revealing that persons under twenty years of age constituted 57 percent of the Algerian population.[2] This age distribution was a result of the sharp decline in the adult male population caused by war casualties and the emigration of workers. An annual birthrate of about 4 percent increased the numerical preponderance of minors in the general population.[3] Since it was predicted that this distribution would not change significantly before

1980, Political Bureau leaders concerned with enlarging the FLN's constituency had to take these statistics into account when contemplating party building.

The Political Bureau also realized that the future political elites of the FLN, as of the country in general, were likely to emerge from the ranks of university students. Even in their present status, students enjoyed a more privileged position than their nonstudent counterparts. "Because of the small size of the educated middle class," Lipset notes in his study on students in underdeveloped societies, "students in certain underdeveloped countries make up a disproportionately large section of the bearers of public opinion; their various affinities of education, class, and kinship with the actual elites give them an audience which students in more developed countries can seldom attain."[4] The students, in other words, were a potentially potent force in Algerian society of the present and the future. This realization prompted the Political Bureau to devise a policy to integrate young people in general, and university students in particular, into the party.

The FLN Youth Section

Early in 1963, the Political Bureau created the JFLN as the vehicle for mobilizing youth in social action programs and for indoctrinating them in the regime's socialist ideology. The JFLN was designed specifically to attract two categories of young people: unemployed lycée dropouts in the towns and illiterate peasant youth in the villages. Others slated for eventual integration into the JFLN included college and lycée students and the Scouts musulmans algériens (SMA). All youths under twenty-five years of age could join the organization; after that age, they graduated to the parent body. JFLN membership was voluntary and often involved certain political and material inducements. FLN leaders, expecting the JFLN to train and produce the FLN militants of the future, dubbed it the nation's "school of socialism."

The activity of a few Algiers' youths who endeavored to organize a party cell shortly after the war had originally suggested the idea of a youth section. This party cell was akin to the embryonic FLN structure that Harbi and Zerdani had organized in Algiers; the youth section also predated the Ben Bella regime. The Political Bureau subsequently used the Algiers model for building a national youth organization. The FLN's Orientation Commission, the party's educational arm, did the main work in setting up the national body.

To mobilize the youths, the Political Bureau promoted social action programs. The main activities were volunteer work projects involving social service activities such as reforestation, literacy programs, village reconstruction, and sundry construction tasks. A training center for the volunteers was established near Algiers at Camp Oued-Fedda on April 4, 1963, as the national site of the JFLN *volontariat*. Some 350 youths congregated there to undergo the practical and theoretical instruction required for volunteer organizers.[5] On the practical side, they learned the essentials of tree planting, road reconstruction, carpentry, language teaching, and the like. For ideological indoctrination, the party drilled them in the tenets of the Tripoli Program, the March decrees, and general Political Bureau policies (which primarily consisted of presidential and ministerial speeches). After the party congress in 1964,[6] the doctrinal instruction was supplemented by the Charter of Algiers, the new party program. Once the youths completed the training program, they returned to their home regions to promote JFLN projects.

Soon after its formation, the JFLN sponsored several work projects across the country. Opération labours, announced by Ben Bella in fall 1962, was the first large-scale project in which youth participated extensively. They worked in great numbers harvesting the crops abandoned by the colons that year, thereby helping to save precious farm produce. Elsewhere, JFLN squads planted thousands of trees (provided by the government) in several coastal regions, arresting the type of soil erosion endemic in the arid and water-imbalanced land shelves of North Africa.[7] The principal volunteer section, known as the Mourad Didouche brigade,[8] regularly sent teams to reforest roadside areas around Algiers.

Literacy programs were the JFLN's most useful contribution. The JFLN organized village and communal teams (of eight to ten youths each) to teach their own illiterate members as well as adults the rudiments of reading and writing. Literacy instruction was conducted mainly in French because almost all the educated youths had received their education in French lycées. (The few madrasat, or Quranic schools, had not produced many arabophones under the colonial regime.[9]) Ben Bella was one of the strongest proponents of the literacy programs, deeming the development of a literate citizenry an essential

to political development: "We well know that there can be no real socialism with ninety-five percent of the population illiterate."[10] The
extent of the JFLN's success in reducing illiteracy cannot be ascertained because of unreliable statistics, but it can be assumed that
their effectiveness was considerable, particularly among the many
peasant volunteers who were unable to read and write in either French
or Arabic.

Volunteer construction and reconstruction teams completed the
activity of JFLN volunteer brigades. In July 1964, the youths cleared
and canalized land areas in the village of Azzefoun, an accomplish-
ment that enabled local farmers to establish a potato farm as a pilot
project in the region. Economically, all projects of this nature, performed through the use of free labor, represented savings to the government.

Volunteer work at the Oued-Fedda dam suggests the economic
significance of the labor of the JFLN brigades. After the youths arrested the erosion and restored the soil of the region, the government
decided to irrigate the land to produce sufficient agricultural goods to
nourish an estimated 50,000 persons.[11] The project required 200,000
workdays, which the free labor of JFLN work teams supplied, and
benefited approximately 1,000 farmers.[12]

Thus, the JFLN made a limited but important contribution to Algeria's overall economic development. Hadj Ben Alla, spokesman for
the Political Bureau, characterized the role of the volunteer work
force as follows:

> The volontariat is to become a powerful instrument for the
> mobilization of our youth and, at the same time, one of the
> means to attack the enormous problems posed in the building of
> a modern country. By combining productive work with political
> and professional training, the volontariat constitutes an exalted
> school of socialism.[13]

Consistent with these goals, the JFLN initiated a program called
"dimanches socialistes" ("socialist Sundays") in which the volunteers
joined trade union workers, soldiers, and other groups who also worked on Sundays to reforest and develop various regions. In certain
areas of cultivation, e.g., grape picking, the youths also toiled on the
self-managed farms. Such activity imbued the youths with a sense of

national purpose and identity because they could literally view themselves as individuals engaged in the development of the country.

The voluntary work brigades were also a response to the legions of nonstudent young people who could neither find regular jobs nor attend school. Unemployment affected about 45 percent of the adult (male) population in 1963; for the most part, lycée and university education remained limited to the sons and daughters of the urban middle class. In the academic year 1963-1964, there were nearly 2,400,000 schoolage youths, that is, youngsters between the ages of six and fourteen—but only 1,300,000 actually attended school.[14] Statistics for university enrollment were even more stunning: fewer than 5,000 students were enrolled at the University of Algiers, the country's sole institution of higher education. After their formation, the JFLN brigades greatly compensated for such inadequacies by siphoning off that significant body of youths excluded from gainful employment and formal education.

Politicization of the youths occurred while they participated in the work projects. The FLN established storefront clubhouses in local areas for youths to congregate on evenings after they finished job assignments. In such settings, the youths discussed party dogma and familiarized themselves with publications and directives from the FLN Orientation Commission, such as the Tripoli Program and the March decrees. Following the 1964 FLN Congress, they were systematically indoctrinated in the teachings of the Charter of Algiers.

JFLN secretary general Abdelmajid Bennaceur, a young militant loyal to Ben Bella and the FLN, conferred with the youths frequently, issuing party orders in his capacity as liaison between the Political Bureau and the JFLN. In 1964, the Political Bureau financed the publication of a JFLN journal, *Jeunesse*, which promulgated FLN doctrine and informed different JFLN sections of pertinent youth activities occurring across the country. The journal also helped to educate the volunteers in party doctrine through its frequent editions on Algerian socialism, agrarian reform, and African decolonization. Much emphasis was placed on allegiance to the Political Bureau (to Ben Bella specifically) and on the necessity of defending the regime against "counterrevolutionaries."

Another form of politicization involved public demonstrations. Ben Bella, whose foreign policy encouraged wars of national liberation in the Third World, staged frequent rallies (usually in Algiers) to incite

public opinion against apartheid in South Africa or in support of liberation movements in Angola and Southwest Africa. JFLN youths
stood in the front ranks of demonstrators at such assemblies, shouting
party slogans and railing against colonialism. When Ben Bella appeared with heads of state or leaders from radical or socialist governments, such as Guinea's Sékou Touré or Cuba's Che Guevara (in
1964), the youths lined the streets to welcome them and applaud the
speechmaking.

The structuring of the JFLN was not completed until the FLN Party
Congress of 1964. The party then created a "satellite camp" at Oued-
Fedda as a model for local sections everywhere. With a group of 475
youth volunteers, the JFLN established four brigades, each consisting
of 100 to 200 members. [15] The brigades were divided into four companies of about thirty members each, every company specializing in
an area of volontariat activity, such as reforestation, literacy, or construction work. A camp commander headed the hierarchy and directed the brigade and company commanders. This structure enabled
the JFLN to expand into rural regions where heretofore it had been
relatively inactive.

At its peak in 1964, JFLN membership amounted to 50,000 to
100,000 regular members and an undetermined number of occasional
adherents.

In an effort to enlarge the JFLN's constituency, the Political Bureau
decided to affiliate it with the SMA, the Boy Scout organization that
had remained autonomous since independence. Like the JFLN, the
SMA engaged in volunteer projects but unlike the JFLN it seemed to
have no special political role save the use of the scouts as applauding
bystanders at political rallies. The SMA did have political potential,
however, and it became an integral component of the "school of socialism." The party sought to restructure it as an agency preparing
youngsters, generally between the ages of six and fifteen, for membership in the JFLN. Its membership totaled about 20,000 in 1964. The
Political Bureau conceived the JFLN as a generational foundation for
the FLN, with the SMA as a feeder to the JFLN.

The FLN provided certain pecuniary inducements to membership
in the youth organizations. A membership card entitled holders to rebates on movie tickets, service at certain cafes and restaurants, and
free entry to cultural festivals or other forms of public amusements.
The JFLN also sent youth delegations abroad; one delegation visited

Cuba and another attended the Maghrib Youth Conference of Casablanca in 1964. The youth were especially inspired by foreign volunteers who came to Algeria in 1964 to form the "international volontariat." For example, the Soviet Union and other East European countries sent their trained young people (i.e., engineers and other technicians) to assist and train the JFLN volunteers in implementing the work projects.[16]

A high point in the JFLN's development occurred at its National Conference which met in Algiers September 10-12, 1964. This conference was convened to lay the groundwork for a national JFLN convention to be held the following year. A total of 634 participants attended, representing JFLN sections from sixteen Algerian towns and rural capitals.[17] The JFLN's constituency had so increased by this time that none of its sections numbered less than 3,000 members.[18] In addition, twenty-four representatives came from the JFLN's affiliate in France, the Association générale de la jeunesse algérienne (AGJA) which had organized 120,000 Algerian youths working or residing on the European continent.

A sociological breakdown of participants showed that 50 percent were laborers, 23 percent salaried office workers, 7 percent lycée graduates, 9 percent peasants, and 3 percent peddlers or craft artisans.[19] These youths formed the elite of the general JFLN constituency, and their involvement indicated that the youth section was not restricted to peasant and unemployed youths.

The JFLN delegates formulated an organizational charter as a basis for future party youth structures. According to paragraph two of the document, the JFLN supervisory committees would be elected by militants and adherents at the section level, and by the section committees at the daira (canton) level, until the next JFLN congress. Article 7 stated that the execution of party decisions necessitated control by the FLN leadership. Article 8 obligated JFLN militants to respect the party hierarchy. A JFLN militant, according to Article 12, could be defined as any Algerian youth, at least seventeen years of age, who had participated in the organization as an adherent for at least six months, and had fulfilled the "conditions of good morality, regular attendance, and activity during the same period."[20] Article 13 affirmed that the Political Bureau considered discipline an essential for labor, effectiveness, and cohesion. All militants had to participate assiduously in JFLN tasks of national interest, i.e., political campaigns, volunteer brigades, and the state-managed farms. The charter also recommended a full-scale institutionalization of the youth organization and its more solid alignment behind the FLN hierarchy.

Interestingly, the demand for autonomy never emerged as an issue in the JFLN. Operating under the Political Bureau's tutelage from the outset, the JFLN did not question the orders it received. In fact Bennaceur admitted that "democracy" did not inhere in the internal functions of the organization. [21] The JFLN rescued most youths from idleness or boredom, thereby stimulating their enlistment into the organization. Furthermore, the perceived benefits of JFLN membership raised the incentive for discipline and obedience. This characteristic of JFLN youths differentiated them greatly from university students and, to some extent, from the SMA.

The most significant question deliberated by the delegates concerned the unification of all youth organizations under the JFLN. Ben Alla conveyed the Political Bureau's directive in mid-1964:

> It is incumbent upon the JFLN to achieve rapidly, in compliance with the wishes of the youths themselves, one of the objectives decided by the party congress: the integration of the different youth organizations into a common unit in order to better utilize the enormous energies which they possess and to transform our youth into a strong and coherent whole. [22]

This objective primarily pertained to the university students who dissociated themselves from the FLN organization after independence. Insisting upon autonomy, they shunned affiliation with the JFLN, fearing that the student movement would be engulfed by the party. The JFLN conference issued a statement affirming that the party youth section did not seek to foist itself on other organizations. Neither the JFLN nor the students knew at that time that the Political Bureau was preparing to subsume the student organization under the JFLN.

Conclusion of the conference climaxed the JFLN's development under the Ben Bella regime. In two years, the organization had grown from a small urban-based party cell to a national constituency. It had distinguished itself by mobilizing a major segment of the country's youths into activities of social relevance and economic benefit. The

JFLN youth had also been politicized so adroitly that some, like Bennaceur, emerged as political spokesmen for the FLN itself. The university students, alone among Algerian youths, were disinclined to
accept the Political Bureau's dispensations.

Students and Party Integration

The evolution of the Algerian student organization the Union générale des étudiants musulmans algériens (UGEMA) contrasted with
the political development of the JFLN. In the first place, Algerian students insisted on an autonomous movement. Second, most students
belonged to the native bourgeoisie and eschewed association with the
unschooled peasant youths of the JFLN. As an educated elite amidst a
predominantly illiterate population, students formed a privileged
class. These factors tended to separate the student movement from
the party and its policy of unification.

The tradition of corporate university autonomy was another colonial vestige. This European tradition originated in the Middle Ages [23]
and was the guiding principle of the Union nationale des étudiants
français (UNEF), the French student movement, when it recruited the
few Muslim students who were enrolled in metropolitan French universities or at the University of Algiers. The UNEF branch in Algiers
vanished along with the colonial regime when Algeria became independent, but the notion of autonomy was fixed in the psyches of
Muslim students before they formed UGEMA. Despite their involvement in the anticolonial struggle, the imprint of acculturation persisted. Somewhat comparable to Algerian trade unionists, university
students reached independence with inveterate ideas and interests
that placed them a priori in opposition to the Political Bureau.

As compared to the JFLN, UGEMA also had a much longer history.
Formed in July 1955 by the FLN, it was instrumental in mobilizing
Muslim students against the French in the war for independence. Two
members of the UGEMA, Mohammed Khemisti (Algeria's first
foreign minister) and Colonel Youssef Khatib (commander of wilaya
IV by 1962), ascended to prominent political or military positions in
the FLN struggle. But UGEMA's principal wartime activity centered
around its diplomatic representations before the International Student Conference (ISC) and the International Union of Students (IUS),

respectively the Western and the Soviet-backed international student organizations.

Two Algerian student leaders—Ahmed Taleb, a medical student and the son of Shaykh Ibrahimi, and Messaoud Ait Chaalal, the son of an affluent Constantine landowner—steered UGEMA away from entanglement in the cold war conflict between the ISC and the IUS. More pragmatists than ideologues, they lobbied both sides for recognition of UGEMA as the legitimate representative of Algerian students, since the French Algerian branch of UNEF was claiming to represent Muslim students as well. When the Sixth International Student Conference met in Ceylon in September 1956, UGEMA leaders gained recognition and international support for the Algerian anticolonial struggle, and numerous scholarships were provided for Algerian students to study abroad. This success qualified as one of UGEMA's major victories during the war. In later years, the organization defended the FLN cause before foreign student forums, but it grew less cohesive as the French police arrested student leaders or forced them and their members into exile or hiding.

The UGEMA came out of the war a severely fragmented organization. Most of its leaders had been victims of French repression. For example, the French police arrested Ahmed Taleb in February 1957 and detained him for the next four years. That same year a similar fate befell Mohammed Khemisti. Near independence, the GPRA contributed to UGEMA's decline by dismissing some of its wartime leaders in an effort to consolidate control of the student movement before the challenge from Ben Bella and the Political Bureau. [24]

Probably the most significant factor in UGEMA's wartime disintegration involved the summer crisis of 1962. As with the politicians and the guerrillas, schisms erupted among the students as they sided either with the Political Bureau or the GPRA. Some students even supported individual leaders within the contending forces. In the same period, hundreds of Algerian students who had studied in the West, Eastern Europe, or Arab countries descended upon the newly liberated country imbued with all the different ideological and cultural orientations that these diverse regions represented.

A total of 2,081 students, to be precise, returned from twenty-two different countries. [25] The location and number of students in each country included: France (500), the United States (21), the United

Arab Republic (150), and Tunisia (26 liberal arts and science students, and 750 in traditional Islamic studies). Many of the students, especially those who had studied in Eastern European countries and had received scholarships from the host governments through UGEMA's diplomacy, were greatly affected by the ideological currents in these countries. This fact was to have great import for the development of UGEMA after independence.

UGEMA's fifth congress met in Algiers on September 5, 1962, and exposed the schisms in the student movement. Four preceding UGEMA conventions had met during the war. All had taken place in exile, usually in Tunis or Switzerland, and none represented the organization's membership or made critical decisions on UGEMA's role after independence. The 1962 convention assembled specifically to restructure the student organization and to determine its new ideological orientation. It failed to consider these issues, however, because conflict immediately ensued among the various delegates. The university section, composed of the Algiers' students who arranged the convention, was accused of granting disproportionate representation to the delegations from Algiers and France which favored party integration. A majority of the 2,000 delegates opposed it. [26] A number of delegates who had arrived from the USSR, the United States, and Tunisia walked out of the meeting, angered by the inordinate delegate quotas. Students fresh from Eastern Europe denounced both the Political Bureau and the GPRA for lacking the radicalism they considered necessary to build a socialist country. The arrivals from Middle Eastern countries raised the additional complaint that UGEMA leaders had omitted proposals for an Arabization program. They argued vehemently that UGEMA's primary interest involved a defense and propagation of traditional Arab-Islamic cultural values. Overwhelmed by this plethora of factions, the UGEMA congress dissolved in the middle of its deliberations.

The students did manage to approve a resolution that maintained the principle of autonomy. They also postponed the decisions on UGEMA's policy and orientation until the next UGEMA convention, scheduled for the following year. A proposed preparatory committee was not authorized to decide these issues in the interim. Hence, they accomplished nothing concrete. In fact, they failed even to agree on the organization of the preparatory committee. With the students in such disarray, the Political Bureau began to plot its strategy for assimilating the UGEMA into the FLN.

About 3,000 students matriculated at the University of Algiers in the academic year 1962-1963. This was more than quadruple the enrollment of Algerian students in 1954, when the Europeans had restricted the registration of Arab-Muslim students. Approximately two-thirds of the student population, or about 2,000 students, had entered the university without the lycée *baccalauréat* which had heretofore been a requirement for acceptance. [27] These students benefited from a new policy called *la promotion sociale* (social promotion) which the government introduced to increase university enrollment. It permitted those who had received some lycée education (but had not completed it) to enroll without the baccalauréat, the commonly accepted standard.

In principle, the social promotion policy democratized university education or assured all youths, more or less qualified, equal access to it. The Ministry of Education offered each student a scholarship of 300 DA ($60) monthly, a sum covering the costs of necessities such as room, board, and books. This stipend also enabled the government to increase the number of UGEMA students amenable to the party line. Thus, social promotion operated as a critical aspect of the Political Bureau's strategy, especially at a time when there were few FLN partisans among university students.

Encouraged by the presence of new students loyal to the FLN, the Political Bureau summoned a national student conference in April 1963 which ousted the current executive committee of UGEMA. A party student, Mustapha Mekideche, headed the new executive, replacing Mokhtar Mokhtefi, a former ALN officer who had recently overturned the UGEMA nine-man committee that the Political Bureau appointed in 1962. The FLN then ordered the formation of a twelve-man control commission to prepare for the reconvened fifth congress.

Ben Bella pressed the students to be active in ameliorating the social and economic conditions of the country's masses, particularly those of the peasantry. Speaking at the university's inaugural convocation in 1962, he declared:

The Tripoli Program calls for the union of the peasants and the

intellectuals. I am convinced it is the university that will give us
the avant-garde. The students have to understand that they
must lead the peasants. They must go into the interior and help
in the reconstruction campaign, just as the students in Cuba
help to cut sugar cane. [28]

In other words, Ben Bella instructed UGEMA to engage in the type of
activity promoted by the JFLN. Politically, the speech meant that the
student organization had to submit to the dictates of the party concerning its purpose and actions.

But two important factors militated against the Political Bureau's
projections for UGEMA. The first was the presence of radical students in the UGEMA leadership—especially Houari Mouffok,
twenty-six years old, a student who had returned from East Germany
where he had studied economics and planning, and Nourredine
Zenine, a leftist student activist, formerly in East Germany, who now
worked as Mouffok's chief assistant. The new leaders, politicized and
doctrinaire, were diametrical opposites to their moderate predecessors such as Taleb (who revered Ferhat Abbas). Mouffok and Zenine
were strongly influenced by Marxism-Leninism and had now adopted
what they referred to as "revolutionary politics," or notions they
fashioned to justify continuing an autonomous student organization.

The second factor was the middle-class backgrounds of most students, which predisposed them to individualist conceptions of their
roles. Laffargue's research on students at the Faculty of Law and Economics in 1963-1964 illustrates the point. [29] By identifying the profes-
sion of the students' fathers, Laffargue discovered that the great
majority of students came from families headed by men who belonged
to the Algerian middle class (employers, merchants, bureaucrats, and
liberal professionals). Very few students had fathers who were cate-
gorized as workers or farmers. To the middle-class group, the university represented "the privileged means of social mobility." [30] It came
as no surprise, therefore, that most students pursued careers in the
professions or some form of administration rather than in agriculture
and related fields that would qualify them for occupations in the
hinterland.

Urban residence further conditioned the attitudes of the students.
Students from Algiers and its environs formed the dominant regional

grouping at the university. About half the students in Laffargue's survey (or 47.5 percent of the male and 42.5 of the female students) resided in or near the capital. [31] A parity appeared to exist in terms of a city-country distribution; that is, 51.3 percent of the student population originated from rural areas and 41.1 percent from urban centers, but this distribution camouflaged the overrepresentation of the Algiers group, and so concealed a major characteristic of the student population.

The radical ideology of student leadership and the socioeconomic backgrounds of most students thus combined to counteract party strategy. The radical leaders who opposed the Political Bureau's plan to incorporate UGEMA into the FLN outmaneuvered the party students in their midst and stacked the Algiers section with enough of their allies to elect Zenine president. The majority of the university students avoided active participation in the organization, but permitted Mouffok and Zenine to speak and act for them. This set of circumstances created the impression that the radicals enjoyed broad support from the student body as a whole. In reality, the activist student arena encompassed only the party students and the radicals.

A mutual interest in maintaining student autonomy, not ideological affinity, linked the student majority to Mouffok and Zenine. If most students were not inclined to participate in the UGEMA, they did indeed applaud the radicals' speeches on student management of the university. The party students resented the middle-class baccalaureates who feared that the party devotees would depreciate the university's academic standards because of the lowered, unexclusive entrance requirements. In an agreement with the Algerian government, France decided to honor degrees awarded by the University of Algiers on a par with French university degrees. To the middle-class student majority, this issue was of far greater importance than the government's policy for democratizing the university. When the Algiers' section assembled on June 9 to elect a delegation for the rescheduled fifth congress, they chose Zenine to head it. The election again demonstrated that class values, not ideology, worked to the advantage of the radical leaders.

UGEMA's fifth congress reconvened on August 10, 1963, with 180 delegates in official attendance. As the ranks of the party students had not increased significantly since the previous convention, a confrontation seemed likely between the Political Bureau and the student radicals. Mouffok and his allies controlled the preparatory committee and the key Algiers section, while the party students had failed to gain access to any of UGEMA's decision-making committees.

Ben Bella, who was not scheduled to address the convention, made a surprise appearance in an effort to mollify the dissident radicals. The party's aim of uniting UGEMA and the JFLN with the peasants had not been renounced, but he expressed it differently: "We have only one program, but no ideology. . . . Your task is precisely to prepare yourselves to work with us, to confront our ideas in order to create something richer, more profound than the Tripoli Program."[32] Ben Bella did not repeat his objection to student autonomy; instead, he invited the students to participate in the formulation of official FLN ideology. He also conceded to certain of the radicals' doctrinal positions, asserting that the Political Bureau favored "scientific socialism" as well. Then, if the radicals refrained from criticizing traditional Islam and its customs, the government would be prepared to implement a "scientific socialism" without precedent. The radicals rebuffed these appeals and manifested their inflexibility by changing the name of the student organization to the Union nationale des étudiants algériens (UNEA). The letter "M" in UGEMA (for Muslim) symbolized a religious association which the radicals disavowed.

The new charter for the UNEA reasserted student autonomy in absolute terms. The party students, like the Political Bureau, retreated behind the show of force made by the radicals. The radicals, in turn, escalated their demands on the government, including student management of university regulations and a student majority on the government's scholarship committee. Moreover, they demanded a substantive role in the university's higher council and university services, the policy-making division of the institution. The regime advised the students that their demands exceeded the concessions it could make at that time, but this response merely inspired the radicals to intensify their pressures.

Following the presentation of UNEA demands and policy, the delegates cast ballots to elect a committee directorate to execute them. The election proved a turning-point in the struggle between the radical and party students as a result of the interplay of political and religious motives. The radicals triggered a dispute over credentials by again stacking the electoral committee with their allies. The forty-eight delegates from Arab countries stormed out of the convention in protest. Of the remaining delegates, only 101 participated in the final vote, including 50 of Mouffok's partisans. The committee directorate appointed Mouffok president and Zenine vice-president of UNEA. Now, however, they were without the support of the student traditionalists. This strategic loss set the scene for a cooptation of the organization's membership and a disclosure of the facade of support that had enabled the radicals to hold sway.

The new leaders distributed a declaration of principles when the convention ended, reiterating the demands for student autonomy and student management of various university functions and services. They agreed that organizational autonomy did not constitute an end in itself but should be utilized to "integrate UNEA into the vast popular movement of a socialist society."[33] Seemingly entrenched in their dominant positions, Mouffok and his clique viewed UNEA as an independent entity, the exclusive sphere of student interests.

The Political Bureau later ordered the JFLN to resume the drive for unification of all youth organizations, revealing that it did not submit to the actions the radicals had taken at the congress. Consequently, the JFLN militants met in Algiers on May 24 to discuss two proposals for a merger: the first consisted of a thorough fusion of the youth organizations within the JFLN; the second entailed the establishment of the JFLN simply as an elite structure for youths pledged to intensive political, economic, and technical activity. A provisional National Youth Council was to coordinate the youth organizations regardless of which plan the students favored.

The outbreak of the Algerian-Moroccan War in October 1963 advanced the party's strategy for unification. Nationalist sentiment impelled even the radicals to overlook their differences with the Political Bureau and to rally to the defense of the regime. Approximately 600 students volunteered to serve as military aides to the ANP. Party leaders exploited student attitudes by confronting the radicals with the proposed merger which, because of the external crisis, they felt constrained to accept. The party announced in late October that "the three great National Youth Organizations—the JFLN, UNEA, and the SMA—have decided to create the National Youth Committee [under the supervision of the FLN's Political Bureau]. This committee will have as its essential task the mobilization of young Algerians—workers, peasants, university and lycée students, and intellectuals."[34] Profiting from passions generated by war nationalism, FLN leaders succeeded in obtaining UNEA's official commitment to an internal political policy that the students had attacked consistently since independence.

UNEA students continued their participation in the National Youth Committee after the war. Though less active in the party structure, some even accepted assignments in JFLN work brigades. When earthquakes devastated the region of Biskra and Touggourt in early 1964, for example, 200 lycée and university students went there from Algiers to assist local residents in the reconstruction of their homes and villages. [35] But only a small percentage of the university student body ever became involved in these projects. Those who volunteered their labor, in fact, were often party students.

As the military crisis grew remote, the middle-class student majority once again became apathetic to domestic politics, concentrating instead on career interests. A study conducted by the Ministry of Education in this period disclosed the students' principal class interests. In questionnaires distributed randomly to 400 students at the University of Algiers, 80 percent identified themselves as active members of UNEA. [36] The breakdown remained fairly consistent when the students were asked why they had joined the organization: 27 percent became members because they were UNEA "militants," 23 percent because of "conformity or duty," 16 percent because of material advantages, and only 5 percent because they aspired to be "political militants."

The most instructive of the students' attitudes related to their preference for study abroad: three-fourths chose a capitalist country. As for UNEA, 60 percent said its function should deal primarily with improving the students' material conditions, while only 14 percent thought it should concern itself with political education. [37] Temporarily mobilized in response to the Moroccan episode, most students promptly abandoned participation in the activities of the National Youth Committee and left UNEA to the radicals.

The UNEA leaders adopted a public stance of solidarity with the party. When the Political Bureau announced its preparations for the first FLN convention in early 1964, Mouffok wrote an important editorial in UNEA's journal reaffirming the students' support:

We share completely the viewpoint of the FLN . . . that all youth organizations must be incorporated into a single leadership and

directed by the party. . . . That is why we endorse the propositions of . . . the JFLN for the creation of a National Council of
Youth which, under the authority of the party, would orient the
youth organizations and coordinate their activities. [38]

He pointed out that UNEA's committee directorate had reviewed and
approved the texts of the proposed merger. A general assembly of the
UNEA membership, composed of more than 400 students, met on
April 15 and ratified the leaders' action. Thus, Mouffok concluded,
there could be no grounds for discord between the radicals and the
party.

Mouffok's statement, with its critical concessions to the Political
Bureau, aroused suspicion, for it came at a time when the radicals'
control of UNEA was deteriorating. Their dominance began to erode
when the students divided into factions at the fifth congress and was
decreased even more in October 1963 by UNEA's alliance with the
party. Afterwards, the radicals' position continued to weaken not so
much because the student majority had deserted the radicals but because they had become apathetic toward UNEA leaders as they had
been earlier toward the FLN.

To regain the support of student traditionalists, Mouffok averred
that the radicals, accused of being anti-Islamic, had been misrepre-
sented:

> The idea is often spread about that the intellectuals and the stu-
> dents are against Islam. The revolutionary intellectuals and the
> revolutionary students are not against Islam. . . . They are the
> flesh of the flesh of their people, sharing in full right their civil-
> ization, their history, their culture, and their Arab-Islamic
> heritage. [39]

Aware that the radicals were on the defensive vis-à-vis the party, he
appealed desperately to the traditionalists because they comprised a
substantial percentage of UNEA's membership. But this statement,
like the concessions to the Political Bureau, concealed the fact that
the radical leaders had no intention of renouncing their positions on
autonomy and discipline.

Mouffok also insisted that the Political Bureau should devise a program for enrolling peasant youths in the university. Instead of going

to the peasants, as Ben Bella proposed, the radical leader reversed the formula so that the initiative came from the peasants and not the students. By this time, however, the Political Bureau had strengthened its position against the radicals. When they aligned with the National Youth Committee, the radicals had unwittingly committed UNEA to the party. This association appeared merely pro forma in October, but party leaders exploited it by packing more party students into the organization. In late 1963, for example, 150 party students infiltrated it; by spring 1964, three party students—Mohammed Berdi, Abdelazziz Bouchaib, and Abdel Sadok—had formed a nucleus within UNEA to pressure for fusion with the JFLN.

A showdown between the radicals and the party appeared imminent at UNEA's sixth congress, which opened in Algiers on August 3, 1964. Mouffok and his allies encountered hostility not only from the pro-FLN faction, but also from two new dissident groups. The delegates from Arab countries and the United States opposed UNEA's Marxist orientation and objected to Mouffok's proposal making allegiance to the Charter of Algiers a requisite of UNEA membership (instead of the existing criterion of simple enrollment in a university). The Paris delegation, which comprised partisans of Ait Ahmed's FFS, impugned both Mouffok and the FLN for undermining the success of the revolutionary struggle. [40]

Ben Bella did not order the party to intervene at the convention, confident that the party students could unseat the radicals. The Political Bureau instead concentrated its efforts on a new wave of underground opposition associated with the FFS. The party students managed to enforce an enlargement of UNEA's committee directorate (from twelve to thirty-one members), but failed to prevent Mouffok's group from retaining a slight majority. Mouffok maintained his position on the UNEA executive. Subsequently, he took advantage of the victory by pushing through a motion instating UNEA as a full member of the IUS, an act confirming that the radicals did not retreat from their earlier ideological commitments.

The Political Bureau was finally prompted to suppress the radical leaders when it received a request from the IUS and its communist-oriented associate, the World Federation of Democratic Youth, to conduct the Ninth World Youth Festival in Algiers in 1965. Ben Bella regarded the convention as a forum that would enhance Algeria's international prestige as a leader of the Third World, thus promoting one of the key objectives of his foreign policy. Since he wanted to have all Algerian organizations represented by the FLN, he decided to break the radicals' hold on UNEA.

In November, the Political Bureau instigated a plan to subjugate Mouffok and the radical faction to party control. A "vigilante committee," composed of party students, was imposed on UNEA. The Political Bureau did not divulge the committee's responsibilities, but the party students assumed arbitrary authority as if they constituted the legitimate executives of UNEA. The radical student leaders soon yielded to a compromise with the party students on the stipulation that Mouffok remain in the UNEA leadership. Bouchaib became the new secretary general and Berdi filled the post of vice-president of foreign relations. Two other party students were promoted to the UNEA's foreign relations bureau to ensure that UNEA's foreign policy declarations coincided with Ben Bella's. These actions resulted in a subordination of the radicals and ended Ben Bella's protracted struggle to control them.

With the authority of Mouffok and Zenine undermined, the Political Bureau assumed direction of the student movement to complete the fusion of all youth organizations under the JFLN. The numbers and influence of the party students were later increased and, as a result, UNEA was further relegated to party control. The middle-class student majority, which had once applauded the radicals' protest actions, looked on impassively at this penetration of university affairs. In the end, UNEA was coopted in much the same way as the UGTA had been incorporated into the FLN.

The unification of the youth organizations appeared to advance significantly the party goals of organizing a mass constituency. The development of the JFLN represented a quantum jump in the FLN's institutional growth, producing as it did a core of politicized, disciplined participants in the political process. Furthermore, the JFLN provided an arena for the recruitment and training of potential party leaders, as indicated by the fact that Ben Bella later promoted Bennaceur, the JFLN chairman, to a consultative capacity on youth affairs under the Political Bureau.

With respect to UNEA, on the other hand, Ben Bella succeeded in acquiring control of the student movement at the cost of alienating the articulate student leadership and the vast body of baccalaureate (i.e., middle-class) students. Although the students were generally divided among themselves at independence, the Political Bureau's interventions had the effect of hardening divisions into factions that either favored or opposed party integration. From the previous diffuse divisions, lines were drawn that appeared to support neither Ben Bella's personal rule nor the long-range interests of the FLN. Like students in all countries, industrial and nonindustrial, the Algerian university students were destined to comprise a significant proportion of the future political and managerial elite. Thus, Ben Bella's developmental approach correctly identified the need for a "school of socialism," but he was not successful in dealing with all of its "pupils."

9

Coup d'Etat: The Fall of
Ben Bella and the FLN

The FLN Congress of 1964 was probably the most significant political event in the party's development under Ben Bella. Whereas the constitution of 1963 sanctioned the one-party system, the convention proposed to provide the FLN with a durable organizational structure and a well-defined program that would make the party an actuality. If Ben Bella succeeded, he would have completed the task of consolidating his regime. The Political Bureau likened the party convention to the Soummam Valley Congress, hoping that it would shape the postindependent FLN as Soummam had made possible the triumph of the wartime FLN.

Through his state-building program, Ben Bella had formalized his political hegemony and indirectly prepared the institutional framework for the consolidation of a mass party. His political authority was also based on the integration or cooptation of mass constituent groups into the party. Boumedienne and the army assisted this process by suppressing the regime's armed opposition. The party congress thus presented a unique opportunity for Ben Bella to redress the excesses of personal rule by reducing his dependency on the army through the formation of a fully institutionalized, autonomous party.

This opportunity was thwarted by events immediately after the party congress. The underground opposition resurfaced, posing a serious peril to Ben Bella's leadership. To defeat it, he was compelled to resort to Boumedienne and the army. This strategy benefited party development in one respect by leveling the FLN's competitors, but weakened it in another by expanding the army's role in the political process. This development tended to cancel out Ben Bella's belated decision to delegate power to the UGTA, the only nonmilitary organization forceful enough to bolster the party and the regime. Ben Bella's dependency on the army remained an independent variable of the political system.

In an attempt to minimize this dependency, Ben Bella appropriated the Ministry of the Interior and established an FLN militia. But fourteen months after the party congress, an ANP *coup d'état* destroyed his government and terminated official efforts at rebuilding the FLN. As will be seen, the actual causes of the party's collapse were rooted in a system of political rule that concentrated personal power at the expense of the party's institutional development.

The FLN Party Congress

Discussions concerning the upcoming party congress were conducted inside the Political Bureau while Khider served as secretary general. The actual form of the congress, however, stemmed from Ben Bella's method of defusing the counterrevolutionary opposition, symbolized most particularly by the FFS. Under Ait Ahmed, the FFS emerged in June 1963 at the head of what the regime called the counterrevolutionary movement, the militant clandestine opposition that aimed to defeat Ben Bella and reverse the "revolutionary" accomplishments of his leadership. When in November 1963 Ben Bella reached an agreement with FFS military leaders, he set in motion the events that favored the full institutionalization of the FLN on the one hand and created the conditions for his downfall on the other.

The FFS insurrection developed from concrete grievances. Kabylia was one of the areas affected most acutely by wartime destruction. Yet, the government had failed to begin reconstruction of the region's devastated schools, home, villages, and public and commercial centers as late as 1964, even though it had undertaken rehabilitation programs in other localities. The Kabyle mountainous terrain, the habitation of two million Berbers and one of the perennially impoverished areas, did not benefit from the government's economic development program.

The FFS drew heavily on the Berber population for its supporters, and received its military backing from Colonel Mohand Ou El Hadj and his 3,000 troops. When the political and military components of the FFS united late in September, the danger the movement posed to the regime was evident. But before the FFS attacked, the outbreak of war between Algeria and Morocco enabled Ben Bella to blunt its challenge. A surge of nationalism then gripped many of the regime's opponents, including dissidents of the FFS. Recognizing this, Ben Bella proposed defense ministry positions to Mohand Ou El Hadj and his lieutenants on the condition that they abandon the underground movement for membership in the ANP. Ou El Hadj was promised a promotion to the ANP's general staff. After the FFS militarists accepted these overtures, Ben Bella acquiesced to their five-point statement of demands, which included convening an FLN party congress in five months and opening up participation in the state-party system to the FFS. By this concession, he managed in one stroke to coopt the FFS militarists and to isolate Ait Ahmed. Shorn of its military support, the FFS disintegrated into impotence.

To organize the party congress, Ben Bella announced on November 16, 1963, that he had established an FLN preparatory commission. The commission's fifty-two members were representatives of the government and the national organizations; they included eleven ministers, eight FLN officials, eighteen deputies, three bureaucrats, three trade unionists, and one UNEA leader.[1] Ben Bella handpicked most of its members for their personal loyalty to him and gave proportionately greater representation to Assembly deputies from the regions where the FFS, and the PRS before it, had agitated.

Seven deputies from the Algiers region joined the commission, three of whom had been marginally associated with Boudiaf's PRS until its defeat a few months before the ratification of the constitution. The three, Omar Ramdane, Omar Mouhoub, and Youssef Khatib (alias Colonel Si Hassan), expressed their opposition to Ben Bella by voting against the draft constitution. They later made amends for this gesture of defiance and apparently won Ben Bella's approval. Thus, with the possible exception of these three deputies, the commission's members were all subject to orders from Ben Bella in accordance with his new authority as secretary general of the Political Bureau.

Mohammed Harbi and his ideological colleague, Abdelazziz Zerdani, dominated the commission's eight-man secretariat which the full membership elected to decide the congress's agenda and the official FLN party program. They proposed three critical, long overdue objectives: the restructuring of the FLN's organizational foundation; the formulation of new concepts for differentiating the party's administrative and leadership functions from the state's; and the creation of a more definitive ideological weapon than the Tripoli Program. Harbi and Zerdani set the ideological tone of the "theses of the congress," or the Charter of Algiers as the new party program was formally identified. The completion of the commission's task was followed by a national campaign to stimulate public interest in the charter and the forthcoming party convention.

Ben Bella and Assembly president Ben Alla, acting as ex-officio members of the commission, designated the party members to attend the congress. Ben Alla played a special role by reorganizing the FLN federations and setting up the local sections which appointed their own delegates. Election procedures provided for one delegate for every 2,000 party militants. On the whole, these delegates consisted of FLN adherents and partisans of Ben Bella. ANP representation, however, was not insignificant.

The extent to which political alliances had been altered since independence was evident at the congress's inaugural session. Among the 1,991 delegates in attendance,[2] only three GPRA leaders appeared: Boussouf, Ben Tobbal, and Belkacem Krim, or the old GPRA triumvirate. Benkhedda distributed a critique of the FLN's recent history just before the convention, but he refused to attend it. His personal analysis emphasized the tendency of postcolonial socialist regimes to substitute a new privileged class for the former colonial overlords. He concluded that this tendency fostered political instability and a cult of personality owing to the absence of internal democracy in the new government.[3] Here was a thinly veiled criticism of the Ben Bella government, but it did not provoke a reaction because a conciliatory mood pervaded the congress's proceedings and because Benkhedda did not attempt a political comeback.

The new alignments were further manifested by the presence as proregime delegates of several men who opposed the Tlemcen group in 1962. The former dissidents included Ben Yahia and Malek, who had accepted ambassadorial positions in the government, and the former wilaya commander, Youssef Khatib, now a member of the National Assembly. The apparent stability that the regime had achieved in two years persuaded a number of former opponents to submit to the authority of the Political Bureau. On the other hand, some of the regime's influential allies of 1962, such as Abbas, Francis, and Bitat, had now turned against Ben Bella and a few, like Boudiaf and Ait Ahmed, had carried their opposition underground.

A board of directors, elected by the convention delegates, presided over the party congress when it opened on April 16, 1964. The directors included Rabah Djermane, the UGTA secretary general, and Amar Ouzegane, a former labor leader whom Ben Bella had designated minister of state. By a unanimous vote, the delegates approved Bachir Boumaza (minister of national economy) as convention president. This vote revealed that the congress's policy-making body, like its preparatory commission, would be controlled by men loyal to the Political Bureau.

In his opening address, Ben Bella elucidated the tasks he envisaged for the FLN congress:

> This congress has as its principal objective the consolidation of a situation. . . : creating the foundations for democratic party structures through an enrichment of the Tripoli Program, and electing officials to all echelons of the party. These are the conditions necessary to overcome the antagonisms of the past. . . . *There can be no question of opening the dossiers of the revolution.* . . . Today, it is possible to regard the FLN as a homogenous party which draws its force from an essentially peasant and worker base while establishing the structures appropriate for our socialist option. . . . *The program presented to you is one of a party in power*. It contains not only what the party wishes to achieve but what it has partly realized already.[4] [Emphasis added.]

Because he prohibited the convention from questioning or modifying the FLN's present ideological orientation, the delegates were limited to considering a ratification of the system as it existed. The address contained Ben Bella's most expansive statement on party institutionalization thus far, and he was emphatic in characterizing the regime as sufficiently consolidated to proceed immediately with a systematic development of the party.

Boumaza closed the proceedings to the public after Ben Bella's presentation, and the congress stayed in semi-secrecy until adjournment. In the discussions that followed, Ben Bella and Harbi dwelled upon the status of Islam under a socialist regime and the role of the army in politics. Actually, the two subjects were related because the ANP representatives, about sixty officers,[5] encouraged and supported the Islamists who opposed the regime's secularist orientation. The army leaders' real opposition, however, was focused on politicians like Harbi who intended to minimize the autonomy of the ANP in relation to the party. Bouteflika articulated the army's position regarding the issues, but, being no intellectual or forensic match for Harbi, failed to win acceptance of a proposition that advocated a role for the ANP similar to that played by the Egyptian army in politics.[6] As a result, ANP partisans were limited to pressing for modifications in the original text. The changes they originated were confined to a new emphasis on Algeria's Arab-Islamic heritage and a deemphasis on Algeria's "revolutionary" orientation in foreign policy.

When the delegates considered the question of party reorganization, they sought to revivify the basic structures that had developed under Khider's leadership. Centralization was adopted as the formula to guide party reorganization. In accordance with this principle, the various components in the party hierarchy became interconnected in such a manner that the FLN assumed the trappings of a highly institutionalized and cohesive political entity.

The new FLN structures consisted of the party cell, the federation, and the kasma.[7] The party cell, composed of twenty to fifty members, formed the base of the party, recruiting members at the village or district level and in certain urban industrial enterprises. Each party cell elected a cell committee which, when organized at the commune (cf. subprefectoral) level, joined with other cell committees to establish the council of the kasma. The federation, the highest expression of party authority at the regional (cf. prefectoral) level, grouped officials of the different kasmas.

To the basic constituency framework, the delegates added a new executive body, the central committee of the FLN. It held a position coterminous with the national party congress and was supposed to act as a substitute for it in the two-year intervals between party conventions. Above the central committee sat the Political Bureau and the secretary general of the FLN, a new title that superseded the past designation of secretary general of the Political Bureau.

In terms of institutional functions, the party cell was primarily responsible for the recruitment of militants. A party militant was defined as any Algerian citizen at least eighteen years of age who had participated in the FLN or the ALN during the revolutionary war, had committed himself to active involvement in postindependent politics, had adhered to the party's socialist orientation, had paid party dues, and was "of good moral character."[8] A party adherent, also inducted into the party via the cell, was defined as any Algerian, sponsored by two regular party members (militants), who committed himself to the "objectives of the socialist revolution."[9] Each cell was required to disseminate party decisions through systematic political education programs (i.e., utilizing the media and party publications), and to mobilize the masses in support of party campaigns.

The kasma, specifically the kasma committee, exercised territorial jurisdiction. It executed directives from the higher echelons of the party and from the council of the kasma. It also had jurisdiction over all party work at the commune or subprefectoral levels. The federation, composed of officials from the kasmas, executed directives from the Political Bureau and directed party work at the level of the region or prefecture. Each federation was directly responsible to the Political Bureau. Presumably, these intermediary entities would improve intraparty lines of communication and enforce the disciplinary capability of the FLN.

The national party congress, the supreme and sovereign organ of the FLN, was the party's parliamentary or deliberative center. Among its numerous prerogatives were the sanctioning of reports from the central committee; defining the party's doctrine and policy on the country's political development; adopting and modifying party statutes; and electing the central committee and the secretary general of the FLN. Apart from the regularly scheduled party conventions, the congress could be convened in extraordinary sessions upon the request of three-fifths of the members of the central committee or by a majority of the federal councils. All decisions of the congress had to be supported by majority vote.

The central committee was composed of eighty members who approved FLN decisions in intervals between party congresses. Twenty-three ex-officio members selected by a majority at the congress met in a nonvoting capacity with the committee's regular members at the ordinary sessions held every four months. The quite substantial powers of the committee encompassed establishing the different party organisms, executing the congress's decisions, and managing party finances. Upon a motion by the Political Bureau, the committee also designated militants who filled key posts in the Assembly, the government, or other positions that derived from party spoils.

The chief executive body, the Political Bureau, implemented the decisions of the central committee. The Political Bureau was responsible to the central committee, but assumed the latter's prerogatives in intervals between central committee sessions. It will be recalled that the original Political Bureau started with seven members in 1962, but was rapidly reduced in membership because of the resignation of Boudiaf and the forced withdrawal of Bitat and Khider. The congress enlarged the Political Bureau to seventeen members and authorized it to execute decisions of the central committee. The secretary general, whom the national party congress elected, was empowered to appoint the members of the Political Bureau and to control its activity. [10]

As a matter of party policy, the congress renounced Khider's broad mass-party concept in favor of "an avant-garde party" intensely associated with the masses. [11] This modification, which reflected Ben Bella's preference for a party vanguard composed of militants and intellectual elites, won acceptance by a large majority.

The revamped party structure was to operate under the organizational principle of "democratic centralism," which was necessary for "centralized direction and discipline." [12] Under this principle the Political Bureau commanded disciplinary mechanisms that reached down to the cells, the lowest levels of party membership. Proposals, demands, and policy data were to be channeled from the base echelons to the policy-making center, the Political Bureau. Information from the mass constituency would be acted on and forwarded back in the form of directives, policy, and recommendations. The new FLN structures, together with the planned flow of directives and agencies of policy implementation, are shown in Figure 3.

Party control over the state administration was discussed extensively by the delegates. The Charter of Algiers, noting that political power had been concentrated in the state after independence, recommended that the party and state structures be differentiated in authority and functions. In the future, party officials were to devote their full energies to party activities, excluding themselves completely from the government and the administration. Nevertheless, FLN members would hold certain key positions in the government in order to assure

Figure 3. The Party System as Revised by the FLN Congress, 1964

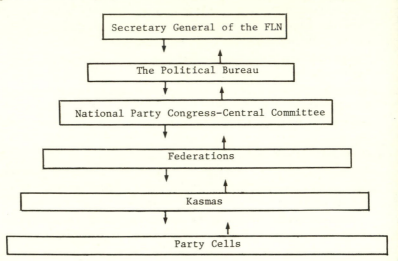

Down arrows indicate the intended flow of output functions. Up
arrows indicate the flow of input functions.

that party programs were implemented. If this was a paradox, it still
served as the rationale for the chief of state to serve also as chief of the
party.

The national organizations continued to be directly responsible to
the FLN but were separated from its structural hierarchy. It should be
recalled that all national organizations had been absorbed into the
FLN by 1964 and that none wielded authority independently of the
Political Bureau. At the congress, the FLN's incorporation of all
national organizations was characterized as a requirement of the one-
party system and of democratic centralism.

After the delegates approved the statutes on party reorganization,
they proceeded to elect new party personnel. The two most important
bodies, the central committee and the Political Bureau, represented
the major decision-making structures that were to function after the
convention. Their composition therefore held great importance for
the party's subsequent development. The conference of party cadres,
predecessor to the central committee, represented 250 members
whom the incumbent Political Bureau nominated. This body, the cen-

tral committee's organizational commission, presented the new Political Bureau nominees to the congress. It appeared that Said Mohammedi did the main work of selecting candidates loyal to Ben Bella for the new eighty-member central committee.

The most striking aspect of the committee's composition was the appearance of numerous former wilaya leaders. Ben Bella's selection of the guerrillas was apparently motivated by a Machiavellian desire to solidify the division between the ANP and wilaya factions at the congress.[13] Army leaders were already embittered toward the wilaya commanders who had been pressing for autonomy from the ANP since independence. Some, like Chaabani, continued to rule their regions independent of ANP control. Thus, the former guerrillas' membership in the same body as the army leaders' scarcely favored the formation of a united military clique within the committee.

As expected, the party congress elected Ben Bella secretary general of the FLN. Personal rule, reaching its crowning moment, was now formalized and tied inextricably to the destiny of the FLN.

The congress culminated its activities on April 23 when it elected the Political Bureau. This new FLN executive held the authority to decide the policies and programs for the FLN's development into a viable, cohesive entity. The key to such an evolution lay in the consensus that prevailed among the members of the Political Bureau.

Understanding the potential threats to the unity of the newly elected leadership requires a scrutiny of the cleavages within it. The FLN-ANP alignment in 1964 largely determined the composition of the new Political Bureau, as can be deduced from an examination of its membership:

1. Ahmed Ben Bella, FLN secretary general and president of the republic
2. Houari Boumedienne, first vice-president and defense minister
3. Said Mohammedi, second vice-president
4. Bachir Boumaza, minister of national economy
5. Abdelazziz Bouteflika, minister of foreign affairs
6. Ahmed Ali Mahsas, minister of agrarian reform
7. Mohammed Seghir Nekkache, minister of social affairs
8. Hadj Ben Alla, president of the National Assembly
9. Ali Mendjeli, vice-president of the National Assembly

10. Omar Benmahjoub, deputy from Orléansville
11. Tahar Zbiri, chief of staff of the ANP
12. Mohand Ou El Hadj, ex-commander of the 7th Military Region (Kabylia)
13. Mohammed Chaabani, ex-commander of the 4th Military Region (Biskra)
14. Youssef Khatib, ex-commander of wilaya IV (Algiers)
15. Hocine Zaouane, representative of the FFLN
16. Ait El Hocine, president of the Association générale des travailleurs algériens (AGTA).
17. Ahmed Medeghri, minister of the interior.

At least eight members could be identified as Ben Bella partisans: Mohammedi, Nekkache, Boumaza, Mahsas, Ben Alla, Benmahjoub, Zaouane, and El Hocine. The remaining members were current or former military officers.

If a distinction could be made between the political and military representatives, one could also be made within the military group itself, i.e., the division between ANP soldiers and wartime guerrilla commanders. The Political Bureau's wilaya faction was composed of Zbiri, Chaabani, Khatib, and Mohand Ou El Hadj; the ANP representatives consisted of Boumedienne, Bouteflika, Medeghri, and Mendjeli. The ANP representatives, who were also members of the government, differed from the wilaya guerrillas not only in their proximity to power but also in their control of the army. The wilaya commanders had incurred the antipathy of Boumedienne in 1962 by resisting the ANP during the summer crisis, but Ben Bella succeeded in pushing through their nominations with the aid of politicians loyal to him.

Meanwhile, the absence of Harbi and Zerdani on the Political Bureau was indicative of the ANP's increasing political influence. Zerdani represented, like Harbi, the party's Marxist intellectual clique and thereby enjoyed a privileged relationship with Ben Bella. He had no independent political standing in the regime, however, and remained relatively unknown until Ben Bella appointed him to the congress's preparatory commission. Harbi, head of the intellectual "braintrust," spurred certain party delegates to criticize Boumedienne during the debates on the issues of Islam and the army. He himself lectured the ANP representatives against encroachments upon party supremacy. These actions contributed to Boumedienne's opposition to Harbi's membership on the Political Bureau. Zerdani did not upbraid the military as vocally but was still vetoed by Boumedienne.

In its final action, the congress approved the Charter of Algiers as amended through the intervention of ANP representatives. The charter represented the first attempt to establish a systematic party program since 1962, the final theoretical and programmatic extension of the Tripoli Program. Much more comprehensive than its predecessor, the charter redefined party goals relative to nationalization, agrarian reform, and Arabization. But it contained few policy proposals that exceeded the programs and policies Ben Bella had adopted since 1962, e.g., the state-building program, autogestion, and the integration of mass organizations into the FLN. The major additions to current policies entailed a demand for reform and "algerianization" of the civil bureaucracy—that is, the replacement of French and other foreign personnel by Algerians[14]—and a new policy of economic austerity so as to curtail the rise in government deficits.

The FLN still did not possess what Moore has termed "total ideology."[15] Until the party congress, the FLN's ideological foundation was broadly described by the constitutional provisions for the party, the March decrees, and the Political Bureau's policies regarding mass mobilization. The Charter of Algiers greatly enhanced party ideology by its refinements in doctrinal precepts.

Still unresolved, however, were the contradictions represented by Ben Bella's rule, ANP interests, and the building of a genuine mass party.

Shortly after the congress, Zerdani summarized what seemed to be its main accomplishments:

> In settling and going beyond the old crises, the congress has sanctioned, as it were, the revolutionary legitimacy of the FLN. It has rightly placed emphasis on autogestion and has endowed the party not only with new forces of leadership—the secretary general Ahmed Ben Bella, the Political Bureau, and the central committee—but also with a basic doctrine: the Charter of Algiers.[16]

Compared to its previous condition, the party now seemed to possess the bases that would make it functional and cohesive. The reorganization systematized the party's hierarchical structure, and through the central committee, established a parliamentary center between the hierarchy and Political Bureau. This change permitted the flow of power from upper to lower echelons and the transmission of communications from the constituent bases to the summit.

The FLN's dues-paying membership of 153,000 indicated that the outlook for the party treasury was favorable, and with 619,000 "adherents" (members undergoing indoctrination), the potential for a generation of disciplined and committed party faithful was quite encouraging. [17] Finally, the Charter of Algiers provided the party with a more identifiable ideological personality. In combination, these factors brightened the FLN's promise as an institutionalized mass political party. Its subsequent consolidation depended on a methodical implementation of the measures adopted at the congress, and the maintenance of unity and stability in its executive leadership.

The "Counterrevolution"

While the party congress met in April 1964, Ait Ahmed rallied other opposition leaders to form a new anti-Ben Bella coalition called the Comité national pour la défense de la révolution (CNDR). A more broadly based body than the FFS, the CNDR united the remnants of Boudiaf's PRS with those of the FFS. Important members of the FFS were Mourad Oussedik and Slimane Dhiles, Berbers who had left the National Assembly at the same time as Ait Ahmed. Dissident wilaya chiefs, Commander Si Moussa and Colonel Chaabani, later allied with the CNDR. The resurgence of the counterrevolutionary movement fixed Ben Bella's attention once more on the underground threat to his leadership. The ANP was reintroduced as the force to combat the opposition, which led in turn to the army's increasingly influential role in the political process.

Although the officers of Ou El Hadj's 7th Military Region in Kabylia returned with him to the ANP, Ait Ahmed retained the support of many of these troops. On May 30, 1964, they attacked the *palais du peuple*, seat of the national government, killing two guards. [18] The gravity of the incident was magnified by its occurrence in broad daylight, within earshot of Ben Bella's residence. Perhaps equally alarming to the regime was the discovery two months later that the CNDR had recruited Moussa Hassani, who had served as minister of telecommunications in the first Ben Bella cabinet and who up to that time had been a deputy in the National Assembly.

During the same period, Mohammed Khider, now situated in Paris, declared his complete rupture with the Ben Bella regime. As spokesman for the CNDR, he emphasized that all of the opposition leaders were agreed on the following major points:

1. Authority in Algeria has been so undermined by cliques in the government that the exercise of power has become incoherent and arbitrary.
2. This situation is leading more and more to the establishment of personal and absolute authority.
3. The present constitution, formulated through antidemocratic procedures, bears no relation to Algerian traditions and national exigencies.
4. Algeria has become a police state with no freedom of expression. The opposition agrees that the present regime is . . . nearly totalitarian, and that it should be abolished. [19]

Khider's announcement, motivated by political and personal grievances, dramatized some of the flaws of Ben Bella's government. But Khider failed to acknowledge the major factor that motivated him to join the CNDR: his desire to have its funds under his control. After he resigned from the Political Bureau in 1963, Khider absconded with the FLN's treasury containing a sum of 6 billion AF (about $12 million). [20] He withdrew the money from Swiss banks, where it had been deposited since independence, and now proclaimed that it would be used to support the opposition.

Given the CNDR's demonstrated capacity to challenge the Ben Bella government openly, questions may be raised about the regime's viability. How was an opposition movement, with a few men and a largely unstructured organization, able to operate in defiance of the FLN and the army? And why did the government fail to retaliate immediately after the May 30 attack?

Ben Bella explained that the government's inaction indicated the regime's hope for reconciliation with the dissidents. No political prisons, he asserted, would be created in Algeria. Beginning late in 1963, he frequently exhorted his opponents to return to the FLN to express their opposition within its framework. Some, like Belkacem Krim and Ali Yahia, accepted the invitation; others, like Boudiaf and Ait Ahmed, denounced it as a design to contain the opposition. For the most part, the dissidents remained with the CNDR, and, as a result, Ben Bella finally decided on armed confrontation.

In a decree of March 7, 1964, he reorganized the army to confront the counterrevolutionary movement. His plan called for the division of the opposition area into five military districts reminiscent of the wartime structure of six wilayat. He also permitted the ANP to exercise more direct control over the country at large by compressing the previous jurisdictional boundaries into smaller units. ANP patrols were increased in Kabylia and in the region south of the Aurès mountains. Ben Bella announced during independence day celebrations (July 5) that the government no longer sought reconciliation with its enemies. It was now prepared to destroy them.

This new policy was concretized in an ordinance empowering a martial court to judge "crimes against the state, discipline of the armed forces, and any related infractions."[21] The court's judgments, which did not require a public hearing, were to be executed promptly. Such actions seemed to corroborate the opposition's indictment of the regime as an authoritarian system.

Amidst these events, Ben Bella escalated his campaign to purge the party and government of suspected subversive elements. He placed two minor members of his original cabinet under surveillance and expelled five directors of the FLN's central committee, the newly instituted policy-making center created by the FLN congress. Twelve National Assembly deputies were forced to resign. Then, on the basis of what appeared to be specious evidence, he had Abbas, Bitat, Fares, and Boualem Oussedik arrested, though none of them belonged to the CNDR. Oussedik had once been associated with Ait Ahmed during previous Assembly debates, and Bitat had resigned from the Political Bureau (in 1963) to criticize the regime's policies and failures as part of the "constructive" opposition. Like the others, Bitat discovered belatedly the cost of such opposition.

To combat the CNDR, Boumedienne sent ANP troops to the Bou-Saada and Biskra regions where Colonel Chaabani had mobilized a major CNDR contingent. Boumedienne deployed two-thirds of the ANP against the CNDR forces, and many who survived the ANP onslaught scurried to join his army. The Defense Ministry reported on

September 4 that Chaabani had been captured with nearly eighty guerrillas. The martial court then tried and condemned him to death.

Such losses diminished the CNDR's strength greatly, but the final collapse did not occur until early October when the ANP apprehended Ait Ahmed. Reports conflict on the details of the interception, but all agree that he and six of his cohorts, including his chief military ally in Kabylia, Colonel Si Sadok, were arrested on October 17, 1964. Ait Ahmed had witnessed a continuous dwindling of FFS forces after the border war, and when arrested he was helpless against the superior ANP troops. Si Moussa, another important FFS guerrilla chief, escaped arrest but surrendered to the government later. In the end, Ait Ahmed, alone, became the scapegoat upon whom the government laid most of the blame for the counterrevolutionary movement. A special "revolutionary criminal court" condemned him and Si Moussa to death in April 1965, but Ben Bella, in a show of magnanimity, commuted the sentences to life imprisonment. By contrast, he let stand the death sentences of Khider, Boudiaf, and six others who were judged in absentia.

Expansion of Military Influence

The defeat of Ben Bella's opposition had the secondary effect of increasing the army's influence in the political process. Until then, the ANP's role evolved slowly and remained restricted to financing military reconstruction. The alliance between Boumedienne and Ben Bella, though strained intermittently, held firm.

From the beginning of the alliance, Boumedienne preoccupied himself with building the army. He aspired to establish a first-rate professional army and spent a good deal of his time seeking the capital to equip, train, and operate it. The Defense Ministry, unlike other ministries, maintained independent access to the Bank of Algeria. Before Ben Bella ordered an austerity policy in early 1963—establishing a composite budget for the first time—total ANP receipts were earmarked at $100 million. [22] This figure compared to $490 million for economic development, and $580 million for the elephantine bureaucracy that Ben Bella erected in his state-building program.

The austerity policy reduced acknowledged ANP spending to $34 million annually. [23] But military expenditures rose again in October 1963 as a result of the border war. By the end of the year, the acknowledged ANP budget reached $66 million.[24] Boumedienne's direct access to the national bank and his singular capacity to bypass finance minister Ali Mahsas expedited his requests for additional financing.

ANP allocations increased gradually in the next two years, returning to a ceiling of about $100 million in 1965. This figure amounted to slightly less than one-eighth of the national budget. Some critics of the army contended that it siphoned off funds intended for economic development, but no evidence has been found to support these charges. After Boumedienne's visit to Moscow in October 1963, the ANP began to receive the bulk of its heavy weaponry on credit terms from the Soviet Union. Together with foreign military assistance, the limited budgetary allocations sufficed to cover the administrative, operational, and related costs of the army. The conclusion can be drawn that Boumedienne satisfied the financial requirements of his establishment.

Building the army also necessitated the elimination of the former guerrillas. By the end of the war, the overall size of military forces was estimated at about 120,000 men, involving 45,000 soldiers (from Tunisia and Morocco) and perhaps 75,000 guerrillas.[25] After independence, Boumedienne began to convert the ANP into a regular professional army with exclusive control of all military activity. Reduction of the military forces resulted partly from the lack of funds to support a large army, but mainly from Boumedienne's desire to demobilize the guerrilla separatists. Most of the guerrillas were forced into instant retirement by being denied access to the ANP.

By deactivating the wilaya contingents, Boumedienne consolidated the armed forces and simultaneously contributed to the regime's stability.

The ANP was relatively small in numbers when viewed in the context of the Algerian population, which totaled 10,453,000 persons in 1963.[26] While the size of the army cannot be stated with precision, it was estimated at roughly 65,000 at this time.[27] The Algerian army contained more personnel and probably exerted more political influence than armies in countries with comparable populations, such as the Sudan's army of about 12,000 or Morocco's 30,000 soldiers.[28]

Boumedienne's response to the presidential election, one week after the constitution was ratified, attested to the durability of the political-military alliance. Ben Bella ran unopposed and received a decisive mandate in all départements except Kabylia, where Berber abstentions corresponded to those recorded in the constitutional ratification of 1963. In an effort to dispel rumors that he opposed Ben Bella's preeminent power, Boumedienne affirmed:

> We have chosen him as candidate for the president of the repub-
> lic because of his faith and confidence in the socialist revolu-
> tion. I make this affirmation . . . to clarify any misunderstand-
> ings and to expose certain maneuvers to dissociate the ANP
> from the FLN. *The choice of . . . Ben Bella by the people and the
> army* was not dictated by mere sentiment. We have decided that
> Ben Bella qualifies for this post because we consider him the
> only man capable of assuming it.[29] [Emphasis added.]

The ANP chief thus confirmed his supportive role. He left the political arena to Ben Bella while practicing what Hurewitz has described as "reactive politics."[30]

There was only a slight increase in the number of ANP representatives when Ben Bella reshuffled the government on September 18, 1963, to form a new seventeen-member cabinet.[31] Among Ben Bella's personal followers were Ouzegane, Bitat, Nekkache, and Boumaza, veterans from the first government. Four new ministers completed the core Ben Bella group: Mohammed Hadj Smain, Ben Bella's former cabinet director; Sadek Batel, an FLN adherent and an Assembly deputy; Said Mohammedi, a vice-president without specified duties; and Ali Mahsas, the new minister of national economy. However, Bitat, reacting to his demotion (from sole vice-president in the first government to third vice-president in the new cabinet), resigned the next day, reducing Ben Bella's voting strength to eight of the remaining sixteen cabinet posts. Both Madani, a veteran retaining his previous portfolio, and Abdelkader Zaibek, a technocrat and one of Algeria's few engineers, operated primarily as political neutrals.

Boumedienne selected four members, including two new appointees, Belkacem Cherif and Ahmed Kaid, as part of the ANP contingent. Cherif, a member of the ALN's general staff in wartime (at Oujda) who entered the Assembly in 1962, had served previously as an informal political advisor to the ANP chief. Kaid, also an Assembly deputy, assisted Boumedienne on the ANP general staff. Boumedienne's widened influence could be inferred from his new position as first vice-president and from Bouteflika's promotion to the Foreign Ministry (which Ben Bella had controlled personally after Khemisti's death in April). The ANP faction commanded all the country's coercive forces since Boumedienne controlled the army, and Medeghri the police through the Interior Ministry. The ANP's representation did not increase over the 1962 cabinet,[32] but the soldiers' new functions, coupled with existing ones, obviously enabled them to exert greater influence in the political system.

Somewhat curiously, the main challenges to the viability of the political-military were made by Ben Bella, not Boumedienne. For instance, Ben Bella appointed Colonel Zbiri chief of the ANP general staff in September 1963 without Boumedienne's knowledge or approval and while Boumedienne was traveling abroad. When he returned, Boumedienne discovered that his former post was held by Zbiri, a former wilaya chief who had expressed loyalty solely to Ben Bella. Later, during the Moroccan border war, Ben Bella again infringed on Boumedienne's domain by assuming personal command of military policy.

Neither event provoked a split between the two leaders. By March 1964, Boumedienne had regained his supremacy over the military establishment; Zbiri stayed on the general staff, but with greatly reduced powers.[33] The Moroccan war and suppression of the counterrevolution had the domestic effect, meanwhile, of restoring the army to the national prominence it held on independence.

New sources of conflict developed between Ben Bella and Boumedienne at the party congress as a consequence of statutes that Harbi introduced to establish party control of the ANP. If implemented, the statutes would have created a "political department" inside the ANP to subject army personnel to political indoctrination.[34] Most importantly, the Political Bureau would have controlled the army. Harbi and Zerdani advanced the proposal for the ANP's subordination to the party, but they voiced Ben Bella's viewpoint, just as Bouteflika spoke for Boumedienne. This conflict was eventually resolved in Boumedienne's favor, as confirmed by a later admendment that deleted from the Charter of Algiers all references to party cells in the ANP.

Ben Bella antagonized Boumedienne again by selecting members for the newly enlarged, seventeen-member Political Bureau. As mentioned earlier, Ben Bella sought to dilute the influence of the ANP officers on the Political Bureau by appointing a faction of four ex-wilaya commanders that included Colonel Chaabani. This divide-

and-rule tactic aborted in summer 1964 when Chaabani denounced the regime and joined the CNDR.

Ben Bella had intended to appoint Harbi and Zerdani to the Political Bureau but did not as a result of vigorous objections from Bouteflika. After the congress, Harbi and Zerdani made fewer appearances before university students, the UGTA, and other groups to mobilize support for subordinating the army to the party; in the past, they had engaged in a seemingly incessant campaign of speechmaking for this program. Ben Bella also removed Harbi from the editorship of *Révolution africaine*. Undoubtedly, the decline of Ben Bella's ideologists was enforced by Boumedienne and Bouteflika.

Ben Bella must certainly have recognized the vulnerability of his regime to a military takeover but often behaved as if he did not. When he formed his third government in December 1964,[35] for example, he dismissed Ahmed Medeghri from the Interior Ministry and assumed direct control of the municipal police forces himself. Boumedienne tolerated the dismissal, even though Medeghri was one of his nominees and Ben Bella annexed a cabinet function that heretofore belonged to the ANP. At the same time, Ben Bella began the process of reducing his dependency on the military by delegating political power to nongovernmental insitutions like the UGTA. Though long overdue, this change tended to alienate the army leaders because it indicated another attempt to minimize their influence in the political system.

The Range of Political Choice

The party congress formally established the FLN's hegemony over the political system. It also revealed the tenuous basis of party authority through the split between Boumedienne's lieutenants and the FLN militants supporting Harbi. Ben Bella, recognizing that the FLN lacked authoritative capability without the army, undertook a personal drive to attract a broad civilian constituency to reinforce the party's supportive base. He focused on the UGTA because it was the only civilian institution with the requisite organizational and group resources. To encourage more active labor support, he permitted the trade unionists to exercise organizational autonomy for the first time, anticipating that an independent labor movement would assist the party as a countervailing force against the army.

Ben Bella's approach was evident in a decree of August 3, 1964, that certified the UGTA company committees as the sole agencies responsible for all training programs and promotions in private business. During a petroleum workers' convention, Ben Bella reassured the workers: "I share entirely the aspiration of your federation to promote managerial syndicalism through which the workers will participate more and more actively in the management of certain enterprises."[36] This prerogative, it will be recalled, was one of labor's prime objectives at the first UGTA congress in 1963. Ben Bella now endorsed another labor demand which the Tripoli Program and the constitution recognized, but which the government had consistently denied before: the workers' right to strike. He thus reversed the Political Bureau's policy of January 1963 when he and Khider overruled these same demands and subjugated the trade union to the FLN.

It was during this period that Ben Bella renewed his appeals to the radical trade unionists. At once he satisfied their demand for a role in agrarian autogestion by authorizing them to participate in the FNTT. Most importantly, he agreed to annul the 1963 UGTA election and to schedule a second UGTA convention that would freely elect a new leadership. The imposition of Djermane and others as leaders at the first convention had resulted in the rise of the radicals over the UGTA's rank and file. This was demonstrated persuasively by a series of aggressive labor strikes that the radicals called during 1963 and 1964 despite Djermane's trumpeting of the Political Bureau's appeal for restraint. Unmistakably, Ben Bella recognized that winning UGTA support hinged upon the radicals' cooperation.

The second UGTA congress opened on March 23, 1965, and was attended by delegates representing all trade union federations. They arrived with the election of a new directorate uppermost in mind. As soon as the assembly convened, delegates from the Algiers local (i.e., the core of radical leaders) denounced Djermane, accusing him of apathy and inaction as the chief executive of the trade unionists. When he presented the incumbents' report for the convention's approval, the delegates rejected it by an overwhelming majority. Thereupon, the radicals demanded the election of a new leadership. Encountering no opposition, they replaced the imposed leadership with a new fifty-one-member executive commission consisting of men selected by the radicals themselves.

In general, the new leaders were young men who had risen to prominence through their local or regional federations. Mouloud Oumeziane, the new secretary general, forty-five years old, typified them. He
belonged to the CGT before the rebellion, leaving it afterwards to become an FLN nationalist and ultimately to lead the hospital workers'
local in his native Constantine. Boualem Bourouiba, a principal leader in the radical group, was named deputy secretary general. Other
independent-minded leaders included Tayeb Djenadi, secretary of
education and volunteer work projects, and Boualem Rebika, secretary of agriculture. [37] They resurrected the principle of managerial
syndicalism and reiterated earlier demands for an acceleration of the
government's nationalization policy.

Manifesting a changed attitude toward the Political Bureau, the
trade unionists unanimously adopted a resolution favoring coexist-
ence with the party:

> The party constitutes the avant-garde of the working masses
> and the nation's leader in accomplishing the socialist revolu-
> tion. In this context, the UGTA, a mass organization, supports
> the objective of mobilizing and involving all the workers behind
> the party to implement the tasks projected by the Charter of
> Algiers. *The UGTA will furnish . . . the party which is still* con-
> solidating itself with the best of its *militants*.[38] [Emphasis
> added.]

This declaration seemed to satisfy Ben Bella's minimal expectations
concerning labor support. However, the general tone of the resolution
made clear the qualified character of labor's support:

> Party members belonging to the UGTA must situate themselves
> among . . . the trade unionists. To them falls the task of giving
> impetus to the trade-union sections, assuring thereby that the
> party's orientation and directives prevail in them. *And all of this
> must be done through explanations and persuasions, for acting
> in an authoritarian manner can only vitiate party prestige.* [39]
> [Emphasis added.]

Thus, it was indicated that a repetition of the first convention's events would be resisted. Cooperation, not coercion, had to replace the Political Bureau's old methods if they were to deal with the new leaders.

To allay the radicals' suspicions, Ben Bella endorsed the resolution promptly. He also made a critical concession by promising that the (urban) socialist sector would dominate the private by the end of 1965. Advocates of total "algerianization," the radical leaders instigated the strikes of 1963 and 1964 specifically to provoke a governmental takeover of the private sector. Ben Bella now acceded to their demands not so much because he favored additional nationalization, but to achieve the more fundamental goal of strengthening the FLN's popular base.

The UGTA claimed a total of 320,000 dues-paying members in 1965.[40] Very few had become active members of the FLN. The party, meanwhile, had a fluctuating, unstable following of several thousand members and adherents. The trade union, more disciplined and better-financed than the FLN, provided a more structured and influential constituency. Djermane had created a mass-elite gap in the rank and file by alienating the radicals, but the free election of Oumeziane and his staff implied that this weakness would be overcome. Together, the party and trade union elements represented a strong mass base that could have significantly advanced party institutionalization.

The development and consolidation of the FLN now seemed to depend less on organizational and human resources, which were adequate, than on securing the necessary time to forge a dynamic party entity. The FLN had already become partially institutionalized, as confirmed by its ability to organize constituencies (cf. the JFLN) and to enforce rule-making and rule-application prescriptions (cf. the March decrees). Credibility also rested on Ben Bella's side, as demonstrated by the resolution affirming the UGTA's adhesion to the Political Bureau. The relevant question was whether party institutionalization could be consummated, not whether it had begun.

These positive developments did not diminish the fragility of the Ben Bella regime. Its vulnerability was tested by the counterrevolution and, as shown above, only the ANP prevented the CNDR's assaults from being effective. In an attempt to void this dependency, the FLN central committee met on June 8, 1964, to organize a popular militia for the party. The militia was staffed by a small group of former guerrillas and was directed by Ben Bella and his followers on the Political Bureau. The militia failed to organize a significant contingency anywhere except in Algiers and did not produce the coercive underpinning needed as a substitute for the army.

A deteriorating economic situation also tended to counteract Ben Bella's new approach. Governmental expenditures after independence were disproportionately allocated to the mammoth bureaucracy that developed in response to his state-building program. Whereas the government managed to more than balance its expenditures against revenues in 1963, a deficit of 424 million DA appeared on its current balance in 1965. [41] Governmental investment expenditures on agriculture declined from 803 million DA in 1963 to 190 million DA in 1965. [42] In the same period, there was a general decline in agricultural production, which was not offset by the marginal growth in industrial output. Though the foreign trade deficit decreased considerably (from 435 million DA in 1963 to 190 million in 1965) because of increased oil and gas production, [43] most export trade still flowed to France.

Unemployment remained high, affecting about half the urban adult (male) population. No data existed to show the extent of rural unemployment; but, owing to the decline in agricultural productivity, together with the dysfunctional aspects of agrarian autogestion, it may be assumed that unemployment also reached certain categories of farmers (i.e., regular as opposed to seasonal or nomadic fallahin). Obviously, the declining economy did not favor Ben Bella's long-term success with the trade unionists.

If Ben Bella could not immediately displace the soldiers or solve the economic crisis, he could still reinforce his position by doing what he had resisted heretofore: namely, he could reduce personal power in favor of popular institutions. The solution to the system's precarious existence seemed directly related to the necessity of generating power in institutions, requiring therefore that the system be decentralized. Power once delegated could flow to civilian institutions and thereby increase the stake of nongovernmental groups in the viability of the system and the party. This perspective seemed to explain why Ben Bella sought to win over the trade unionists, the only pillar of durable support apart from the army.

Notwithstanding Ben Bella's efforts to expand party support in the first quarter of 1965, the reality that the ANP constituted the system's

mainstay could not be ignored. At the same time, it should be noted
that the political-military alliance continued virtually intact. Boumedienne did have an interest in bringing his men into governmental
activity. Despite the increase in the soldiers' political participation,
however, he did not seek a parity in army-party representation within
the regime's general decision-making agencies. Furthermore, he tolerated the popular militia from the outset, though it was organized
specifically to counterpose the soldier's growing political influence.

While Boumedienne restricted himself to army affairs, Ben Bella
increased his prestige among the trade unionists and in the country
generally. After the FLN congress, he gained immense popularity
among party adherents, urban workers, FNTT peasants, and particularly among the youth. Even UNEA radicals, who still opposed Ben
Bella on ideological grounds, defended him.

An index to public opinion could be derived from the results of the
National Assembly election of September 20, 1964. Ballots showed
that slightly more than 85 percent of the registered voters approved
the Political Bureau's single list of candidates. Specifically, the electorate cast 5,164,846 affirmative votes out of a total of 5,177,631, including numerous blank ballots. [44] The votes did not signify opinions
on the Assembly, which had become commonly known as an instrument of personal rule, and can reasonably be interpreted as an endorsement of Ben Bella and his policies. This approval was significant because Ben Bella eliminated several soldiers from the candidate
slate before the election. Boumedienne's acceptance of this action
attested to Ben Bella's political dominance. Since the public dimension of party support was overwhelmingly positive, Ben Bella's capacity to command allegiance could be questioned only with respect to
the internal structure of the regime itself.

In the final analysis, the locus of conflict persisted in the relation
between Ben Bella and Boumedienne. Any successful effort to extend
the parameters of party organization and support depended on their
joint action. Zolberg's remarks on the political development of West
African states equally applied to the Algerian political system:

> [A major trend has been toward] a steady drive to achieve great-
> er centralization of authority in the hands of a very small num-
> ber of men who occupy top offices in the party and the govern-
> ment, and even more in the hands of a single man at the apex of

both institutions. Since the opposition was eliminated, the major source of political tension has stemmed from the contest between the paramount leader and important lieutenants. [45]

This contest erupted in Algiers in June 1965 when Ben Bella attempted to expel another of Boumedienne's men from the government, foreign minister Bouteflika.

Bouteflika had tendered his resignation before this conflict, indicating that his control of the ministry had been undermined. The Foreign Ministry was annexed to the presidency upon the death of Khemisti (April 1963), and Ben Bella retained most of its powers when Bouteflika became foreign minister in September 1963. Ben Bella was on the point of declaring Bouteflika's resignation when Boumedienne intervened, insisting that Bouteflika remain in office. Ben Bella had already dismissed Medeghri in a calculated effort to ease the soldiers out of the government. He saw the opportunity to accelerate the process when Bouteflika submitted a second resignation. Again, Boumedienne intervened. This time Ben Bella retorted that he would not reconsider the resignation and, if necessary, would dismiss the army chief too. This last defiance shattered the three-year-old alliance completely.

On the night of June 18, 1965, ANP troops surrounded the presidential residence and effected the coup that resulted in Ben Bella's abrupt disappearance. The coup occurred while Ben Bella was making elaborate preparations for the Second Afro-Asian Conference, which was scheduled to convene in Algiers on June 25. He welcomed it as a forum for advancing his ambitions for leadership of the Third World. The chiefs of state from more than sixty African and Asian nations, as well as the United Nations secretary general, were supposed to attend the conference. Ben Bella had hoped to demonstrate absolute mastery over his own government in order to preside confidently over the foreign dignitaries. This plan, like his new preparations for the FLN, became a footnote to history.

Virtually without bloodshed, the army overturned the regime and replaced it with a military directorate headed by Boumedienne. He encountered hardly any significant resistance in establishing army rule. The FLN was still a relatively impotent political movement and the UGTA had not yet coalesced with it. The fragile system of personal rule was finally strained to the breaking-point.

The collapse of the FLN accompanied Ben Bella's downfall. Once vaunted as the hope of the postindependent system, the party was fatefully linked to his regime of his personal rule. For that reason, the FLN did not survive after him. At the time of the coup, Ben Bella held the presidency and direct control of three different ministries (Interior, Finance, and Information). He was also head of the FLN. Thus, what began as one of the most exciting experiments in party building among postrevolutionary societies culminated in disaster.

Conclusion

The coup of 1965 produced a decisive shift in Algeria's post-independent history. With the disappearance of Ben Bella, the party system and all the institutions which the FLN had represented were dismantled. New power, under the aegis of the army, effectively replaced the old institutions. After more than a decade of successful military government, there has been no indication that the coup's termination of party politics was anything but permanent.

Immediately after the coup, army officers created the Council of the Revolution as the leadership of the newly militarized political system, headed by Colonel Boumedienne. The council's twenty-six members soon established firm control of state and society. As for Ben Bella, it is almost universally believed that he was not killed and has since been kept under secret house detention. A year after the coup, the old headquarters of the FLN was reduced to a small office located inside an ANP facility. The fact that Ahmed Kaid, a former army officer and an ANP stalwart, supervised the FLN bureau was an indisputable confirmation of the emergence of military rule in the post-Ben Bella era.

Yet, despite the dramatic reversals in political leadership and organization, there has been some continuity in political policy, roles, and philosophy from the Ben Bella regime to the military government. In foreign policy, for instance, the Boumedienne leadership has maintained a generally aggressive position vis-à-vis the Western powers, especially France and the United States. The Algerians have also continued to provide material and diplomatic support to Africans now engaged in liberation struggles against such colonial survivors as the white minority regimes of Southern Africa. To this extent, it can be said that "Benbellism" lives on in the absence of Ben Bella.

Despite its demise as a political entity, the FLN has continued to interest scholars of African politics as a prime example of the possibilities for the success of political party systems in new nations. Because of the FLN's wartime difficulties, it has sometimes been compared to other African nationalist parties, especially those of Angola. Because of independent Algeria's spectacular experiment at party building, the FLN has been viewed as a prototype of the failures that have beset African political parties in their postindependent development.[1]

This concluding chapter focuses on the changes in political policy, roles, and philosophies described in this analysis, and it also seeks to show what lessons the analysis may hold for the study of other parties of national liberation.

Continuity and Change Since Ben Bella

"In the new era," Boumedienne declared a year after the coup, "Algeria cannot continue to live under the old structure."[2] Among the first institutions eliminated from the FLN party system, the "old structure," was the Political Bureau, the erstwhile party executive. The governmental powers and functions that had belonged to the Political Bureau were subsumed under the Council of the Revolution. The locus of the decision-making authority was thus established in the new, militarized system. But since the council, like the Political Bureau before it, was not a duly constituted government, governmental authority in Algeria continued to be controlled by an extragovernmental agency. Although the structure of governmental power underwent a basic alteration after the coup, its form remained very much the same.

The unique foundation of the Boumedienne regime, of course, was the army. Not only did the ANP replace the FLN as the central institution of the political system, but it became the only popular institution with nationwide standing: the collapse of the FLN was also accompanied by the decline of its national organizations (such as the influential UGTA) and the immobilization of its constituency. While they existed, the civilian (party) institutions provided useful contributions to Algeria's political development through the FLN's programs and instrumentalities for mass participation, mobilization, recruitment of leaders, leadership mobility, and the like. The organizational vacuum left by the defunct party institutions has since been filled entirely by the army.

For the formulation of policy, the Boumedienne regime made another major change of entrusting certain governmental functions to civilian technocrats and bureaucratic specialists. As head of state, Boumedienne began, in July 1965, to reorganize the central government for order and efficiency, seeking to duplicate at the governmental level the ANP's example of smooth, efficient administration. This decision led him to dismiss a number of politicians who remained at the head of certain ministries, such as Mahsas and Boumaza,[3] in order to make room for new technocrats like Dr. Ahmed Taleb, who was appointed minister of education. Management of the oil industry was made the essential responsibility of a new state-owned corporation, the Société nationale pour la recherche, la production, le transport, la transformation et la commercialisation des hydrocarbures (SONATRACH).[4] A new class of administrative elites, distinguished by their professionalism rather than personal or ideological commitments, came to the fore as a result of this effort. The upshot of these changes was the emergence of a rational and efficient administrative system composed of middle-class technicians who did not belong to the army but who served the army's ends by regularizing governmental operations.

Ideology has vanished as an issue of official concern in the post-Ben Bella era. The Boumedienne regime has maintained a formal attachment to socialism but has made no effort to develop an ideological synthesis to theoretically explain and justify governmental decision-making. Like Ben Bella, Mohammed Harbi, perhaps Algeria's leading Marxist ideologist, was carted off to an undisclosed area where he was to remain under permanent house arrest. Boumedienne has not sought an ideological counterpart to Harbi to articulate the policies of his regime. The promise of the Charter of Algiers for a definition of the nature and content of Algerian socialism was not to be realized.

Instead, efficiency and productivity have emerged as the prime motivating factors of the new government's policies and actions. For example, Boumedienne spoke only of Algeria's economic self-interest in February 1971 when he nationalized 51 percent of the French oil companies together with the totality of natural gas concessions, petroleum operations, and gas and oil transport facilities. By this unilateral act, Boumedienne withheld a majority share of revenues from the

French companies exploiting Saharan oil fields and completely terminated Algeria's commitment to the Evian Accords. During the time
that these actions were taking place, Boumedienne negotiated a
twenty-five-year contract with El Paso Gas of Texas for the exporta-
tion of 10,000 million cubic meters of natural gas to the United States
annually.[5] The implementation of such decisions was usually left in
the charge of the new state-owned corporation or specialized governmental agencies. The government has retained central planning as
the organizing principle of the economic system, but the fact that the
new state institutions like SONATRACH structually resemble the
former French-owned enterprises has led some critics to describe the
new economy as a system of "state capitalism."[6]

The problem of divisiveness in political leadership, which plagued
Algerian political development in wartime and then later under the
Ben Bella regime, was alleviated considerably by the coup of 1965.
With the consolidation of the military government and the elimination of politicians from the decision-making arena, politics became
the principal concern of military officers, members of the Council of
the Revolution. Major Bouteflika, for instance, assumed control of
the Foreign Ministry after the coup and has since played the leading
role in the formulation of foreign policy. Any new reversals in governmental leadership can be expected to derive from competition among
the chief army leaders because leadership conflict would be effectively
circumscribed within the military hierarchy.

Because of the apparent collegiality of leadership in the Council of
the Revolution, the FLN's wartime principle of collective rule has
been restored to a limited extent. The previous regime of personal rule
has been formally replaced by the coterie of ANP chieftains. However,
it is still possible to regard power as personal under the new government because it is wielded only by Boumedienne and the subordinate
officers and technocrats to whom he has delegated decision-making
authority. Compared to the Ben Bella system, this limited dispersion
of executive power represents a dramatic and substantial change in
the political process. At the same time, the authoritarian control of
the military government has foreclosed the possibility of public dissent, and thus it is not surprising that Boumedienne has not encountered opponents or critics of "personal power."

In retrospect, it can be seen that Ben Bella's system of personal rule
certainly contradicted the FLN's development, but this study suggests

that personal or authoritarian rule is not intrinsically inimical to political development in new societies. The war of liberation thrust to the forefront a charismatic leader hailed by the people as chief of state on independence. As a national hero, Ben Bella held the power to build political institutions by channeling the energies of the masses into constructive organization and by delegating authority to promote the organization. For effective party development, the leader's personal goals must correspond to the institutional interests of the party he heads. Ben Bella disregarded this principle in the first few years of his administration, as evidenced by his domination of the state administration, the National Assembly, and the drafting of the constitution. In contrast, Mao Tse-Tung in China and Julius Nyerere in Tanzania have succeeded in large part by promoting personal aspirations and ideologies that have been conducive to the party institutionalization process. [7]

This study has also revealed that the army's participation in the political arena is not inherently antithetical to institutionalizing a party system. Indeed, it has been suggested that military involvement is temporarily functional if accompanied by broad-based participation of civilian interest groups together with aggressive party leadership at all levels. Ben Bella, preoccupied with state building as a means of consolidating his monopoly of power, made only modest efforts in the first years after independence to relieve his dependency on the ANP for enforcement of policy decisions. The ANP suppressed the opposition to the FLN and enforced the Political Bureau's policies throughout the party's gestation period. Nonetheless, it could be seen that staunch backing from powerful organizations like the UGTA would probably have enabled the party eventually to outgrow its dependence on the army. Ben Bella's neglect of party building had as a consequence the army's gradual and ultimately dominant influence in the political process.

Party building in new nations, as witnessed in this study, demands both manipulation and accommodation of diverse socioeconomic groups. Khider, as secretary general of the Political Bureau, pointed the way to building a cohesive party structure by integrating nongovernmental interest groups into it. The authoritarian approach he used in coopting the UGTA did not solely explain the subsequent alienation of the trade unionists, particularly the radical trade unionists. Rather, the authoritarian tactics, uncompensated by benefits in other areas of the workers' interests, accounted for their antagonism toward the FLN. The failure of the government to temper its authoritarianism with policy concessions and material rewards explains the persistent antiparty militancy of the workers.

Unattributable to the excesses of Ben Bella's leadership were vestiges of colonialism that contributed to those forces resisting the emergence of socialism under his regime. Many of the bureaucrats in the governmental civil service, especially in the ONRA, had served in the colonial administration; most of them maintained the practices and values of the colonial era. Given the general societal collapse upon independence, Ben Bella was compelled to rehire them to revive government and administration. The indispensability of these bureaucrats was magnified by his state-building priority.

Though in diminishing form, the colonial structure of the Algerian economy endured after the defeat of the colonial regime. It represented a certain danger to Algerian economic independence, posing as it did the possibility of a "neocolonial" relationship.[8] Trade and commerce during colonialism developed essentially as a series of economic relations between the French in Algeria and the French in the métropole. Such domestic staples as grapes (for wine production) were produced primarily for consumption at the tables of Paris, Marseille, and Bordeaux. Internal trade and commerce were relegated to correspondingly subordinate importance. When Ben Bella came to power he inherited this economic structure and, despite his protestations, discovered that it was virtually impossible to terminate it, at least in the short run. The structure still characterized Algerian-French relations at the time of the coup.

Such aspects of the colonial heritage, coupled with Ben Bella's own failures as a leader and builder of socialism, have been interpreted by some writers as indicative of the defeat of the Algerian revolution,[9] or else as evidence that no revolution ever took place.[10] The first assessment is premature, but the second is inaccurate. Ben Bella was in power for only three years, and it is difficult to conceive how socialism or any form of economic independence could have been consummated in such a short time, even if he had endeavored unequivocally to do so. Given Algeria's considerable economic resources, particularly oil, its economy was bound to become strong in the long run, regardless of the prevailing political leadership. This interpretation has been borne out by Algeria's increasing movement toward economic independence since the coup, not to mention an acceleration of the process in the wake of the 1973 Arab oil boycott.

To argue that the anticolonial struggle did not produce a revolution in Algeria is to ignore the substantive socioeconomic changes that resulted from that struggle. The most critical changes were the reversals in social and economic relations caused by the FLN's mobilization and control of the Muslim population in the early years; the rise to power, through the ANP or the FLN, of Algerians from peasant backgrounds; the changes in property ownership following the exodus of the French; and the new sense of self-esteem and positive identity among independent Algerians, i.e., a psychological transformation that Fanon regards as indispensable to revolution.[11] With the petroleum nationalization of 1971, Boumedienne established Algeria's majority control of the country's main capital resource and thus seemed to preclude the emergence of neocolonialism. As a symbolic gesture of Algeria's growing economic independence, in 1971 the government initiated a campaign to uproot Algeria's vineyards, the old symbol of colonial association and dependency.[12]

Rise and Fall of the Liberation Party

A prominent characteristic of the liberation party in Africa has been its inability to harness all nationalist forces into a single, unified movement from rebellion to independence. In his useful study of African movements, Gibson found that the outcome of liberation wars showed Africans pitted against Africans for numerous reasons—ethnic, ideological, and personal—despite the fact that the basic conflict was between Africans and Europeans, the colonized and the colonizers.[13] Repeatedly, the fratricidal struggle grew out of movements lacking in developed political institutions and ideology, from deficiencies that were exacerbated by potential or actual divisiveness in the political leadership. The battle between the Political Bureau and the GPRA upon independence exemplified this woeful conclusion of anticolonial war.

In the case of the FLN, it became quite clear during the early stages of the war that the acquired nationalist unity was founded almost exclusively upon common opposition to the French. What the FLN leaders were for, what they aimed to create and establish after victory, remained unknown and undecided. They could not decide this question because they had not defined the political objectives of their struggle before 1954 and failed to do so throughout the war. Lacking a party program, they were unable to advance policies for the FLN's wartime and future development; lacking an ideology, they did not have a doctrinal and instructive context from which policies are suggested and made.

Because of this omission, divisions within the FLN leadership developed and continued unabated through the wartime era. The intra-leadership divergencies were both personal and political. In light of the movement's programmatic and ideological vacuum, they often appeared merely as personality conflicts or as egoistic struggles for power. The FLN leaders were without political guidelines for their actions. As a consequence, the personal divisions hardened and became imbedded as more or less permanent elements in the revolutionary organization.

The forcible separation of the internal from the external leaders was not an insurmountable problem. Likewise, the conflicts among the internal leaders were not necessarily unsusceptible to solution. Lenin helped to stage part of the Bolshevik revolution from abroad, and Kenyatta, in jail, maintained leadership of the Kenyan nationalist forces.[14] The internal and external leaders of the FLN failed to maintain a joint front because they were not able to reach common agreement on the political objectives that their struggle was presumed to promote. The absence of an ideology, the transcendent medium, made their problems and conflicts insurmountable.

Quite apart from the divisiveness among FLN leaders, the failure of the party movement to develop viable political insitutions in wartime was severely hampered by the absence of guidelines for political and economic objectives that could be advanced during the struggle. Lacking an ideology, the FLN could not provide its followers with clues as to what concrete programs and benefits party leaders would produce for them. This deficiency explains why the nationalist leaders did not organize political (as distinguished from military and personal) constituencies, and why they could not build the institutions necessary for managing a peaceful transition from war to independence.

In contrast to the wartime disintegration of the FLN, the Chinese Communist party, led by Mao Tse-Tung, undertook a protracted and painstaking campain to build political institutions under the pressure of military exigencies that were at least as arduous as those encountered by the Algerian leaders. The Chinese party-building process, which took form in 1934, enabled the Communists to achieve military success by 1950, and, later, to establish a viable and authoritative party system.[15] The Chinese example supports the conclusion that party insurgents should concentrate on building political institutions, even if it necessitates restraining the military effort, because nationalist unity is not likely to endure when party objectives are limited to ousting the imperialists.

The revolution in Angola has been the most recent example of the deficiencies that afflicted the FLN. In Angola, however, the problem of leadership divisiveness was compounded by intractable conflicts among three different parties, each organized around discrete ethnic groups, leaderships, and geographic milieu. The triumphant Angolan party, the Movimento popular de libertação de Angolo (MPLA), began to organize in 1956 but did not succeed in developing a broad-based national constituency or in containing its rivals, the Frente nacional de libertação de Angola (FNLA), organized in 1962, and the União nacional para a independência total de Angola (UNITA), organized in 1966.[16] Unlike the FLN, no single Angolan party managed to defeat, coopt, or otherwise eliminate its rivals before independence. None of the parties, moreover, was able to claim all the credit for compelling the Portuguese to accept the negotiated settlement that brought Angola to independence in November 1975.

Independence in Angola, as in Algeria, ignited the flame of civil warfare, rapidly replacing the war against the external enemy with the war that pitted African against African. Thanks in part to the intervention of an estimated 10,000 Cuban troops on the side of the MPLA,[17] this party, under the leadership of Dr. Agostinho Neto, sacked its rivals and established control of the newly independent nation. This victory was won at the expense of fratricide, the casualties of which have been put in the thousands, and the possibilities of renewed civil conflict have not disappeared. Unlike the Algerians, the Angolans never acquired nationalist unity during the liberation struggle, and the search for national unification has been left to a distant and uncertain future by the crisis at independence.

Given intense wartime disunity among the Angolan factions, it would be mere speculation to suggest that common agreement on a particular ideology would have transcended the various ethnic, regional, and political differences and warded off leadership divisiveness during the anticolonial struggle. It is clear, however, that the Angolans had no common element of agreement except a general consensus that the colonial system had to be eliminated. Societal heterogeneity was far more acute in Angola than in Algeria; hence, it could be argued that social conflict would have prevailed in varying degrees regardless of any unity achieved in the nationalist leadership. On the other hand, Angola could have been spared a great deal of political and social hardships upon independence if the wartime movement had already introduced the general population into participation through effective political institutions created in response to lines offered by a systematic ideology.

Indeed, it could be argued that the post-1958 disintegration of the FLN was minimal compared to the profound divergencies among the Angolan parties. The specter of civil war did not appear in Algeria until after the nationalist objective had been achieved, but this ugly phenomenon was quite apparent in Angola long before independence. A quest for a monopoly of political power outweighed all other considerations in both countries. This fact suggests that a functioning party system will scarcely materialize in postindependent Angola just as the FLN finally failed in Algeria.

The Angolans have also imitated the Algerians by seeking to establish political legitimacy through the single-party system. After the defeat of its two rivals, the MPLA emerged as the central political institution, the only legal political party. Governmental decisions are made and implemented in the name of the party. After he came to power, Ben Bella used the FLN to sustain the popular legitimacy of his government, and he rationalized his authoritarian practices by referring to the needs of the one-party system. Kwame Nkrumah played a similar role as the head of the Convention People's party in Ghana. [18] It is no surprise that the Angolan leaders have identified the MPLA as the validating basis of their new power.

As shown in this study, the one-party system may generate the potentiality for its own disintegration. At first, Ben Bella's prohibition of competitive political groups appeared to favor a progressive consolidation of the FLN. However, this policy led ultimately to the restriction of all forms of dissent, with the result that opposition leaders resorted to the maquis to redress what they considered to be legitimate grievances. A party system tolerating some dissent diminishes the probability of insurrection and at the same time is more likely to facilitate integration and to moderate conflict. The one-party system still seems the best mechanism for coalescing manifold political divisions into political organization after independence, but the evidence of this study indicates that party politics in Africa, so important in the independence euphoria of the 1960s, is fast becoming an attraction of the past.

Appendix I

Members of Ben Bella's First Government
(September 1962)

 1. Ahmed Ben Bella, premier and president of the Council of Ministers
 2. Rabah Bitat, deputy premier and council vice-president
+ 3. Houari Boumedienne, minister of national defense
 4. Mohammed Khemisti, minister of foreign affairs
+ 5. Ahmed Medeghri, minister of the interior
 6. Ahmed Francis, minister of finance and economics
 7. Omar Bentoumi, minister of justice
 8. Amar Ouzegane, minister of agriculture and agrarian reform
 9. Mohammed Khobzi, minister of commerce
+10. Abdelazziz Bouteflika, minister of youth and sports
 11. Abderrahmane Benhamida, minister of education
 12. Mohammed Nekkache, minister of public health
 13. Ahmed Boumendjel, minister of reconstruction and public works
 14. Bachir Boumaza, minister of labor and social affairs
 15. Mohammed Hadj Hamou, minister of information
+16. Laroussi Khalifa, minister of industrialization and energy
+17. Moussa Hassani, minister of telecommunications
 18. Tewfik El Madani, minister of *Habous* (religious trusts)
 19. Said Mohammedi, minister of war veterans and victims

+ Indicates ANP representatives or appointees of Boumedienne.

Appendix   2

Members of Ben Bella's Second Government
(September 1963)

1. Ahmed Ben Bella, president of the republic and the Council of Ministers
+ 2. Houari Boumedienne, minister of defense and council vice-president
3. Said Mohammedi, second vice-president of the council
4. Rabah Bitat, third vice-president of the council
5. Amar Ouzegane, minister of state
+ 6. Ahmed Medeghri, minister of the interior
+ 7. Abdelazziz Bouteflika, minister of foreign affairs
8. Mohammed Nekkache, minister of social affairs
9. Bachir Boumaza, minister of national economy
10. Ahmed Ali Mahsas, minister of agriculture
11. Ahmed Boumendjel, minister of public works
12. Mohammed Hadj Smain, minister of justice
13. Tewfik El Madani, minister of *Habous*
+14. Ahmed Kaid, minister of tourism
+15. Belkacem Cherif, minister of national orientation
16. Abdelkader Zaibek, minister of postal service and telecommunications
17. Sadek Batel, state undersecretary for youth and sports

+ Indicates ANP representatives or appointees of Boumedienne.

Appendix 3

Members of Ben Bella's Third Government
(December 1964)

+ 1. Ahmed Ben Bella, president*
+ 2. Houari Boumedienne, vice-president and minister of defense
  3. Said Mohammedi, vice-president
+ 4. Abdelazziz Bouteflika, minister of foreign affairs
  5. Abderrahmane Cherif, minister delegated to the presidency
  6. Ahmed Ali Mahsas, minister of agriculture
  7. Bachir Boumaza, minister of industry and energy
  8. Safi Boudissa, minister of labor
  9. Amar Ouzegane, minister of tourism
 10. Mohammed Bedjaoui, minister of justice
 11. Mohammed Hadj Smain, minister of reconstruction and housing
 12. Mohammed Nekkache, minister of health, war veterans and social affairs
+13. Belkacem Cherif, minister of education
 14. Sadek Batel, minister of youth and sports
 15. Tedjini Heddam, minister of *Habous*
 16. Abdelkader Zaibek, minister of posts and telecommunications
 17. Said Amrani, minister of administrative reform
 18. Ahmed Ghozali, undersecretary for public works

* Ben Bella also attached the Ministries of the Interior, Finance, and Information to the presidency in this government.
+ Indicates ANP representative or appointees of Boumedienne.

Notes

INTRODUCTION

1. See Nevill Barbour, *A Survey of North West Africa* (London: Oxford University Press, 1962), p. 212.

2. L. Gray Cowan, *The Dilemmas of African Independence* (New York: Walker and Co., 1964), p. 124.

3. For a study of guerrilla warfare, the reader is recommended Kenneth W. Grundy, *Guerrilla Struggle in Africa* (New York: Grossman Publishers, 1971).

CHAPTER 1

1. Nevill Barbour, *A Survey of North West Africa* (London: Oxford University Press, 1962), p. 203.

2. For an analysis of the distinctions between Arab Bedouins and city dwellers, see Pierre Bourdieu, *The Algerians* (Boston: Beacon Press, 1962), Chapter 4.

3. Generally, the Sunni sect of Islam is distinguished by its adherence to the first four caliphs (spiritual leaders of Islam) as the legitimate successors of Mohammed the Prophet, and by its emphasis on the words and acts believed to derive from him.

4. Boudieu, op. cit., p. 106.

5. For a discussion of Islam as a religion and a totality regulating the life of a Muslim, see Joseph Schacht, *An Introduction to Islamic Law* (Oxford: Clarendon Press, 1964).

6. Bourdieu, op. cit., p. 56, Bourdieu's study contains a very scholarly sociological analysis of the Algerian population as a whole.

7. Raymond Aron, *Les Origines de la guerre d'Algérie* (Paris: Fayard, 1962), p. 38.

8. Charles-Robert Agéron, *Histoire de l'Algérie* (Paris: Presses Universitaires de France, 1966), p. 27.

9. Adam Smith, *The Wealth of Nations* (New York: Cannan edition, 1937), p. 538.

10. David and Marina Ottaway, *Algeria: The Politics of a Socialist Revolution* (Berkeley: University of California Press, 1970), p. 39.

11. Agéron, op. cit., p. 55.

12. For an examination of the new administrative system, see Roger Le Tourneau, *Evolution politique de l'Afrique du nord musulmane* (Paris: Librairie Armand Colin, 1962), p. 303.

13. Ageron, op. cit., p. 51. One hectare equals 2.471 acres.

14. Barbour, op. cit., p. 216.

15. In 1830, Algeria consisted primarily of cities on the Mediterranean and belonged to the North African territories known as the Barbary States. The current geographic boundaries of the country were established mainly by the French, who in the late nineteenth century brought Morocco and Tunisia under protectorate status. The French, controlling the three countries, moved between them freely and did not lay out exact boundaries. The imprecise frontiers were a factor in 1963 when Morocco and Algeria went to war over Saharan territory which both countries claimed as part of their patrimony.

16. Roger Le Tourneau, "Implications of Rapid Urbanization," in *State and Society in Independent North Africa*, ed. by Leon Carl Brown (Washington, D.C.: Middle East Institute, 1966), p. 63.

17. Thomas Hodgkin, *Nationalism in Colonial Africa* (New York: New York University Press, 1957), p. 63.

18. For a thorough study of the *bidonvilles*, see R. Descloitres, et al., *L'Algérie des bidonvilles: le tiers-monde dans la cité* (Paris: Mouton, 1961).

19. Le Tourneau, "Implications of Rapid Urbanization," loc. cit., p. 124.

20. Joseph Kraft, "Settler Politics in Algeria," *Foreign Affairs*, No. 4 (July 1961): 593.

21. Le Tourneau, "Implications of Rapid Urbanization," loc. cit., p. 125.

22. Ageron, op. cit., p. 81.

23. Frantz Fanon, *The Wretched of the Earth* (New York: Grove Press, 1963), p. 35.

24. Bourdieu, op. cit., p. 57.

25. No reliable figures have been found to show the size of the PCA's membership. Humbaraci estimated that there were 5,550 card-carrying members in 1964. However, this figure relates almost exclusively to European members, and it appears inordinately high. In the 1920s, PCA membership was surely much lower and probably did not contain more than 200 Muslim members. For a discussion of Algerian communists as of 1965, see Arslan Humbaraci, *Algeria: A Revolution That Failed* (New York: Praeger, 1966), p. 170.

26. Mohamed Farès, "L'Histoire du travail algérien" (Unpublished manuscript, University of Algiers, 1967). No pagination.

27. A history of the PCF can be found in Philip Williams, *Politics in Post-War France* (London: Longmans, Green and Co., 1958), pp 44-59.

28. Edgar O'Ballance, *The Algerian Insurrection: 1954-1962* (Hamden, Conn.: Archon Books, 1967), p. 29.

29. As translated from Le Tourneau, *Evolution politique de l'Afrique du nord musulmane*, p. 314. The article appeared in *L'Entente*, the assimilationists' journal, on February 23, 1936.

30. Richard and Joan Brace, *Ordeal in Algeria* (New York: Van Nostrand, 1960), p. 29.

31. The marabouts were Muslim priests who practiced saint-worship, mysticism, and forms of superstition. Orthodox Muslims regarded them as heretics, a status that

placed them consistently under the attack of the ulama. The marabouts usually resided in the countryside, and the French sometimes supported them against the ulama as a means of dividing the general Muslim population.

32. Agéron, op. cit., p. 80.

33. Le Tourneau, *Evolution politique de l'Afrique du nord musulmane*, p. 329.

34. See ibid., p. 339, for details of this incident.

35. Brace, op. cit., p. 50.

36. O'Ballance, op. cit., p. 32.

37. Le Tourneau, *Evolution politique de l'Afrique du nord musulmane*, p. 350. The figure cited by the Algerians seems excessively high and contrasts sharply with the official French source, which reported about 1,500 Muslim losses. The exact count probably lies somewhere between these two extremes.

38. Michael K. Clark, *Algeria in Turmoil* (New York: Grosset and Dunlap, 1960), p. 43.

39. Brace, op. cit., p. 70.

40. A very informative and provocative analysis of Algerian leaders has been made by Quandt. He explains the cause of divisiveness in Algerian leadership as "a discontinuous process of political socialization whereby each political generation was exposed to radically different experiences while at the same time reacting to what was widely perceived as the failures of the preceding generation to achieve any of its major political goals." See William B. Quandt, *Revolution and Political Leadership: Algeria, 1954-1968* (Cambridge, Mass.: The MIT Press, 1969), p. 14.

41. Clark, op. cit., p. 57. For Ben Bella's own account of this exploit, see Robert Merle, *Ben Bella* (London: Michael Joseph, Ltd., 1967), pp. 81-83.

42. Clark, op. cit., p. 58.

43. For an analysis of Nasser's accession to power, see Joachim Joesten, *Nasser: The Rise to Power* (London: Odhams Press Ltd., 1960).

44. "Maghrib" is the Arabic term for Northwest Africa, which refers to Morocco, Algeria, Tunisia, and sometimes to Libya.

45. Brace, op. cit., p. 85.

46. Ibid.

47. Joan Gillespie, *Algeria: Rebellion and Revolution* (New York: Praeger, 1960), p. 67.

48. Brace, op. cit., p. 83.

49. Agéron, op. cit., p. 78.

50. Barbour, op. cit., p. 241.

51. Ibid., p. 250.

52. Ibid.

53. Fanon, op. cit., p. 33.

CHAPTER 2

1. As this study is not concerned with the strictly military aspects of the Algerian revolution, the reader is recommended Jacques C. Duchemin, *Histoire du FLN* (Paris: La Table Ronde, 1962); Edgar O'Ballance, *The Algerian Insurrection* (Hamden, Conn.: Archon Books, 1967); and Jules Roy, *The War in Algeria* (New York: Grove Press, 1960).

2. Ferhat Abbas, *Guerre et révolution d'Algérie* (Paris: Juilliard, 1962), p. 219.

3. For an account of this event by a participant, see Mohammed Boudiaf, *Où va l' Algérie?* (Paris: Editions Librairie de l'Etoile, 1964).

4. Joachim Joesten, *The New Algeria* (Chicago: Follett, 1964), p. 27.

5. FLN, "Proclamation to the Algerian People and to All Who Fight for the National Cause," Algiers, November 1954. English edition.

6. Ibid.

7. Ibid.

8. Ibid.

9. Ibid.

10. Ibid.

11. Ibid.

12. Sources differ on the number of FLN guerrillas in 1954. For instance, Joan Gillespie, *Algeria: Rebellion and Revolution* (New York: Praeger, 1960), p. 95, offers the estimates of 2,000 to 3,000 men; Arslan Humbaraci, *Algeria: A Revolution That Failed* (New York: Praeger, 1966), p. 34, asserts that there couldn't have been more than 500; and William B. Quandt, *Revolution and Political Leadership: Algeria, 1954-1968* (Cambridge, Mass.: The MIT Press, 1969), p. 93, reports his sources' estimates ranging from 900 to 3,000.

13. Joseph Kraft, *The Struggle for Algeria* (Garden City, N.Y.: Doubleday, 1961), p. 73.

14. Assigned by CRUA leaders at a secret meeting held in Algiers on July 10, 1954, the command posts with their respective chiefs were as follows:

Wilaya I   : The Aurès. Chief: Mustapha Ben Boulaid
Wilaya II : The northern part of the Constantine département.
             Chief: Rabah Bitat
Wilaya III : Kabylia. Chiefs: Belkacem Krim and Amar Oumrane
Wilaya IV : The central and western parts of the Algiers département.
             Chief: Mourad Didouche
Wilaya V   : The Oran département. Chief: Larbi Ben M'Hidi
Wilaya VI : The Sahara. No chief then designated

15. Joesten, op. cit., p. 27.

16. Michael K. Clark, *Algeria in Turmoil* (New York: Grosset and Dunlap, 1960), P. 86.

17. Alim is the singular of ulama (i.e., doctors of Islamic laws).

18. As cited by Amar Ouzegane, *Le Meilleur combat* (Paris: Juilliard, 1962), p. 183.

19. Humbaraci, op. cit., p. 172.

20. Ibid.

21. Ouzegane, op. cit., p. 185.

22. See Henri Alleg, *The Question* (New York: George Braziller, Inc., 1958).

23. For a study of French trade unions, see Val R. Lorwin, *The French Labor Movement* (Cambridge, Mass.: Harvard University Press, 1954).

24. As cited by Mohammed Farès, "Histoire du travail algérien" (Unpublished manuscript, University of Algiers, 1967). No pagination.

25. The other founding officers of the UGTA were Boualem Bourouiba, in charge of

the railway trade; Rabah Djermane, in charge of the dockers union; Ali Yahia Majid, secretary of social securities; and Attalah Benaissa, in charge of the hospital workers.

26. Jeanne Favret, "Le Syndicat, les travailleurs, et le pouvoir en Algérie," *Annuaire de l'Afrique du nord* (1964): 46.

27. Quandt, op. cit., p. 100.

28. Duchemin, op. cit., p. 179. UGEMA, the Algerian student organization, is discussed later in this chapter.

29. The seventeen regular members of the CNRA are listed below:

1. Ramdane Abane+
2. Ferhat Abbas+
3. Hocine Ait Ahmed *
4. Ahmed Ben Bella *
5. Mustapha Ben Boulaid *
6. Benyoussef Benkhedda +
7. Larbi Ben M'Hidi *
8. Rabah Bitat *
9. Mohammed Boudiaf *
10. Saad Dahlab +
11. Mohammed Khider *
12. Belkacem Krim *
13. Mohammed Lamine Debaghine +
14. Tewfik El Madani +
15. Amar Oumrane x
16. Mohammed Yazid +
17. Youcef Zirout x

* Indicates the surviving "historic chiefs," principal organizers of the CRUA.
x Also founding members of the CRUA.
+ Indicates the new members who had risen to positions of leadership in the FLN since 1954.

30. Among the substitute members, those who were, or would become, politically significant included Lakhdar Ben Tobbal, deputy commander of wilaya II; Mohammed Ben Yahia, former secretary general of UGEMA: Abdelhafid Boussouf, commander of wilaya V; Slimane Dhiles, deputy commander of wilaya IV; Ahmed Francis, former deputy leader of the UDMA and Abbas' closest ally; Ahmed Ali Mahsas, an FLN militant; Said Mohammedi, commander of wilaya III; and Aissat Idir, secretary general of the UGTA.

31. Quandt, op. cit, p. 101.

32. Ibid., p. 100.

33. *La Plateforme de la révolution algérienne*, Resolutions of the Soummam Valley Congress, August 1956.

34. Ibid.

35. Gillespie, op. cit., p. 132. (Note: According to one of Quandt's sources, Ben Bella and the external delegation may not have even been informed of the Congress, although this seems most unlikely. See Quandt, op. cit., p. 94.)

36. Duchemin, op. cit., p. 180.
37. Serge Bromberger, *Les Rebelles algériens* (Paris: Librairie Plon, 1958), p. 108.
38. *L'Ouvrier algérien,* November 1, 1958.
39. Op. cit.
40. Quandt, op. cit., p. 122; Farès, op. cit., estimates that there were 400,000 Algerian workers at this time.
41. Ibid.
42. Farès, op. cit. A hundred AF (old French francs) equals 10 NF (new French francs) or about $2.
43. Op. cit. According to Farès, op. cit., the contributions from the Algerian workers in France exceeded the monetary assistance from the United Arab Republic and other Arab countries combined.
44. David B. Ottaway, "Algeria," in *Students and Politics in Developing Nations,* ed. Donald K. Emerson (New York: Praeger, 1968), p. 4.
45. As translated from *La Plateforme de la révolution algérienne.*
46. For a discussion of the Meurice-Challe Line, see Humbaraci, op. cit., pp. 41-42. According to his source, nearly 4,500 ALN troops were killed within six months during 1958 as they attempted to cross the barricade; ibid., p. 42. It cannot be doubted that many Algerians met death trying to return to the battlefield, but this figure is probably exaggerated.
47. The French seemed to retaliate militarily against Bourguiba when, in February 1958, they bombed the Tunisian border town of Sakiet Sidi Youssef. Morocco, which became independent in 1956, was also concerned about French reprisals.

CHAPTER 3

1. According to Arslan Humbaraci, *Algeria: A Revolution That Failed* (New York: Praeger, 1966), p. 64, the FLN rebels killed more Muslim inhabitants than the French. No figures have been discovered on the Algerian fratricidal casualties, but the generally accepted view is that they were very high.
2. As cited in *The Manchester Guardian,* July 13, 1957.
3. Women were particularly involved as saboteurs during the "Battle of Algiers," discussed in this chapter.
4. Joan Gillespie, *Algeria: Rebellion and Revolution* (New York: Praeger, 1960), p. 145.
5. Ibid.
6. James S. Coleman and Carl G. Rosberg, Jr., *Political Parties and National Integration in Tropical Africa* (Berkeley: University of California Press, 1964), p. 2.
7. As cited by Michael K. Clark, *Algeria in Turmoil* (New York: Grosset and Dunlap, 1960), p. 315.
8. Ibid., p. 318.
9. For a fuller discussion of the "Battle of Algiers," see ibid., pp. 314-320.
10. Estimates vary on the number of ALN soldiers stationed in Tunisia and Morocco, but range from 35,000 to 45,000. For example, David and Marina Ottaway, *Algeria: The Politics of Socialist Revolution* (Berkeley: University of California Press, 1970), p. 15, suggest 40,000 altogether; Humbaraci, op. cit., states that there were

30,000 in Tunisia (p. 132) and 10,000 in Morocco (p. 135). The figure of 35,000 (25,000 in Tunisia and 10,000 in Morocco) is offered by I. William Zartman, "L'Armée dans la politique algerienne," *Annuaire de l'Afrique du nord* 7 (1967): 269.

11. Those loyal to Abane and Krim included Lamine Debaghine, Oumrane, Bous-, souf, Ben Tobbal, and Mahmoud Cherif (an officer in the French army during World War II and currently the cohort of Oumrane). The Abbas faction included Francis and Mehri.

12. As cited by Gillespie, op. cit., p. 154. Emphasis added.

13. For a discussion of the death of Abane, see William B. Quandt, *Revolution and Political Leadership: Algeria, 1954-1968* (Cambridge, Mass.: The MIT Press, 1969), p. 135.

14. The Arab states consisted of Iraq, Libya, Morocco, Sudan, Tunisia, the United Arab Republic, and Yemen.

15. For a discussion of the fall of the Fourth Republic and the rise of de Gaulle, see Phillip M. Williams and Martin Harrison, *De Gaulle's Republic* (London: Longmans, 1962), Chapters, 3 and 4.

16. Quandt, op. cit., p. 139.

17. Clare Hollingworth, "The Struggle for Power in Algeria," *The World Today* 17 (October 1962): 436.

18. *Jeune Afrique*, July 4, 1965.

19. For a translation of De Gaulle's offer of Algerian self-determination, see *The New York Times*, September 17, 1959. The French president issued the declaration on September 16, 1959.

20. Benyoussef Benkhedda, "Contribution à l'historique du FLN," mimeograph, April 1964.

21. The French invested heavily in prospecting for and extracting Saharan oil and natural gas from 1954 to 1961. Oil exports exceeded 25 million tons after 1963. See Samir Amin, *The Maghreb in the Modern World* (London: Cox and Wyman, Ltd., 1970), pp. 122-123.

22. *Révolution africaine*, October 23, 1965.

23. An abridged translation of the French texts of the *Accords d'Evian* can be found in Joachim Joesten, *The New Algeria* (Chicago: Follette, 1964), pp. 229-246.

24. Pierre Bourdieu, *The Algerians* (Boston: Beacon Press, 1962), p. 163.

25. See Humbaraci, op. cit., p. 55.

26. *Jeune Afrique*, July 13, 1964.

27. Quandt, op. cit., p. 143.

28. Research failed to reveal the exact numerical distribution between GPRA and Ben Bella supporters. The FLN members whom I interviewed—and who had either participated in or were intimately familiar with the Tripoli Conference—gave me conflicting accounts. Most held that the Benbellists formed the majority, but others insisted that Benkhedda could have thwarted the Ben Bella challenge had he provoked a showdown at the meeting. The CNRA met in complete secrecy and little has since been divulged of its proceedings.

29. As cited in the translation of the *Tripoli Program* in Joesten, op. cit., pp. 206-207.

30. Frantz Fanon, who drew the provocative conclusions of his analysis on colonization from the Algerian war, notes that "revolutionary elements" from the towns initiate

revolutionary political organization; but he argues that peasants eventually "come to show themselves capable of directing the people's struggle." Fanon, *The Wretched of the Earth* (New York: Grove Press, 1963), p. 114. Although individuals of peasant origin rose to positions of leadership in the FLN, the evidence of this study shows that peasants as a class were induced into the struggle through a variety of techniques, including terror, moral suasion, and the influence of Islam.

31. Joesten, op. cit., p. 208.

32. Ibid., p. 209.

33. Ibid., p. 215.

34. Ibid., p. 217.

35. The Tripoli Program also stated that the FLN should seek to "nationalize all forms of transportation." Ibid., p. 218.

36. Ibid.

37. Ibid., p. 226.

38. Ibid., p. 227.

39. Gérard Chaliand, *L'Algérie, est-elle socialiste?* (Paris: Editions Maspero, 1969), p. 18.

CHAPTER 4

1. The referendum was ratified on July 1, 1962.

2. Joachim Joesten, *The New Algeria* (Chicago: Follett, 1964), p. 60.

3. For a discussion of the "regroupment centers," see Nevill Barbour, *A Survey of North West Africa* (London: Oxford University Press, 1962), p. 380.

4. I. William Zartman, *Government and Politics in North Africa* (New York: Praeger, 1963), p. 47.

5. For a study of the OAS, the reader is recommended Morland et al., *Histoire de l'organisation de l'armée secrète* (Paris: Juilliard, 1964).

6. As cited in Clare Hollingsworth, "The Struggle for Power in Algeria," *The World Today* 17 (October 1962), p. 436. Boumendjel was defense attorney for Ben Bella in wartime.

7. *Le Monde*, July 6, 1962.

8. The GPRA signed the cease-fire agreement with the OAS on July 17, 1962.

9. As cited in Arslan Humbaraci, *Algeria: A Revolution That Failed* (New York: Praeger, 1966), p. 76.

10. *Jeune Afrique*, July 11, 1962.

11. As cited in *Révolution africaine*, October 23, 1965.

12. Estimate of Mohamed Farès, "L'Histoire du travail algérien" (Unpublished manuscript).

13. William M. Lewis, "Algeria: The Plight of the Victor," *Current History* 44 (January 1963): 26.

14. Humbaraci, op. cit., p. 76.

15. Mostefa Lacheraf, *L'Algérie: nation et société*, (Paris: Editions Maspero, 1965), p. 292. In wartime, Lacheraf served as an FLN information officer. He was arrested in 1956 in the company of Ben Bella and the exterior leaders.

16. A similar typology has been presented by Clement Henry Moore in *Tunisia Since*

Independence (Berkeley: University of California Press, 1965), p. 1. Moore lists the following syndrome of traits to characterize an established mass party system:

1. After winning independence, the party exercises a virtual monopoly of power, either directly or indirectly through the new state administration that it staffs, though weak opposition parties may persist.
2. While depending for its cohesion after independence mainly upon the personal power and prestige of a leader-hero, the party is a national symbol sharing his prestige as founder of the new state.
3. The party is open to (almost) all nationals.
4. Its leaders and cadres are selected primarily on the basis of their loyalty and political achievements rather than social position.
5. Its well-articulated structure, supplemented by a network of ancillary organizations, actively sustains a mass following and aims at integrating the society.
6. Though the party does not have a total ideology, it communicates a broad message of social and economic modernization.

Moore's useful typology omits the important criterion for the regulation of membership discipline, and leadership of the mass party is not necessarily limited to a single "leader-hero." For an examination of political parties generally, the reader is also recommended (1) Maurice Duverger, *Political Parties* (New York: John Wiley and Sons, 1959); and (2) Roy C. Macridis, *Political Parties: Contemporary Trends and Ideas* (New York: Harper & Row, 1967).

17. As cited in Hervé Bourgès, *L'Algérie à l'épreuve du pouvoir* (Paris: Editions Bernard Grasset, 1967), p. 44.

18. For a detailed list of the individual candidates, see *Le Monde*, September 15, 1962.

19. *Le Monde*, September 22-24, 1962.

20. For the text of Ben Bella's speech, see *Le Journal officiel de la république algérienne démocratique et populaire*, Parliamentary Debates, October 1, 1962.

21. The text of the speech can be found in Hocine Ait Ahmed, *La Guerre et l'après-guerre* (Paris: Editions de Minuit, 1964), pp. 115-124.

22. *Le Journal officiel de la république algérienne*, October 1, 1962. Mahiouz cast the negative vote.

23. The nineteen members of the new government are listed in Appendix I.

24. See *Jeune Afrique*, July 13, 1964.

25. It will be recalled that the "historic chiefs" consisted of nine men. By 1962, there were six survivors: Ben Bella, Bitat, Khider, Boudiaf, Ait Ahmed, and Krim. The first three were members of the Political Bureau, i.e., before the resignation of Boudiaf.

26. David and Marina Ottaway, *Algeria: The Politics of a Socialist Revolution* (Berkeley: University of California Press, 1970), p. 83.

27. Ibid.

28. Algerian Government, Ministry of National Orientation, *L'An II, 1962-1964* (Algiers, 1964).

29. Bourgès, op. cit., p. 67.

30. Khemisti was assassinated by a mentally deranged individual. His death did not appear to be politically motivated.

31. In the course of research, the author talked to several Algerians, usually (male) heads of household, who stated that they gave money and often jewelry to the government after independence. The number of such persons, and the monetary amounts they contributed, have not been determined. Also, it was not clear whether the donations went to the rebuilding of the FLN or for some governmental purpose.

CHAPTER 5

1. See the typology of the essential elements for a mass-party system discussed in Chapter 4.

2. As cited in François Borella, "La constitution algérienne: un régime constitutionnel de gouvernement par le parti," *Revue algérienne des sciences juridiques, politiques, et économiques*, No. 1 (January 1964): 53.

3. Ibid., p. 55.

4. As cited in Hervé Bourgès, *L'Algérie à l'épreuve du pouvoir* (Paris: Editions Bernard Grasset, 1967), p. 43.

5. As cited in Borella, op. cit., p. 60. In public life, Madame Bitat used her maiden name.

6. Statement of deputy Djazouli as quoted in ibid., p. 61. Emphasis added.

7. The Algerian government listed a total of 6,391,818 registered voters and 5,283,974 who actually voted. The slight discrepancies between these figures and those in Table 2 result from incomplete figures from Batna, Medea, and Sétif. (Figures for these areas were not discovered through research.). Source: *Le Journal officiel de la république algérienne démocratique et populaire*, No. 64, September 10, 1963, p. 887.

8. See Chapter 4 for a more detailed discussion of Boudiaf's PRS.

9. *The New York Times*, September 30, 1963.

10. Ibid.

11. A total of 5,303,661 Algerians voted in favor of the Assembly election as compared to 5,166,185 (the official figure) who approved the constitution. The source of the latter figure is *Le Journal officiel de la république algérienne*, No. 64, September 10, 1963, p. 887.

12. Borella, op. cit., p. 72.

13. Algerian Government, *La Constitution de la république algérienne démocratique et populaire*, September 1963. The official French version can be found in ibid., pp. 888 ff. The English translation in Joachim Joesten, *The New Algeria* (Chicago: Follett, 1964), pp. 192-301, inaccurately enumerates the articles of the constitution.

14. Article 57 of the "official draft from the conference of FLN leaders" proposed that: "The FLN defines the nation's policy and inspires the state's action. It controls the action of the ANP and the government." The Assembly amended the proposal, in the final version of the constitution (Article 24), to read: "The FLN defines the nation's policy and inspires the state's action." Borella, op. cit., p. 89.

15. J. C. Hurewitz, *Middle East Politics: The Military Dimension* (New York: Praeger, 1969), p. 196.

16. Manfred Halpern, *The Politics of Social Change in the Middle East and North Africa* (Princeton: Princeton University Press, 1963), p. 262n.

17. Writing on the importance of legitimacy, Apter explains that "a particular form of government is institutionalized only when it becomes morally valid," or accepted. See David Apter, *The Politics of Modernization* (Chicago: University of Chicago Press, 1965), p. 236.

18. *Le Monde*, November 19, 1962.

19. *Le Journal officiel de la république algérienne*, September 1962.

20. Bourgès, op. cit., p. 94.

21. See *Les Discours du Président Ben Bella* (Annaba: Imprimerie Centrale Auto-géreé, 1964), pp. 75-77 and 211-213.

22. As cited in Bourgès, op. cit., p. 82.

23. Ibid., p. 84.

24. Ibid., p. 81.

25. Arslan Humbaraci, *Algeria: A Revolution That Failed* (New York: Praeger, 1966), pp. 286-287.

26. Ibid.

27. As quoted in Joesten, op. cit., p. 112.

28. *L'Observateur du Moyen-Orient et de l'Afrique* 8 (September 25, 1964): 10.

29. Immanuel Wallerstein, *Africa: The Politics of Independence* (New York: Vintage Books, 1961), p. 96.

30. *Alger républicain*, November 27, 1962.

31. See Clement Henry Moore, *Tunisia Since Independence* (Los Angeles: University of California Press, 1965), for a discussion of the involvement of women in Tunisian politics.

32. *Maghreb Labor Digest*, 1, No. 3 (March 1963): 13.

33. Despite their considerable role in the war for independence, Algerian women encountered great resistance to liberation from the traditional patriarchal system after independence. It appeared that the Algerians' psychological reaction against French society and social standards caused a retrenchment of inveterate Muslim customs. Speaking for Algerian women, Fadela M'rabet, an Algerian author, has made the following assessment:

> The great number of marriages are still forced unions; fathers are still all-powerful, and can interrupt at will the studies of their daughters (in order to marry off or cloister them), and husbands have complete freedom to repudiate their wives or to marry four. . . . Let those who accuse us of invading the ministries look at the statistics. In the PTT [the telephone, telegraph, and post office administration], which employs by far the greatest number of women, female personnel total only one-eighth of the whole, numbering about 1,400; 110 women work in the administration of the Ministry of Education, 18 in the Ministry of Foreign Affairs, 26 in that of Youth (out of 200), and 20 in that of Tourism. And most of these are either charwomen or typists. (As cited in Humbaraci, op. cit., pp. 250-251.)

For a comprehensive account of the contemporary conditions of Algerian women, see Fadela M'rabet, *La Femme algérienne* (Paris: Editions Maspero, 1965).

34. The Political Bureau dissolved the FFFLN on November 22, 1962, and replaced it with the Association générale des travailleurs algériens (AGTA), the new organization to represent Algerian workers in France. The AGTA was affiliated with the UGTA. See Monique Laks, *Autogestion ouvrière et pouvoir politique en Algérie (1962-1965)* (Paris: Etudes et Documentation Internationale, 1970), p. 167.

35. David and Marina Ottaway, *Algeria: The Politics of a Socialist Revolution* (Berkeley: University of California Press, 1970), p. 115.

36. Bourgès, op. cit., p. 116.

37. *Les Discours du Président Ben Bella*, loc. cit., pp. 51-52.

38. As cited in *Révolution africaine*, April 20, 1962.

39. Ibid., November 9, 1963.

40. Halpern, op. cit., pp. 281-282.

CHAPTER 6

1. Jeanne Favret, "Le Syndicat, les travailleurs, et le pouvoir en Algérie," *Annuaire de l'Afrique du nord* 3 (1964): 47.

2. Ahmed Eqbal, "Trade Unionism," in *State and Society in Independent North Africa*, ed. Leon Carl Brown (Washington, D.C.: The Middle East Institute, 1966), p. 181.

3. See Val R. Lorwin, *The French Labor Movement* (Cambridge, Mass.: Harvard University Press, 1954), Chapter 3, for a discussion of syndicalism.

4. This biographical sketch and the following one are taken from Mohammed Farès, "L'Histoire du travail algérien" (Unpublished manuscript, Algiers, 1967).

5. The FO (Force ouvrière) and the CFTC (Confédération francaise des travailleurs chrétiens) are discussed in Chapter 3.

6. Interview with Raymoun Dekkar, UGTA official, Algiers, January 15, 1967.

7. The March decrees formed the foundation of Ben Bella's policy of socialism and are discussed in the next chapter.

8. Jean Meynaud and Anisse Salah-Bey, *Le Syndicalisme africain* (Paris: Payot, 1963), p. 104.

9. Favret, op. cit., p. 50.

10. See Manfred Halpern, *The Politics of Social Change in the Middle East and North Africa* (Princeton: Princeton University Press, 1963), p. 51.

11. Frantz Fanon, *The Wretched of the Earth* (New York: Grove Press, 1963), p. 87.

12. Meynaud and Salah-Bey, op. cit., p. 102.

13. *L'Ouvrier algérien*, August 17, 1962.

14. *La Dépêche d'Algérie*, August 20, 1962.

15. Farès, op. cit. The amount of AGTA monetary contributions has not been determined, but they were surely less than FFFLN wartime contributions (discussed in Chapter 3).

16. The CGT supported the program of Blum's Popular Front but rejected active participation or ministerial posts in it.

17. Favret, op. cit., p. 48. The exclusion of the trade union leaders from FLN leadership after 1958, as explained in Chapter 3, resulted from the ascendancy of the wilaya

separatists in the movement.

18. Ibid.

19. *L'Ouvrier algérien*, August 17, 1962.

20. *L'Ouvrier algérien*, November 17, 1962.

21. *The Tripoli Program*, as cited in Joachim Joesten, *The New Algeria* (Chicago: Follette, 1964), p. 227.

22. *Le Monde*, September 14, 1962.

23. Ibid.

24. Ibid.

25. *L'Ouvrier algérien*, October 19, 1962.

26. The figure here is the one cited by the Algerian government to account for the size of the farmlands vacated by the Europeans. See Algerian Government, Ministry of Information, *Documents on Self-Management (Autogestion)*, March 1963.

27. *L'Ouvrier algérien*, October 19, 1962.

28. Ibid., November 1, 1962.

29. Ibid.

30. Ibid., December 7, 1962.

31. Ibid., November 30, 1962.

32. Ibid., December 21, 1962.

33. *Les Discours du Président Ben Bella* (Annaba: Imprimerie Centrale Autogérée, 1964), pp. 8-9.

34. The Tripoli Program stated that the "Party has banished from its midst the co-existence of differing ideologies." As cited in Joesten, op. cit. p. 225.

35. Ibid., p. 9. The sum of 20,000 AF equals 200 NF.

36. Ibid., p. 10.

37. The First UGTA Congress, *Rapport d'orientation* (Algiers, January 1963), p. 9.

38. Ibid.

39. Ibid.

40. Ibid.

41. As quoted in Favret, op. cit., p. 50.

42. *Alger républicain*, January 21, 1963.

43. *Jeune Afrique*, January 28-February 23, 1963.

44. *Alger républicain*, January 21, 1963.

45. Favret, op. cit., p. 51.

46. Ibid., p. 52.

47. The forcible inclusion of the UGTA in the FLN corresponded closely with a trend Millen has observed in newly independent nations seeking to establish a mass-party system: "The direct involvement of trade unions in the total political process has gone hand-in-hand with the all-important efforts of political leaders to introduce the mass of workers rapidly to the politics of "independence" (which may or may not mean "freedom" as defined in the West)." See Bruce H. Millen, *The Political Role of Labor in Developing Countries* (Washington, D.C.: The Brookings Institution, 1963), p. 37.

48. Werner Plum, "Les Problèmes du syndicalisme algérien," *Confluent* (June-July 1963): 528.

49. *Alger républicain*, January 21, 1963.

50. *Jeune Afrique*, January 28-February 3, 1963. Emphasis added.

CHAPTER 7

1. Secrétariat Social d'Alger, *Emploi et sous-emploi* (Algiers: February 1965), p. 19.

2. Jean Meynaud and Anisse Salah-Bey, *Le Syndicalisme africain* (Paris: Payot, 1963), p. 84.

3. An exception was the Sahara oil region where the French erected modern oil exploitation facilities.

4. *Emploi et sous-emploi*, p. 8.

5. Algerian Government, Ministry of National Orientation, *Une Année de révolution socialiste*, July 1963.

6. David and Marina Ottaway, *Algeria: The Politics of a Socialist Revolution* (Berkeley: University of California Press, 1970), p. 52.

7. Ibid., p. 53.

8. One Algerian dinar (DA) corresponded approximately to $0.20.

9. As cited in Algerian Government, Ministry of Information *Documents on Self-Management (Autogestion)*, March 1963, p. 29. English edition.

10. Ibid.

11. Ibid., Article 23, pp. 61-62.

12. Ian Clegg, *Workers' Self-Management in Algeria* (New York: Monthly Review Press, 1971), p. 67.

13. See Frantz Fanon, *The Wretched of the Earth* (New York: Grove Press, 1963), p. 48.

14. For an empirical assessment of the role of peasants in revolutionary and insurrectionary movements, the reader is recommended Eric R. Wolf, *Peasant Wars of the Twentieth Century* (New York: Harper and Row, 1969).

15. *Emploi et sous-emploi*, op. cit., p. 9.

16. Algerian Government, Ministry of National Orientation, *La Revue du plan et des études économiques*, April 1964, p. 17.

17. Clegg, op. cit., p. 85.

18. *Emploi et sous-emploi*, op. cit., p. 9.

19. For a discussion of disguised unemployment, see Hla Myint, *The Economics of the Developing Countries* (New York: Praeger, 1964), pp. 85-96.

20. *Emploi et sous-emploi*, p. 5.

21. *La Revue du plan*, p. 17.

22. Samir Amin, *L'Economie du maghrèb* (Paris: Editions de Minuit, 1966), p. 285.

23. Ibid., p. 284.

24. *Le Monde*, December 22-23, 1963.

25. Secrétariat Social d'Alger, *Dossier sur l'entreprise agricole autogérée*, November-December 1964, p. 43.

26. *Le Monde*, May 7, 1964.

27. Clegg, op. cit., p. 113.

28. *Révolution et travail*, October 31, 1963.

29. As cited in Clegg, op. cit., p. 122.

30. Ibid., p. 109.

31. Charles F. Gallagher, "North African Problems and Prospects," American Universities Field Staff, *Reports Service*, North Africa Series, 10, No. 2 (February 1964):24.

32. Everett E. Hagen, *On the Theory of Social Change* (Homewood Ill.: Dorsey Press, 1962), p. 70.

33. *Le Monde*, December 20, 1963.

34. David and Marina Ottaway, op. cit., p. 65.

35. Algerian governmental wages for directors ranged between 1,500 and 2,000 F monthly. Private firms, such as the Algiers branch of the Shell Oil Corporation, offered Algerian technicians salaries that nearly doubled that amount. See Monique Laks, *Autogestion ouvrière et pouvoir politique en Algérie (1962-1965)* (Paris: Etudes et Documentation Internale, 1970), p. 65.

36. *France observateur*, December 19, 1964.

37. For the workers' decision-making prerogatives, see *Documents on Self-Management (Autogestion)*, subsection II (the Workers' Council) of Article 14, and subsection III (the Management Committee) of Article 16.

38. Yves Sartan, "Perspectives de l'autogestion en Algérie," *Autogestion: études, débats, documents*, No. 1 (December 1966): 82.

39. See Clegg, op. cit., p. 177.

40. Ibid., p. 66.

41. *Révolution et travail*, October 31, 1963.

42. Ibid., May 17, 1963.

43. David and Marina Ottaway, op. cit., p. 134n.

44. François Weiss, "Les Conflits de travail en Algérie dans le secteur privé non-agricole," *Revue algérienne des sciences juridiques, politiques et économiques*, No. 1 (March 1966): 19ff.

45. Ibid.

46. *Alger républicain*, December 25 and 26, 1964.

47. Réne Dumont, et al., *Socialisms and Development* (London: Andre Deutsch, Ltd., 1973), p. 258.

48. See George L. Beckford, *Persistent Poverty* (New York: Oxford University Press, 1972), p. 47 and Chapter 7.

49. As cited in François Weiss, "Less Conflits de travail en Algérie dans le secteur privé non-agricole," *Revue algérienne des sciences juridiques, politiques, et économiques*, No. 2 (June 1966): 299-300.

50. In June 1964, the Algerian government reached an agreement with Berliet by which 40 percent of the firm's profits would be retained by the government. (Weiss, op cit., p. 339).

CHAPTER 8

1. David and Marina Ottaway, *Algeria: The Politics of a Socialist Revolution* (Berkeley: University of California Press, 1970), p. 128.

2. Algerian Government, Ministry of National Orientation, *La Revue du plan et des études économiques*, April 1964, p. 27.

3. Secrétariat Social d'Alger, *Orientations pour une politique de population*, March-April 1964, p. 7.

4. Seymour Martin Lipset, "University Students and Politics in Underdeveloped Countries," in *Student Politics*, ed. Seymour Martin Lipset (New York: Basic Books, Inc., 1967), p. 6.

5. *Révolution et travail,* April 9, 1964.

6. The Charter of Algiers is discussed in Chapter 9.

7. See *Oxford Regional Economic Atlas: The Middle East and North Africa* (London: Oxford University Press, 1960), pp. 18, 22, 24, 26, and 28.

8. The section was named after Mourad Didouche, one of the "historic chiefs."

9. See David C. Gordon, *North Africa's French Legacy* (Cambridge, Mass.: Harvard University Press, 1962), Chapters 5 and 8.

10. *Jeunesse,* November 1964.

11. *Révolution et travail,* February 6, 1964.

12. Ibid.

13. Ibid., April 2, 1964.

14. Ibid., October 3, 1963. Article by Mohamed Farès.

15. *Jeunesse,* June 23, 1964.

16. Ibid., August 11, 1964.

17. JFLN, *Jeunesse-Documents (enquêtes, études, documentation)* (Algiers: September 1964).

18. Ibid.

19. Ibid.

20. JFLN Conference, *La Constitution provisoire de la JFLN* (Algiers: September 1964).

21. Speech of JFLN secretary general Abdelmajid Bennaceur, JFLN National Conference, Algiers, September 1964.

22. Speech of Hadj Ben Alla, member of the FLN's Political Bureau, JFLN National Conference, Algiers, September 1964.

23. See Lipset, op. cit., pp. 7-8.

24. Clement H. Moore, et al., "Student Unions in North African Politics, *Daedalus* 97, No. 1 (Winter 1968): 27.

25. David B. Ottaway, "Algeria," in *Students and Politics in Developing Nations,* ed. by Donald K. Emerson (New York: Praeger, 1968), p. 33n.

26. Ibid., p. 15.

27. Ibid., p. 16.

28. As quoted in ibid., pp. 17-18.

29. R. Laffargue, "Les Etudiants de la faculté de droit et des sciences économiques: quelques chiffres et commentaires," *Revue algérienne des sciences juridiques, politiques, et économiques,* No. 2 (June 1966): 367-375. .

30. Ibid., p. 372.

31. Ibid., p. 371.

32. *Les Discours du Président Ben Bella* (Annaba: Imprimerie Centrale Autogérée, 1964), pp. 131-132.

33. *Maghreb Labor Digest,* 1, No. 10 (October 1963): 8.

34. *Révolution africaine,* October 19, 1963.

35. Ibid., April 2, 1964.

36. As cited in David B. Ottaway, "Algeria," loc. cit., p. 36n.

37. A UNEA membership entitled holders to the same monetary benefits enjoyed by JFLN members, viz., rebates at movies, restaurants, festivals, etc.

38. *Révolution à l'université,* April 1964, p. 3.

39. Ibid.

40. *Le Monde*, August 8 and 10, 1964.

CHAPTER 9

1. *Maghreb*, No. 1 (January-February 1964): 24. See ibid. for the complete list of commission members and the organizations they represented.

2. Ibid., No. 3 (May-June 1964): 19.

3. Benyoussef Benkhedda, "Contributions à l'historique du FLN" (Unpublished article, April 1964). Mimeographed.

4. *Révolution africaine*, April 18, 1964.

5. *L'Express*, April 23, 1964.

6. For an analysis of the Egyptian army's role in politics, see P. J. Vatikiotis, *The Egyptian Army in Politics: Pattern for New Nations* (Bloomington, Ind.: University of Indiana Press, 1961).

7. FLN, Central Commission of Orientation, *La Charte d'Alger* (Algiers: April 1964), Article 24, p. 122.

8. Ibid., Article 4(e), p. 118.

9. Ibid., Article 11, p. 120.

10. Ibid., Article 36, p. 125.

11. Ibid., Article 1, p. 118.

12. Ibid., Article 12, p. 121. This provision probably indicated the Political Bureau's attempt to adapt the model of the Soviet Communist party in restructuring the FLN.

13. *Maghreb*, No. 3 (May-June 1964): 19.

14. In 1964, Frenchmen worked under a Franco-Algerian agreement called "la coopération" (technical assistance), and comprised 43 percent of the Algerian civil service in administrative grade A, the highest level of the governmental bureaucracy; in the senior executive grade B, the next highest level, they constituted 77 percent of the personnel. See Arslan Humbaraci, *Algeria: A Revolution That Failed* (New York: Praeger, 1966), p. 197, and Chapter 7 of this study.

15. See Clement Henry Moore, *Tunisia Since Independence* (Los Angeles: University of California Press, 1965), p. 1.

16. *Démocratie nouvelle* (June 1965), p. 42. Special edition.

17. David and Marina Ottaway, *Algeria: The Politics of a Socialist Revolution* (Berkeley: University of California Press, 1970), p. 116. The figures here show a slight decline in party membership from the period when Khider was secretary general of the Political Bureau. The decline probably resulted from the purges Ben Bella made later in attempting to build an elite mass party.

18. *Le Monde*, June 22, 1964.

19. Ibid., July 12-13, 1964.

20. *Jeune Afrique*, July 13, 1964.

21. Algerian Government, *Le Journal officiel de la république algérienne democratique et populaire*, July 30, 1964.

22. Charles F. Gallagher, "The Algerian Year," American Universities Field Staff, *Reports Service*, North Africa Series,10, No. 6 (July 1963): 11.

23. Ibid.

24. *Africa Report* 9, No. 1 (January 1964): 4.

25. I. William Zartman, "L'Armée dans la politique algérienne," *L'Annuaire de l'Afrique du nord* 7 (1967), p. 269, estimates that there was a total of 130,000 troops in 1962, 35,000 of them in the ALN.

26. Algeria, Ministry of National Orientation, *La Revue du plan et des études économiques* (April 1964), p. 29.

27. J. C. Hurewitz, *Middle East Politics: The Military Dimension* (New York: Praeger, 1969), p. 197.

28. Ibid., pp. 169 and 343.

29. *El Djeich*, September 1963.

30. Hurewitz, op. cit., p. 198.

31. The members of Ben Bella's second government can be found in Appendix II. Members most closely associated with Boumedienne are indicated.

32. See Appendix I for the composition of Ben Bella's first government. Members most closely associated with Boumedienne are indicated.

33. Hurewitz, op. cit., p. 197.

34. *La Charte d'Alger*, Article 24, p. 124.

35. The composition of Ben Bella's third government, identifying the ministers closest to him, can be found in Appendix III.

36. *Alger républicain*, October 2, 1964.

37. For a complete list of the new UGTA leaders, see *Alger républicain*, March 29, 1965.

38. Ibid.

39. Ibid.

40. Mohamed Farès, "L,Histoire du travail algérien" (Unpublished manuscript, Algiers, 1967).

41. Ian Clegg, *Workers' Self-Management in Algeria* (New York: Monthly Review Press, 1971), p. 221.

42. Ibid., p. 222.

43. Ibid.

44. *Le Monde*, September 22 and 23, 1964. There was a total of 6,091,991 registered voters.

45. Aristide R. Zolberg, *Creating Political Order* (Chicago: Rand McNally and Co., 1966), p. 135.

CONCLUSION

1. In 1966 alone, military coups overthrew civilian regimes in Ghana, Upper Volta, Central African Republic, and Nigeria.

2. Algeria, Ministry of Information. *Discours du Président Boumedienne*, June 1966, p. 28.

3. When Ben Bella formed his third government in December 1964, he appointed Mahsas to head the Ministry of Agriculture and Boumaza the Ministry of Industry and Energy. Both men hastily declared their allegiance to Boumedienne at the time of the coup, and so were able to retain their posts for a while longer.

4. The SONATRACH was actually created toward the end of the Ben Bella regime but did not begin full operations until Boumedienne took over.

5. See Middle East Research Project, "State Capitalism in Algeria," *MERIP REPORTS* 35 :February 1975): 8.

6. See, for example, Ian Clegg, *Workers' Self-Management in Algeria* (New York: Monthly Review Press, 1971), p. 90 ff.

7. The effective union of personal leadership and ideology in China is explained in Franz Shurmann, *Ideology and Organization in Communist China* (Berkeley: University of California Press, 1968), pp. 58-104 and 534-557. A similar examination of party development in Tanzania is made by Henry Bienen, *Tanzania* (Princeton: Princeton University Press, 1970), Chapter 6.

8. For a definition and general examination of neocolonialism, the reader is recommended Kwame Nkrumah, *Neo-Colonialism* (New York: International Publishers, 1970); for a specific case study, see Colin Leys, *Underdevelopment in Kenya: The Political Economy of Neo-Colonialism, 1964-1971* (Berkeley: University of California Press, 1974).

9. See Arslan Humbaraci, *Algeria: A Revolution That Failed* (New York: Praeger, 1966).

10. See Clegg, op. cit., pp. 177-179.

11. See Frantz Fanon, *The Wretched of the Earth* (New York: Grove Press, 1963).

12. Middle East Research Project, op. cit., p. 7.

13. Richard Gibson, *African Liberation Movements* (London: Oxford University Press, 1972), p. 327. The word "ethnic" is my substitute for Gibson's "tribal" in the cited reference. I have avoided use of this word throughout the study because of its value-laden, pejorative connotations (which also derive from European colonialism). For a critical discussion of the negative applications of "tribal," the reader is recommended Mazi Okoro Ojiaku, "European Tribalism and African Nationalism," *Civilisations*, 22, No. 3 (1972), pp. 387-404.

14. For a discussion of Kenyattta's success despite his imprisonment, see Carl G. Rosberg, Jr., and John Nottingham, *The Myth of Mau Mau: Nationalism in Kenya* (New York: Praeger, 1966).

15. For a discussion of party building in China after the "long march," see Eric R. Wolf, *Peasant Wars of the Twentieth Century* (New York: Harper and Row, 1969), Chapter 3, especially pp. 152-155. Wolf's study (Chapter 5) also contains a brief but useful discussion of the Algerian insurrection.

Franz Schurmann, op. cit., presents an extraordinary analysis of the successful establishment of the one-party system in China after 1950. See Chapters 2 and 3 especially.

16. A good summary of these Angolan parties can be found in Gibson, op. cit. For an excellent account of the historical background to the Angolan war of liberation, and the divisiveness among leaders and parties, see John Marcum, *The Angolan Revolution*, Vol. 1 (Cambridge, Mass.: The MIT Press, 1969).

17. *Africa* No. 55 (March 1976): 88.

18. A discussion of the causes of the Ghana coup can be found in Robert Fitch, *Ghana: End of an Illusion* (New York: Monthly Review Press, 1966).

Glossary of Abbreviations

AGTA: L'Association générale des travailleurs algériens. An affiliate of the UGTA, established in November 1962 to represent some 800,000 Algerian workers in France.

ALN: L'Armée de libération nationale. The regular army organized in 1954 by the CRUA to spearhead the military strategy of the nationalist struggle.

AML: Les Amis du manifeste et de la liberté. A Muslim integrationist party, founded by Ferhat Abbas in 1944 to promote legal, political, social, and economic reforms for Algeria's Arab-Muslim population.

ANP: L'Armée nationale populaire. The new name of the ALN as changed after independence.

CCE: Le Comité de coordination et d'exécution. The executive organ of the FLN in war, established by the Soummam Valley Congress in August 1956.

CFTC: La Confédération française des travailleurs chrétiens. A French labor organization allied with the PCF.

CGT: La Confédération générale du travail. The dominant French labor organization allied with the PCF.

CNDR: Le Comité national pour la défense de la révolution. An anti-Ben Bella underground movement that emerged in April 1964 coalescing various opposition elements which the Ben Bella regime called the "counterrevolution."

CNRA: Le Conseil national de la révolution algérienne. The wartime parliamentary body of the FLN, created by the Soummam Valley Congress.

CRUA: Le Comité révolutionnaire d'unité et d'action. The paramilitary force composed of the nine "historic chiefs" who initiated the rebellion in November 1954.

ENA: L'Etoile nord-africaine. The first important Muslim political party
                    and early nationalist movement, founded by Hadj Abdelkader in
                    1924 but more popularly associated with his successor Messali Hadj.

FEMA: La Fédération des élus musulmans d'Algérie. An assimilationist
                    party of Muslim middle-class elites, formed by Dr. Mohammed
                    Salah Bendjelloul in the 1920s.

FFFLN: La Fédération de France du FLN. The wartime FLN organization in
                    France that mobilized an estimated 600,000 Algerian migrant work-
                    ers there in support of the nationalist struggle. The AGTA replaced
                    the FFFLN after independence.

FFS: Le Front des forces socialistes. A clandestine party opposed to the
                    Ben Bella regime, organized by Hocine Ait Ahmed in June 1963.

FLN: Le Front de libération nationale. Successor to the CRUA, the party
                    of the nationalist revolutionary struggle formed in November 1954.
                    It became Algeria's only political party after independence.

FNTT: La Fédération nationale des travailleurs de la terre. The state bureau
                    that Ben Bella organized in 1964 to regulate the peasants' activity on
                    state-owned farms.

FO: La Force ouvrière. A French labor Movement generally aligned with
                    metropolitan socialist parties.

GPRA: Le Gouvernement provisoire de la république algérienne. The Alge-
                    rian provisional government created in September 1958 by the
                    CNRA, operated in exile until the proclamation of independence in
                    July 1962.

ICFTU: The International Confederation of Free Trade Unions. The inter-
                    national trade union organization of the West.

ISC: The International Student Conference. The international student
                    organization of the West.

IUS: The International Union of Students. The Soviet-sponsored inter-
                    national student organization.

JFLN: La Jeunesse du FLN. The FLN's youth section, created by the party
                    as part of its mobilization policy in 1963.

MNA: Le Mouvement national algérien. The Messalist party organization,
                    formed in 1954 by Messali to vie with the FLN for control of the na-
                    tionalist movement.

MTLD: Le Mouvement pour le triomphe des libertés démocratiques. A mili-
                    tant nationalist party organized by Messali in 1946.

OAS: L'Organisation de l'armée secrète. A clandestine force organized in
                    1961 by die-hard French generals, residents of Algeria, who sought
                    to prevent Algerian independence.

ONRA: L'Office national de la réforme agraire. The agrarian reform administration that Ben Bella formed in 1963.

OS: L'Organisation spéciale. A Muslim paramilitary force that preceded the CRUA, created by Algerian revolutionaries in 1947.

PCA: Le Parti communiste algérien. The Algerian communist party, composed largely of Algeria's European residents. An adjunct of the PCF, the party was banned after independence.

PCF: Le Parti communiste français. The communist party of France.

PPA: Le Parti du peuple algérien. Messali's party, which succeeded the ENA, founded in 1937 to promote the goal of national independence.

PRS: Le Parti de la révolution socialiste. A splinter opposition party, organized by Mohammed Boudiaf in September 1962 to overturn the Ben Bella regime. The government abolished the party early in 1963.

RFMA: Le Rassemblement franco-musulman algérien. An assimilationist party formed in 1938 by Dr. Bendjelloul to intensify demands for Muslim equality and participation in the French system.

SMA: Les Scouts musulmans algériens. The Algerian Boy Scout organization which the government sought to integrate into the JFLN after 1963.

SONATRACH: La Société nationale pour la recherche, la production, le transport, la transformation et la commercialisation des hydrocarbures. A state-owned corporation whose chief function was the administration and development of independent Algeria's petroleum resources.

UDMA: L'Union démocratique du manifeste algérien. An integrationist party created by Ferhat Abbas in 1946 to seek an autonomous Algerian republic within the French system.

UGEMA: L'Union générale des étudiants musulmans algériens. The Algerian nationalist student movement that the FLN organized in July 1955 to support the internal struggle through diplomatic and nonmilitary means.

UGTA: L'Union générale des travailleurs algériens. The Algerian labor organization that the FLN formed in February 1956 to unify the Muslim working classes in support of the nationalist struggle on the labor front.

UNEA: L'Union nationale des étudiants algériens. The new name of UGEMA, adopted by a student congress in August 1963.

UNFA: L'Union nationale des femmes algériennes. The Algerian women's organization, created by the FLN late in 1962.

UPA: L'Union populaire algérienne. Predecessor to the AML, the integrationist party organized by Abbas in 1938 to promote assimilationist goals.

USTA: L'Union syndicale des travailleurs algériens. The labor component of MNA, established by Messali Hadj in February 1956 to rival the FLN.

ZAA: La Zone autonome d'Alger. A military zone formed inside wilaya IV (Algiers) during the war.

Bibliography

PRIMARY SOURCES

Abbas, Ferhat. *Guerre et révolution d'Algérie*. Paris: Juilliard, 1962.

Ait Ahmed, Hocine. *La Guerre et l'après-guerre*. Paris: Editions de, Minuit, 1964.

Algeria. *La Constitution de la république algérienne démocratique et populaire*. September 1963.

―――. *Les Discours du Président Ben Bella*. Annaba: Imprimerie Centrale Autogéreé, 1964.

―――. *Documents on Self-Management (Autogestion)*. March 1963, English edition.

―――. *Le Journal officiel de la république algérienne démocratique et populaire*. Débats parlementaires. 1962-1965.

―――. Ministry of Information. *Discours du Président Boumedienne*. June 1966.

―――. Ministry of National Orientation. *L'An II: 1962-1964*. 1964.

―――. Ministry of National Orientation. *Une Année de révolution socialiste*. 1963.

―――. Ministry of National Orientation. *La Revue du plan et des études économiques*. April 1964.

Alleg, Henri. *The Question*. New York: George Braziller, Inc., 1958.

Benkhedda, Benyoussef. "Contribution à l'historique du FLN." Unpublished article distributed in Algiers. April 1964 (Mimeographed).

Boudiaf, Mohammed. *Où va l'Algérie?* Paris: Editions Librairie de l'Etoile, 1964.

The Evian Conference. "Les Accords d'Evian." Joint declaration drawn up by the delegations of the government of the Fifth French Republic and the Algerian Front of National Liberation. Evian, Switzerland. March 18, 1962.

Farès, Mohamed. "L'Histoire du travail algérien." Unpublished manuscript, Algiers, 1967. (Typewritten).

Le Front de libération nationale. *La Charte d'Alger*. Algiers: April 1964.

―――. *La Plateforme de la révolution algérienne. Resolutions of the Soummam Valley Congress*, August 1956.

―――. "Proclamation to the Algerian People and to All Who Fight for the National Cause." Political tract distributed on November 1, 1954. English edition.

―――. *Le Programme de Tripoli*. Tripoli: June 1962.

Harbi, Mohammed. "Les Paysans dans la révolution." *Démocratie nouvelle* (June 1965): 56-62. Special edition.
La Jeunesse du FLN. JFLN Conference. *La Constitution provisoire de la JFLN*. Algiers: September 1964.
————. Jeunesse-Documents (enquêtes, études, documentation). Algiers: September 1964.
Lacheraf, Mostefa. *Algérie: nation et société*. Paris: Editions Maspero, 1965.
Ouzegane, Amar. *Le Meilleur combat*. Paris: Juilliard, 1962.
Secrétariat Social d'Alger. *Dossier sur l'entreprise agricole autogérée*. Algiers: November-December 1964.
————. *Emploi et sous-emploi*. Algiers: February 1965.
————. *Orientations pour une politique de population*. Algiers: March-April 1964.
L'Union générale des travailleurs algériens. First UGTA Congress. *Rapport d'Orientation*. February 1963. (Mimeographed).

INTERVIEWS

Algeria. Consulate (Washington, D.C.). Interview with the Chargé d'affaires. April 1966.
————. Mission to the United Nations (New York). Interviews with departmental secretaries, May 1966 and October 1967.
Centre de recherches sur les affaires méditerranéennes. University of Aix-en-Provence, France. Interviews with the editors of *Annuaire de l'Afrique du nord*. June 1967.
Dekkar, Raymoun. UGTA official. Algiers. January 1967.
Farès, Mohamed. Secretary of the UGTA's teachers' federation. Algiers. January-March 1967.
Kired, Hossein. UGTA official. Algiers. October 1966-May 1967.
Laffargue, R. Professor, University of Algiers. November 1966 and May 1967.

(Note: Several individuals whom the author interviewed requested anonymity; that request has been observed here.)

Secondary Sources

STUDIES ON ALGERIA

Agéron, Charles-Robert. *Histoire de l'Algérie*. Paris: Presses Universitaires de France, 1966.
Aron, Raymond. *Les Origines de la guerre d'Algérie*. Paris: Fayard, 1962.
Bourdieu, Pierre. *The Algerians*. Boston: Beacon Press, 1962.
————. *Travail et travailleurs en Algérie*. Paris: Mouton, 1963.
Bourgès, Hervé. *L'Algérie à l'épreuve du pouvoir*. Paris: Editions Bernard Grasset, 1967.
Brace, Richard, and Brace, Joan. *Ordeal in Algeria*. New York: Van Nostrand, 1960.
Bromberger, Serge. *Les Rebelles algériens*. Paris: Librairie Plon, 1958.
Chaliand, Gérard. *L'Algérie, est-elle socialiste?* Paris: Editions Maspero, 1964.

Clark, Michael K. *Algeria in Turmoil.* New York: Grosset and Dunlap, 1960.
Clegg, Ian. *Workers' Self-Management in Algeria.* New York: Monthly Review Press, 1971.
Descloitres, R., et al. *L'Algérie des bidonvilles: le tiers-monde dans la cité.* Paris: Mouton, 1961.
Duchemin, Jacques C. *Histoire du FLN.* Paris: La Table Ronde, 1962.
Estier, Claude. *Pour l'Algérie.* Paris: Editions Maspero, 1964.
Favrod, Charles-Henri. *Le FLN et l'Algérie.* Paris: Librairie Plon, 1962.
Gillespie, Joan. *Algeria: Rebellion and Revolution.* New York: Praeger, 1960.
Humbaraci, Arslan. *Algeria: A Revolution That Failed.* New York: Praeger, 1966.
Joesten, Joachim. *The New Algeria.* Chicago: Follett, 1964.
Julien, Charles-André. *Histoire de l'Algérie contemporaine.* Paris: 1964.
Kraft, Joseph. *The Struggle for Algeria.* Garden City, N.Y.: Doubleday, 1961.
Laks, Monique. *Autogestion ouvrière et pouvoir politique en Algérie (1962-1965).* Paris: Etudes et Documentation Internale, 1970.
Mandouze, André (ed.). *La Révolution algérienne par les textes.* Paris: Editions Maspero, 1961.
Merle, Robert. *Ben Bella.* London: Michael Joseph, Ltd., 1967.
Morland, et al. *Histoire de l'organisation de l'armee secrète.* Paris: Juilliard, 1964.
M'rabet, Fadela. *La Femme algérienne.* Paris: Editions Maspéro, 1965.
O'Ballance, Edgar. *The Algerian Insurrection: 1954-1962.* Hamden, Conn.: Archon Books, 1961.
Ottaway, David, and Ottaway, Marina. *Algeria: The Politics of a Socialist Revolution.* Berkeley: University of California Press, 1970.
Quandt, William B. *Revolution and Political Leadership: Algeria, 1954-1968.* Cambridge, Mass.: The MIT Press, 1969.
Tillion, Germaine. *Algeria, the Realities.* New York: Knopf, 1958.

GENERAL WORKS

Amin, Samir. *L'Economie du maghreb.* Paris: Editions de Minuit, 1966.
———. *The Maghreb in the Modern World.* London: Cox and Wyman, Ltd., 1970.
Apter, David. *The Politics of Modernization.* Chicago: University of Chicago Press, 1965.
Barbour, Nevill. *A Survey of North West Africa.* London: Oxford University Press, 1962.
Beckford, George L., *Persistent Poverty.* New York: Oxford University Press, 1972.
Bienen, Henry. *Tanzania.* Princeton: Princeton University Press, 1970.
Brown, Leon Carl (ed.). *State and Society in Independent North Africa.* Washington, D.C.: The Middle East Institute, 1966.
Coleman, James S., and Rosberg, Carl G., Jr., *Political Parties and National Integration in Tropical Africa.* Berkeley: University of California Press, 1964.
Cowan, L. Gray. *The Dilemmas of African Independence.* New York: Walker and Co., 1964.
Dumont, René, et al. *Socialisms and Development.* London: Andre Deutsch, Ltd., 1973.

Duverger, Maurice. *Political Parties*. New York: John Wiley and Sons, 1959.

Emerson, Donald K. (ed.). *Students and Politics in Developing Nations*. New York: Praeger, 1968.

Fanon, Frantz. *The Wretched of the Earth.* New York: Grove Press, 1963.

Fitch, Robert. *Ghana: End of an Illusion*. New York: Monthly Review Press, 1966.

Gallagher, Charles F. *The United States and North Africa*. Cambridge, Mass.: Harvard University Press, 1964.

Gibson, Richard, *African Liberation Movements*. London: Oxford University Press, 1972.

Gordon, David C. *North Africa's French Legacy*. Cambridge, Mass.: Harvard University Press, 1962.

Grundy, Kenneth W. *Guerrilla Struggle in Africa*. New York: Grossman Publishers, 1971.

Hagen, Everett E. *On the Theory of Social Change*. Homewood, Ill.: Dorsey Press, 1962.

Halpern, Manfred. *The Politics of Social Change in the Middle East and North Africa*. Princeton: Princeton University Press, 1963.

Hodgkin, Thomas. *Nationalism in Colonial Africa*. New York: New York University Press, 1957.

Hurewitz, J. C. *Middle East Politics: The Military Dimension*. New York: Praeger, 1969.

Janowitz, Morris. *The Military in the Political Development of New Nations*. Chicago: University of Chicago Press, 1964.

Joestern, Joachim. *Nasser: The Rise to Power*. London: Odhams Press Ltd., 1960.

Julien, Charles-André. *L'Afrique du nord en marche: nationalismes musulmans et souveraineté française*. Paris: Juilliard, 1952.

La Palombara, Joseph, and Weiner, Myron (eds.). *Political Parties and Political Development*. Princeton: Princeton University Press, 1966.

Le Tourneau, Roger. *Evolution politique de l'Afrique du nord musulmane*. Paris: Librairie Armand Colin, 1962.

Leys, Colin. *Underdevelopment in Kenya: The Political Economy of Neo-Colonialism, 1964-1971*. Berkeley: University of California Press, 1974.

Lipset, Seymour Martin (ed.). *Student Politics*. New York: Basic Books, Inc., 1967.

Lorwin, Val R. *The French Labor Movement*. Cambridge, Mass.: Harvard University Press, 1954.

Macridis, Roy C. (ed.). *Political Parties: Contemporary Trends and Ideas*. New York: Harper and Row, 1967.

Marcum, John. *The Angolan Revolution*, Vol. 1. Cambridge, the MIT Press, 1969.

Meynaud, Jean, and Salah-Bey, Anisse. *Le Syndicalisme africain*. Paris: Payot, 1963.

Michaud, Charles A. *Tunisia: The Politics of Modernization*. New York: Praeger, 1964.

Michaels, Robert. *Political Parties*. New York: Hearst's International Library, 1915.

Millen, Bruce H. *The Political Role of Labor in Developing Countries*. Washington, D.C.: The Brookings Institution, 1963.

Moore, Clement Henry. *Tunisia Since Independence*. Berkeley: University of California Press, 1965.

Myint, Hla. *The Economics of the Developing Countries*. New York: Praeger, 1964.

Nkrumah, Kwame. *Neo-Colonialism.* New York: International Publishers, 1970.

Pye, Lucien W. *Aspects of Political Development.* Boston: Little Brown and Co., 1966.

————, and Verba, Sidney (eds.). *Political Culture and Political Development.* Princeton: Princeton University Press, 1965.

Rosberg, Carl G., Jr., and Nottingham, John. *The Myth of Mau Mau: Nationalism in Kenya.* New York: Praeger, 1966.

Schacht, Joseph. *An Introduction to Islamic Law.* Oxford: Clarendon Press, 1964.

Schurmann, Franz. *Ideology and Organization in Communist China.* Berkeley: University of California Press, 1968.

Vatikiotis, P. J. *The Egyptian Army in Politics: Pattern for New Nations.* Bloomington, Ind.: University of Indiana Press, 1961.

Wallerstein, Immanuel. *Africa: The Politics of Independence.* New York: Vintage Books, 1961.

Williams, Philip M. *Politics in Post-War France.* London: Longmans, Green and Co., 1958.

Williams, Philip M., and Harrison, Martin. *De Gaulle's Republic.* London: Longmans, Green and Co., 1962.

Wolf, Eric R. *Peasant Wars of the Twentieth Century.* New York: Harper and Row, 1969.

Zartman, I. William. *Government and Politics in North Africa.* New York: Praeger, 1963.

Zolberg, Aristide R. *Creating Political Order.* Chicago: Rand McNally and Co., 1966.

ARTICLES

Borella, François. "La constitution algérienne: un régime constitutionnel de gouvernement par le parti," *Revue algérienne des sciences juridiques, politiques, et économiques,* No. 1 (January 1964): 53.

Deutsch, Karl W. "Social Mobilization and Political Development." *The American Political Science Review* 3 (September 1961): 493-514.

Favret, Jeanne. "Le Syndicat, les travailleurs, et le pouvoir en Algérie." *Annuaire de l'Afrique du nord* 3 (1964): 45-62.

Gallagher, Charles F. "The Algerian Year." American Universities Field Staff, *Reports Service,* North Africa Series, 10 No. 6 (July 1963): 1-19.

————. "North African Problems and Prospects." American Universities Field Staff, *Reports Service,* North Africa Series, 10, No. 2 (February 1964): 1-28.

Hollingworth, Clare. "The Struggle for Power in Algeria." *The World Today* 17 (October 1962): 428-437.

Huntington, Samuel P. "Political Development and Political Decay." *World Politics* 17 (April 1965): 386-430.

Kraft, Joseph. "Settler Politics in Algeria." *Foreign Affairs* No. 4 (July 1961): 591-600.

Laffargue, R. "Les Etudiants de la faculté de droit et des sciences économiques: quelques chiffres et commentaires." *Revue algérienne des sciences juridiques, politiques, et économiques* No. 2 (June 1966): 167-374.

Lewis, William M. "Algeria: The Plight of the Victor." *Current History* 44 (January 1963): 22-28.

———. "The Decline of Algeria's FLN." *The Middle East Journal* 20, No. 2 (Spring 1966): 161-172.

Middle East Research Project. "State Capitalism in Algeria." *MERIP REPORTS* 35 (February 1975).

Moore, Clement H. et al. "Student Unions in North African Politics." *Daedalus* 97, No. 1 (Winter 1968): 21-50.

Ojiaku, Mazi Okoro. "European Tribalism and African Nationalism." *Civilisations* 22, No. 3 (1972): 387-404.

Plum, Werner. "Les Problèmes du syndicalisme algérien," *Confluent* (June-July 1963): 528.

Sartan, Yves. "Perspectives de l'autogestion en Algérie." *Autogestion: études, débats, documents,* No. 1 (December 1966): 81-88.

Silvert, K. M. "Parties and Masses." *The Annals of the American Academy of Political and Social Science* 358 (March 1965): 101-108.

Weiss, Francois. "Les Conflits de travail en Algérie dans le secteur privé non-agricole," *Revue algerienne des sciences, juridiques, politiques, et économiques* 1 (March 1966): 17-77; 2 (June 1966): 299-345.

Zartman, I. William. "L'Armée dans la politique algérienne." *L'Annuaire de l'Afrique du nord* 7 (1967): 266-278.

NEWSPAPERS AND JOURNALS

Alger republicain, passim 1962-1964.
El Djeich, passim 1963-1965.
L'Express, passim 1962-1965.
Jeune Afrique, passim 1962-1965.
Jeunesse, passim 1963-1965.
Manchester Guardian, The 1957.
Middle East Journal, passim 1965-1966.
Le Monde, passim 1954-1965.
El Moujahid, passim 1962-1965.
The New York Times, passim 1962-1965.
L'Ouvrier algérien, passim 1963-1965.
Le Peuple, passim 1964-1965.
Revolution africaine, passim 1962-1965.
Révolution à l'université, passim 1964-1965.
Révolution et travail, passim 1962-1965.

Index

About the Author

Henry F. Jackson is an assistant professor in the Afro-American Studies Department, University of California, Berkeley. Specializing in the political and economic development of Africa and the Middle East, he has written for the *Pan-African Journal* and is currently preparing material for a book on the ideas of Frantz Fanon.